'Ethiopia in Theory deserves the widest readersh̲ [...] tual and political enterprise of the last three Ethiopian generations through a dazzling method at once archival, literary, and auto/ethnographic. Second for illuminating a dark space in Twentieth-century global history: how intellectuals outside Europe, or in diasporas, put Marxism and 'Western' social sciences to work. Historians of elsewhere in the Tricontinent will find a valuable lens in this portrait of the intellectual origins, climax and aftermaths of the Ethiopian Revolution. For it was not just in Ethiopia that the emancipatory promise of c. 1960 collapsed through its own contradictions and yet, like the anchor to a blues chord, stubbornly persists.'
–*Richard Drayton, Rhodes Professor of Imperial History, King's College London, author of* Nature's Government: Science, Imperial Britain, and the "Improvement" of the World.

'*Ethiopia in Theory* is an ambitious, surprising book. Its focus is the Ethiopian student movement of the 1960s and 1970s in Addis Ababa and across the globe, and its relationship to the great upheavals of revolutionary Ethiopia. It gives us a highly original analysis of the ideas produced by this movement based on a close reading of its texts, but does much more than that too. It offers not just an analysis of the social science ideas of the students themselves and the ways in which they shaped and were shaped by Ethiopian history, but also of the categories used to study those ideas. This double move reflects a deep interest in understanding the politics of knowledge production in Ethiopia and Africa, and gives us a novel means of doing so. It is a move that is also rooted in Zeleke's own life story, and is thus an act of self-recovery too. This crossing of disciplines, genres and viewpoints has produced an extraordinarily productive and engaging account of a momentous time.'
–*Jocelyn Alexander, Professor of Commonwealth Studies, University of Oxford, author of* The Unsettled Land: The Politics of Land and State-making in Zimbabwe, 1893–2003.

'This superb book will transform all discussions concerning the production of knowledge. Ranging through the archives, moving across philosophy and critical theory, and traversing social history, *Ethiopia in Theory* frames a stunningly original account of the Ethiopian student movement of the 1960s and '70s as a site for the production of radical social science. Rather than the mere reception of revolutionary theory in an African context, Zeleke shows us the dynamics of its *generation*. There is truly nothing in the literature that comes close to the depth of this multi-leveled, interdisciplinary study. Zeleke's outstanding book deserves the widest possible readership in social history, African studies, post-colonial analysis, and Marxist and critical theory in general.'
–*David McNally, Cullen Distinguished Professor of History, University of Houston, author of* Monsters of the Market: Zombies, Vampires and Global Capitalism

'Political research on the period from roughly 1966 to the mid-1970s often fail to artic-ulate the global dimensions of student movements in African countries. This much-overdue study of the Ethiopian example offers, with nuance, rich historical evidence, and wonderfully clear prose, the revolutionary situation in which, as its author Elleni Centime Zeleke aptly puts it, the bandit is transformed into "a guerilla or leader." In response to those who cry "illiberalism," this work reveals an alignment with other movements of what is at times called "the black radical tradition" through which the response, echoed with explanatory force and defiance through the corridors of history, is that those at the bottom cannot *and should not* wait. As such, this extraordinary book also illuminates the complexity, strengths, and shortcomings of revolutionary forms of knowledge and praxis in Afro-modernity.'
—*Lewis R. Gordon, Professor of Philosophy, University of Connecticut, author of* Existentia Africana *and* What Fanon Said.

'An original and pathbreaking study of the ideology and the intellectual traditions that informed the Ethiopian revolution of 1974. *Ethiopia in Theory* provides sophisticated analysis of the ideas of the Ethiopian student movement of the 1960s and the way in which these ideas have continued to shape state policies in contemporary Ethiopia. This meticulously researched book offers a unique perspective for the study of revolu-tions and the socialist experience in Africa as well as the process of local knowledge production. It will undoubtedly appeal to a wide range of scholars beyond the field of African studies.'
—*Ahmad Sikainga, Professor of African History, Ohio State University, author of* City of Steel and Fire: A social History of Atbara, Sudan's Railway Town, 1906–1984.

Ethiopia in Theory

Historical Materialism Book Series

The Historical Materialism Book Series is a major publishing initiative of the radical left. The capitalist crisis of the twenty-first century has been met by a resurgence of interest in critical Marxist theory. At the same time, the publishing institutions committed to Marxism have contracted markedly since the high point of the 1970s. The Historical Materialism Book Series is dedicated to addressing this situation by making available important works of Marxist theory. The aim of the series is to publish important theoretical contributions as the basis for vigorous intellectual debate and exchange on the left.

The peer-reviewed series publishes original monographs, translated texts, and reprints of classics across the bounds of academic disciplinary agendas and across the divisions of the left. The series is particularly concerned to encourage the internationalization of Marxist debate and aims to translate significant studies from beyond the English-speaking world.

For a full list of titles in the Historical Materialism Book Series
available in paperback from Haymarket Books, visit:
https://www.haymarketbooks.org/series_collections/1-historical-materialism

Ethiopia in Theory

*Revolution and Knowledge
Production, 1964–2016*

Elleni Centime Zeleke

Haymarket Books
Chicago, IL

First published in 2019 by Brill Academic Publishers, The Netherlands
© 2019 Koninklijke Brill NV, Leiden, The Netherlands

Published in paperback in 2020 by
Haymarket Books
P.O. Box 180165
Chicago, IL 60618
773-583-7884
www.haymarketbooks.org

ISBN: 978-1-64259-341-9

Distributed to the trade in the US through Consortium Book Sales and
Distribution (www.cbsd.com) and internationally through Ingram
Publisher Services International (www.ingramcontent.com).

This book was published with the generous support of Lannan
Foundation and Wallace Action Fund.

Special discounts are available for bulk purchases by organizations and
institutions. Please call 773-583-7884 or email info@haymarketbooks.org
for more information.

Cover art: "Mahzoum - Defeat 1963" by Hamed Abdalla. Copyright
Hamed Abdalla Estate.
Cover design by Jamie Kerry and Ragina Johnson.

Printed in the United States.

10 9 8 7 6 5 4 3 2 1

Library of Congress Cataloging-in-Publication data is available.

Contents

PART 2
Theory as Memoir

Foreword

The Ethiopian revolution – that cultural earthquake that produced at once progressive social measures, prodigious killing, and the spewing forth of millions into what is now the Ethiopian diaspora – continues to haunt scholars, if not indeed all Ethiopians. Elleni Zeleke grew up in exile and begins this wide-ranging study – part philosophy, part history, part anthropology – with an account of a genre of song in the post-revolutionary era called *tizita*, 'memory'. To Elleni as a child, such songs seemed only to rub salt into raw wounds. She wanted to cure the adults of their backward-looking nostalgia. But as she grew older, she discovered increasing layers of complexity in any such 'cure'. This book is the product of that journey.

The focus that Elleni brings to the revolution involves the Ethiopian student movement that began in the 1960s in Addis Ababa, as well as among Ethiopians studying abroad in North America and Europe. It has long been appreciated that these students were critical actors in the 1974 revolution, and the present work is preceded by two other distinguished books on the Ethiopian student movement, by Randi Balsvik in 1985 and by Bahru Zewde in 2014. What sets Elleni's approach apart from both of her predecessors is an imaginative and productive identification with the early leaders of the student movement and, more importantly, with the kind of social theory they wielded, Marxism. This leads, through an examination of what Elleni calls knowledge production, to a way of understanding historical materialism that is different to that of the revolutionaries themselves.

Since the late nineteenth century, Ethiopian intellectuals have studied the rest of the world in order to understand their own society's 'backwardness', but that form of knowledge typically took the West (including its Marxism) on the West's terms. By the 1970s, one could even say that the Western university had played an essential role in the Ethiopian revolution. Perhaps the most original aspect of Elleni's work is her exploration of how these themes interrelate and her consequent attempt to construct a form of Marxism from a postcolonial point of view.

This book led me to look back at some of the writings of Ethiopian students in the late 1960s. I was, as they say, blown away by pieces like that of Walleligne Mekonnen. But Walleligne, like many others, was soon dead. In conversing with the ghosts of the students, Elleni aims to reinvigorate revolutionary theory. Virtually all the great issues of the Ethiopian student movement – land, nationalities, the meaning of democracy – continue as critical questions in the country in 2019. Can Ethiopians now somehow redeem the sufferings of the dead, escape their mistakes, while honouring their vaunting ambitions? That, for me, is the final question this book poses.

Donald L. Donham
Distinguished Research Professor of Anthropology
University of California, Davis

Acknowledgements

The research questions in this book were first raised through conversations with my aunt Tutu (Ruphael) Imru. Tutu had spent most of her career working as both an image archivist at Ethiopian Television and a librarian at the *Ethiopian Herald*. She was also the first person to teach me how to read the sediments of the past in the present. She blew beautiful smoke rings and once revelled with Nina Simone. This manuscript was written in memory of her life and for my aunts Hirut and Yodit too. They all made that extra effort to teach me something about living well.

Over the years many colleagues have read much of my writing and debated many of the ideas contained within this book. In my home department, Middle Eastern, South Asian and African Studies at Columbia University, I have found a warm home for the ongoing development of my ideas: Tim Mitchell paid close attention to my writing style and helped me see where I needed to revise the manuscript; both Tim Mitchell and Mamadou Diouf also asked crucial questions about my project that helped me reformulate the entire framing of the book; Gil Anidjar provided good advice about how to move through the publishing process, while conversations with Mahmood Mamdani allowed me to clarify the stakes of my project. At Whitman College, where I spent two years as an assistant professor, Timothy Kaufman-Osborn read my entire manuscript when I was at a loss as to how to begin revisions, and Arash Davari was a formidable interlocutor who helped me build the confidence to believe in my project as a useful contribution to post-colonial political theory. Dagmawi Woubshet at the University of Pennsylvania provided inspiration, instruction and conversation on living the academic life while also speaking to multiple audiences. Lee Cassanelli, the General Editor of the *Journal of North East African Studies*, provided useful editorial advice when I submitted an early version of Chapter Four for review and eventual publication. Jonathan Adjemian not only read every chapter of this book multiple times but also helped enter bibliographic information into Zotero and basically sped up the process for getting the manuscript into a presentable form. I want to thank Erin MacLeod for demonstrating a way to effectively bring together modern citation systems and the Ethiopian naming system. I have followed Erin MacLeod's example in this book. Sebastian Budgen and Danny Hayward, two of the editors at the Historical Materialism book series, have been patient and generous with me throughout the revision process.

This book project began as a PhD dissertation in the Graduate Program in Social and Political Thought at York University (Toronto). Everything I learnt in those years was with a vibrant community of thinkers including Travis Fast, Rade Zinaic, Rob Heynen, Sue Brophy, Bojana Videkanic, Neil Braganza, Gabe Levine, Kathy Kiloh, Aaron Kamugisha, Ayesha Hameed, David McNally and Pablo Idahosa. During my time at York I was grateful to have received a Doctoral Research Award from the International Development Research Centre (Canada) in order to conduct field research in Ethiopia. During my time in Ethiopia I was affiliated with the Institute of Ethiopian Studies (IES) at Addis Ababa University. Elizabeth Wolde-Giorgis, who was the Director of IES at the time, made resources easily available to me and generally welcomed me with open arms. This manuscript could not have been completed without her assistance. At the IES, I also taught a class on theory and method in African Studies. Through this class I was given the opportunity to meet many inspiring students, some of whom have now gone on to write interesting dissertations of their own. In the end we became a community of supportive learners who taught each other so much about critical thinking in the Horn of Africa. In this regard I would especially like to thank Netsanet Michael and Serawit Bekele. Lastly, other communities of support must also be acknowledged, especially my childhood friends from Courida Park in Georgetown, Guyana, as well as those friends who brought me food and money when both were running short. This includes Asafa George, Loza Seifu, Monique Tamrat, Loulou Cherinet, Hillina Seife, Aisha Green, Marie-Jolie Rwigema, and Mohan Mishra, amongst many others.

Abbreviations

AAU	Addis Ababa University
ADLI	Agricultural Development-Led Industrialization
AMC	Agricultural Marketing Corporation
AESM	All Ethiopia Socialist Movement (English acronym for Me'ison Mala Ityopya Socialist Neqnaqe)
CUD	The Coalition for Unity and Democracy
EEA	Ethiopian Economics Association
EPLF	Eritrean People's Liberation Front
EPRDF	Ethiopian People's Revolutionary Democratic Front
EPRP	Ethiopian People's Revolutionary Party
ESANA	Ethiopian Students Association North America
ESM	Ethiopian Student Movement
ESUE	Ethiopian Student Union Europe
ESUNA	Ethiopian Student Union North America
GTP	Growth and Transformation Plan
FDRE	Federal Democratic Republic of Ethiopia
HSIU	Haile-Selassie I University
NUES	National Union of Ethiopian Students
ODF	Oromo Democratic Front
OPDO	Oromo Peoples Democratic Front
PNDR	Program of the National Democratic Revolution of Ethiopia
PASDEP	Plan for Accelerated and Sustained Development to End Poverty
TPLF	Tigrayan People's Liberation Front
UEDF	United Ethiopian Democratic Front
WWFES	World Wide Federation of Ethiopian Students
WWUES	World Wide Union of Ethiopian Students

Note on Citations

In Ethiopia, a family name system is not used. Individuals have a given name and their father's name is used for the second name. I have used both names at first mention but first names at subsequent mentions in the text. For the sake of citation, and to stay in keeping with author-date reference style, I have used the Ethiopian second names. In this way I avoid inconsistency between Ethiopian authors and everyone else.

Introduction

This book tells a story of how to tell the story of revolution in the Third World. Taking the Ethiopian student movement of the 1960s and 1970s as a complex and concrete case study, I begin by asking: What does it mean to write today about the appropriation and indigenization of Marxist and mainstream social science ideas in an Ethiopian and African context; and, importantly, what does the archive of revolutionary thought in Africa teach us about the practice of critical theory more generally? Between the years 1964 and 1974, Ethiopian post-secondary students studying at home, in Europe, and in North America produced a number of journals where they explored the relationship between social theory and social change within the project of building a socialist Ethiopia. In this book I examine the literature of this student movement, together with the movement's afterlife in Ethiopian politics and society. Moving beyond both popular and academic accounts of political protests in Ethiopia, I show how the intellectual culture and persons that animated the Ethiopian student movement in the 1960s and 1970s continued to impact political processes in the country up to 2016 and beyond. I then connect the different historical practices related to knowledge production within the Ethiopian student movement with ongoing debates on knowledge production in Africa. Attending to the ongoing crisis in African studies regarding what constitutes decolonized knowledge production, I propose that this impasse can only be addressed by situating knowledge production in Africa within the historical processes that have led to contemporary political forms.

1 Revolutionary Ethiopia

The year 1974 in Ethiopia is indelibly marked by a major social revolution which was led in part by the Ethiopian student movement of the 1960s and 1970s. The major demands of both the students and the revolution more generally were the abolition of multiple 'indigenous' land tenure systems that were often also described as 'feudal'; the right to self-determination for the various nations and nationalities that exist within the modern boundaries of Ethiopia; and the abolition of the monarchy then headed by Haile-Selassie I. The Ethiopian revolution of 1974 marked the culmination of a process of agitation and organising whereby Haile-Selassie was deposed as head of state, feudalism came to an end, and a 'land to the tiller' programme was initiated. 'Scientific socialism' was adopted as the overall method of governance by the first revolutionary regime (popularly known as the Derg regime) that followed the downfall of Haile-Selassie's regime in 1974. At the same time, many members of the Ethiopian student movement began to have significant policy differences with the Soviet-backed regime that was installed after 1974, and as early as 1975 a number of rebel fronts and political parties initiated a series of civil wars against the new revolutionary government.[1] Many of these rebel groups operated in the name of building a more broadly based ethno-nationalist and peasant-based socialism. Importantly, the Ethiopian People's Revolutionary Democratic Front (EPRDF), which has been in power in Ethiopia since 1991, was formed from some of these rebel groups (including the Tigray People's Liberation Front and remnants of the Ethiopian People's Revolutionary Party). Despite much in-fighting between the various revolutionary forces in the 1970s and 1980s, the coalition of rebel groups that finally took over the Ethiopian state through force of arms after the cold war came to an end in 1991 represented another side of the Ethiopian student movement (ESM), and led to the opening of a second phase of the Ethiopian revolution after 1991.[2] Rather than abandon many of the gains won through the revolution of 1974 (such as the Land to the Tiller programme and the establishment of peasant associations), when the EPRDF regime came to power in 1991 they built on the legacy of the 1974 revolution by establishing a developmental state often esteemed to have made significant gains on the human development index, but also seen as too illiberal in orientation and thus authoritarian and anti-democratic in nature.

Before the Ethiopian student movement shifted the country's direction by launching the 1974 revolution, class formation in Ethiopia involved a peasant-based agrarian economy along with a nascent bourgeoisie. Gebru Tareke has argued that this so-called bourgeoisie never developed their own collective and coherent political outlook, nor were they owners of the means of production.[3] Although agrarian capitalism was beginning to alter the structure of the economy in the period before 1974, producing a new class of tenant farmers and private property owners, in terms of strategic location within the national economy bourgeois class formation in Ethiopia before 1974 was limited to the creation of a mere 'transitional class' (Gebru Tareke's term) of professionals who had been trained by the state and were embedded in the state bureaucracy in professional positions as doctors, lawyers, college and school teachers, bank

---

1   For a detailed description of the nature of these civil wars, see Tareke 2013.
2   Gebru Tareke prefers to call the victory of the EPRDF in 1991 a second revolution, even though he also details the roots of the EPRDF in the Ethiopian Student Movement of the 1960s and 1970s.
3   Tareke 2013.

representatives, and military officers. Other scholars including Messay Kebede and Bahru Zewde have described this new transitional class as the 'educated elite'.[4]

Despite efforts towards modernisation, no officially recognised political parties and very few modern civil society organisations existed in the country.[5] As Gebru Tareke has pointed out, where there was social critique it came from the likes of novelists, playwrights, and poets who belonged to this transitional class of newly educated persons. Until the Ethiopian students based in Ethiopia and abroad organised themselves into a protest movement, critique did not come from organisations as such but from individuals embedded within this class.[6] Yet by the 1960s these newly educated students, in opposition to the developmental trajectory of Haile-Selassie's regime, expressed an anti-capitalist and anti-imperialist position. In particular, university students proposed that public space be expanded to include the masses into politics. The student movement made this demand through street demonstrations, primarily in the capital Addis Ababa, and through the production of a number of highly theoretical journals including *Be Ready* (Tatek), *Struggle*, and *Challenge*.[7] From 1964 onwards these journals took on a committed radical social agenda which in turn shaped the debates and policy outcomes of the 1974 revolution and its aftermath.

The Ethiopian student movement was often dominated by sloganeering at the expense of detailed discussion. Sarah Vaughan has argued that the movement generally saw revolution as a shortcut to development and social justice, and understood its primary task as using concepts derived from the university setting to popularise an alternative path to national development. The goal was to transform the shape and size of the Ethiopian state in the image of knowledge provided by the newly educated.[8] Gebru Tareke reminds us that neither the immediate post-revolutionary Derg regime nor the rebel fronts that launched a civil war in 1975 were led by an insurgent peasantry. Instead, in each case an intellectual vanguard of educated persons led the peasantry and urban masses, linking the various needs of the population to larger political grievances through narratives of class conflict, state-led nationalism and often ethno-nationalism. These groups attempted an alliance between radical intel-

---

4 The educated elite have been discussed in numerous works on Ethiopia, most especially in the works of Messay Kebede. See Kebede 2008; see also Zewde 2001.
5 Balsvik 1994.
6 See the discussion in Chapter One of Tareke 2009.
7 See Kifle 1994.
8 Vaughan 2003, p. 284.

lectuals and ordinary people so that '"consent and the active aid of the people" transformed the bandit into a guerrilla or leader'.[9] In each case, these narratives were developed in the urban classroom and in student-run revolutionary journals.

The 1974 revolution and the subsequent civil wars embedded new institutions and social relations in Ethiopia (and Eritrea). Despite this, opponents of the presently ruling EPRDF (and, I would add, also of the Derg regime) have tended to strip both regimes of their 'ideological pedigree'.[10] Opponents of the EPRDF have more often than not claimed that the party's legacy of democratic centralism cannot stand in the context of global liberal democracy; they claim, in other words, that the Ethiopian regime has been inherently anti-democratic.[11]

The EPRDF regime, against accusations of its being too illiberal, has argued that for democracy to have substantive meaning in a peasant-based economy the state must fuse a class analysis with a national (ethnic) analysis. Only at this institutional level can historical injustices be addressed and fair distribution of resources ensured (access to land being the key issue in this case).[12]

---

9   Tareke 2009, p. 46.
10 I have borrowed this phrase from Vaughan 2003, p. 130.
11 Interestingly, in an interview given in 2009 by Yacob Haile-Mariam, a leading opposition member of the CUD blames the political culture of the ESM for why the current opposition is unable to overcome differences today. He says, 'we brought a culture where differences could only be resolved through elimination'. He further insists that this Marxist hangover must end, thus: 'This is a time of liberal-democracy'. See Haile-Mariam 2009.
12 For example, in the Introduction to the 2006 Basic Program issued by the EPRDF there is an extensive but somewhat confused discussion as to why democracy is unable to fully play a part towards development in the context of an agrarian society. First is the claim that democratic objectives are fulfilled only if they trigger successful economic growth, so that the most important thing is to overcome structural problems and defects in the agricultural system. There is a need to link agriculture to industry, but in such a way 'as to not leave the bulk of the population as spectators of a well endowed few ... [T]he people must be the real beneficiaries (the country must become really self-sufficient)'. In this discussion the party concedes that a robust market economy is necessary for this kind of development, but there is still need to 'ensure that multitudes are the real beneficiaries of growth'. Thus, for democracy to work it must be demonstrated that democracy is an instrument of development in practice. But then in Section 13 of the Introduction it appears that democracy cannot be defined as respecting human and democratic rights of the individual. Thus, parallel to individual rights are group rights (rights of self-determination of nations): 'We must ensure that Ethiopians are all beneficiaries of all entitlements in an equal basis'. Section 14 then states that these objectives can only be met through mobilising the peasantry: 'The front is fundamentally an organization of the peasantry, which is the main force behind revolutionary democracy'. See Ethiopian People's Revolutionary Democratic Front 2006.

This was based on an updating of Lenin through the Maoist principles of mass mobilisation: the ethnic nation is seen as the best social institution through which to organise political participation and representation.[13] The EPRDF has argued, given the agrarian nature of the country, that one can 'only speak of the democratization of society and social relations'; indeed, in their language, 'we seek a coalition with the people'. To speak of pluralism for the sake of pluralism is to speak ahistorically and 'apolitically'.[14] Accordingly, many of the various EPRDF political programmes have emphasised establishing fraternity amongst the peoples of Ethiopia. For example, in many sections of the 6th EPRDF party programme there is an emphasis on 'mutual interest and fraternity'.[15] This language is echoed in the Ethiopian constitution, which declares that the role of the state is to promote 'self-rule and fraternity amongst the peoples of Ethiopia'.[16]

The language of fraternity seems to be derived from the political philosopher Andreas Eshete, a principal theoretician and activist in the Ethiopian student movement who was actively involved in discussions leading up to the constitutional commission that formulated the post-Derg constitution of 1994. As a political philosopher who lived in exile during the Derg regime and who taught on a number of US campuses, Andreas Eshete has written about the idea of fraternity, proposing that it is a key but under-clarified concept in the revolutionary triad of liberté, égalité, and fraternité.[17] The present constitution that frames political behaviour in Ethiopia, in this respect and others, is then the partial culmination of the work of social theorists tied to the student movement, the 1974 revolution, and the concomitant civil wars. As Gebru Tareke has pointed out, interpreting the civil wars and the revolution is a question not only of how and when centralised state power was claimed, but also of asking who was mobilised for the various revolutionary wars.[18] To the keen observer, the process of establishing revolutionary institutions provided a continuous passage for intellectual persons and their ideas to travel between the student movement, the military field, state institutions, and law-making, all the while mobilising concepts gathered from the university setting as objective arbiters

---

13   See Vaughan 1994, p. 171.
14   Meles quoted in Vaughan 1994, p. 171.
15   See Article 4, Ethiopian People's Revolutionary Democratic Front 6th conference statutes, 2006.
16   Federal Democratic Republic of Ethiopia 1995.
17   On Andreas Eshete's role within the ESM, see Woubshet 2010. For Eshete's academic work on fraternity see Eshete 1981. To glean the pragmatics of how Eshete connects fraternity to the Ethiopian constitution see Eshete 1993.
18   Tareke 2009, p. 82.

of social conflict. This pattern of resolving social conflict has been reproduced in every political crisis since 1974.

This book is centred on an examination of the form and content of the literature produced by the Ethiopian student movement, tracing the passage of ideas from the student movement into state-driven policy documents in the aftermath of the 1974 Ethiopian revolution and up until the federal elections of 2005. It then turns to look at the 2014–16 protests in the peri-urban areas surrounding the capital city of Ethiopia, Addis Ababa, one of whose main goals was to prevent the implementation of the government's proposed master plan for the city. The new master plan sought to expand the boundaries of Addis Ababa into densely populated smallholder farming areas in order to transform some of those areas into zones of light manufacturing and urban condominium projects. Since all land in Ethiopia is vested in the state, expropriation for the purposes of state-led development could be easily justified. Discourses in support of the 2014–16 protests often appealed to ideas and notions first introduced by the student movement, including the usufruct rights of peasant farmers and the idea of ethnic self-determination. In many ways, through the revolutionary process, these ideas have become enshrined in the federal constitution as well as regional and local legislation, and so their meaning and implementation now shape the claims made by both the state and the protests against it. It is this multiple, contested history that I seek to understand in this book, aiming to restore the link between theory and practice by examining the ideas that shaped policy outcomes and political practice in Ethiopia, and vice versa.

But this raises complicated questions about how one begins to recognise theory as something distinct from practice. I attend to this problem as an issue that plagues the processes of knowledge production in the student movement as much it effects the writing about the student movement, including my own. Specifically, I trace how the intellectual culture and persons who animated the Ethiopian student movement in the 1960s and 1970s are part of a larger story about the role played by the social sciences in reproducing local processes of knowledge production and political practice in Ethiopia and Africa. This makes it possible to illustrate the ways in which explanatory models in the social sciences filter down and affect local knowledge production and practice, and vice versa. In this book I thus raise the question of how one can characterise and understand the influence of the social sciences on actual social forces in a particular historical context and this becomes an important part of how I seek to examine the historical processes that have led to contemporary political forms.

2   Background to the Project

The initial research for this book began in my attempt to make sense of the blogs, newspaper articles and academic accounts that discussed the 2005 federal elections in Ethiopia. This was particularly pressing for me, since observers of Ethiopian politics saw the 2005 elections as a founding event, being the first to be contested by multiple parties.[19] Accounts of the election focused on technicalities associated with the election process at the expense of discussing more substantive issues. I found this remarkable given that the electoral platforms of the competing political parties offered different views of what constituted the democratic process. Each party had a different perspective on how democratic processes were linked to substantive issues such as land privatisation, capital controls, and national self-determination. Given that these issues were at the heart of the manifestos offered by competing political parties, and had previously pushed the country into war and revolution, I was interested in asking why these substantive issues were relegated to the background in accounts of the election period. Had these issues been discussed in an Ethiopian context prior to the elections, and if so, were those who had raised these substantive issues in the past partially responsible for the way in which the 2005 elections came to be characterised both locally and internationally?

Working intuitively, I began to consider the pre-history of the 2005 elections by, first, reading through the manifestos of each competing political party, and second, launching an investigation into the journals, brochures, and pamphlets produced by the Ethiopian student movement in the period leading up to the Ethiopian revolution of 1974. As I read, I began to notice that the debates, ideas, and writings produced by the Ethiopian student movement had in fact become the dominant discourse that shaped state-driven policy outcomes in the post-revolutionary period up until the federal election of 2005. These same debates, ideas and writings were being fundamentally contested by the opposition parties in the 2005 elections. Examining the literature of the student movement in tandem with the history of the movement's aftermath became a window through which to reflect on the connection between theory and practice in the context of dramatic social change. This shifted the focus of my study. Methodologically, I wanted to rub the elections of 2005 against the grain of the 1974 revolution by tracing how the debates of the Ethiopian student movement played out in the revolutionary struggles of the post-1974 period. Accord-

---

19   See Clapham 2005.

ingly, I reinterpreted the body of literature produced by the Ethiopian student movement as the pre-history of the Ethiopian revolution, and then posited the period of 1974–2005 as the after-history of the Ethiopian student movement. I wanted to discover not only how the hopes, gains and contradictions of the student movement shaped the post-1974 period but also, more importantly, how they could provide a measure of the failures and gains of the post-revolutionary period. Lastly, I wished to understand the continuing appeal of the student movement's discourses to various sections of the Ethiopian population, hoping to discover what was at stake in the 2005 election and its aftermath. I also wanted to understand how the tragic and complicated outcomes of the 2005 elections set the stage for the unfolding of politics in the period leading up to the protests of 2014–16.

Many of the journals, brochures and pamphlets that ended up forming the corpus of the student movement literature were published on the university campus of what was then called Haile-Selassie I University College, located in Addis Ababa. The evolution of the locally-based Ethiopian student movement was also importantly influenced by Ethiopian students studying in North America, Europe, Lebanon, Algiers, Moscow, and elsewhere. The premier English-language journal of the Ethiopian student movement, *Challenge*, was published by the Ethiopian Student Union of North America (ESUNA). The Ethiopian Student Union Europe (ESUE) also published a number of newsletters and journals, including the well-known *Tiglachen* (Our Struggle); however, between 1964 and 1974, *Challenge* was the journal published most consistently. In this journal we can begin to trace the debates and resolutions that eventually shaped the ideas of Ethiopia's most important political parties, including the Ethiopian People's Revolutionary Party (EPRP) and the All Ethiopia Socialist Movement (AESM) or *Mela Ethiopia Sosialist Niqinaqē* (ME'ISON), both of which were founded by students who contributed to *Challenge*.

The Ethiopian student movement was a plural movement with multiple branches, but each branch often referred to the other as part of a single movement. Throughout this book I refer to the Ethiopian student movement in the singular, even as I try to delineate the contested nature of that singularity. It is clear that each branch of the movement was well aware of what the other was doing, and always operated in relation to the resolutions and decisions of the other branches. Each branch also participated in a variety of transnational meetings to bring together a movement often perceived by its members to be splintered.

In the journals, brochures and pamphlets produced by the Ethiopian student movement one can find essays that address the debates and conflicts that ended up shaping the Ethiopian revolution, as well as resolutions from the meetings that would shape so much of the violent conflict of the revolutionary period. Nearly every Ethiopian who has written directly about the Ethiopian student movement was a participant in the movement and, in some way or another, is seeking to explain their own role in its activities. This means that much of the literature on the student movement is concerned with personal redemption.[20] On the other hand, the more formal scholarly literature that examines the roots of the Ethiopian revolution tends to frame the causes of the revolution in military terms or as a conflict between modernity and tradition.[21] Although the student movement contributed to establishing many of the terms and goals of the revolution, the secondary literature takes the fact of the revolution for granted, without analysing its outcomes in terms of the contestation within the literature of the student movement. The questions and answers posed by the student movement are hardly ever linked to longer social, political, or economic trajectories that have framed Ethiopian, African, or even global history, and neither the student movement nor the revolution is analysed in terms of policy impacts or continuities with other African or third world countries.[22]

The question that then emerged for me was: Why is the multi-layered transnational aspect of the Ethiopian student movement so often ignored, and what does this fact tell us about how the story of the history of ideas in Ethiopia is told? When we examine the journals, policy documents and brochures produced by both the Ethiopian student movement and the post-revolutionary regimes, we note that the realities that shaped and influenced them diverge significantly from the methodology that is used to tell their story.[23] Not only was the Ethiopian student movement a transnational social movement, it was influenced by social movements and a social science literature that were in turn deeply influenced by the events of the day (Vietnam, the cold war, Black power struggles, and decolonisation). The literature of the Ethiopian student

20 Over the past few years, a number of new works have been published by academics who were members of the Ethiopian student movement during the 1960s and 1970s. Major texts in this group include Kebede 2008; Tareke 2009; and Zewde 2014. Collectively, these works help us rethink the social roots of the Ethiopian revolution by demonstrating the impact of the student movement on both policy outcomes and state formation in the period following the 1974 revolution. Even more striking is that each author's reinterpretation of the Ethiopian revolution can be understood as a retrospective analysis of a political project launched by his cohort of student colleagues. See also Tadesse 1993. I discuss these works in more detail in Chapter 2 of this book.
21 See, for instance, Clapham 1990; Ottaway and Ottaway 1978. Also see Donham 1999.
22 See Chapter 2 of this book for more on this.
23 A classic in the field is Balsvik 1994.

movement was in dialogue with international Marxism, Maoism, and decolonial discourses as much as it took its cues from homegrown events.

Ironically, in trying to situate the literature of the Ethiopian student movement within a broader history of ideas, I realised that I faced the same sense of lack that the students themselves must have faced when producing knowledge about Ethiopia for the sake of social transformation. In wrestling with the question of knowledge production as it related to scholarship on the Ethiopian student movement, I had to simultaneously identify and think through the limits and contradictions of the social sciences in Ethiopia. Given the late arrival of the social sciences in Ethiopia, it seems to me that the Ethiopian student movement also represents one of the first large-scale systematic attempts in Ethiopia to apply the methods of the social sciences to a set of social problems in Ethiopia. The Ethiopian student movement is as such a major component of the history of the social sciences in Ethiopia. To confront the lack of knowledge about the Ethiopian student movement is then to confront the history of the social sciences in Ethiopia, of which the Ethiopian student movement has been both victim and constitutive player. Any critical history of the Ethiopian student movement needs to examine the use of social science concepts by the Ethiopian student movement, and to connect that case with the historical and philosophical problems related to social science knowledge production in Ethiopia and Africa.

There is a link between the history of social sciences and the history of social policy development by both state and non-state actors in Ethiopia. At the heart of social science practice in Ethiopia is a positivist over-investment in the meaning of concepts. Because the social sciences have been pushed to produce a direct benefit for society rather than being understood as a space that opens up a critical and philosophical dialogue on social reality, these concepts have been overly politicised.[24] For Ethiopia, this has meant that discourses coming out of the social sciences have been accompanied by war and social conflict directly articulated around whatever social engineering project currently dominates social science practice in the country. Even though the social sciences have always been linked to social policy development in Ethiopia, the manner in which social science practitioners advocate on behalf of those whom they research and study becomes bound up in complicated political and social processes. Social science practice in Ethiopia must be understood as a site where academic practice, government policy, civil society activism, and the social needs of local communities are brought together and recombined

---

24   See Zeleza 1997, 2002.

in very fraught ways. When social science practitioners work in the Ethiopian field they play a crucial role in framing which local issues, communities and individuals will become dominant. The practice of policy-making becomes, at best, unclear, and at its worst is wrapped up in purposeful bewilderment.

In my reading of the literature of the student movement I discovered that its members in Ethiopia consistently referred to the knowledge they produced as scientific. I take this self-representation at its word, and have little concern with proving whether that appellation is justified or not. Instead, I show how the students' self-understanding of who and what they were became part of the process of creating a wider vocabulary to describe social problems in Ethiopia. I also argue that the secondary social science literature on the Ethiopian revolution mirrors the debates and social questions raised by the student movement, without subjecting the language of the student movement to critique. Consequently, much secondary social science literature also became a battlefield in the revolutionary process. The social sciences in Ethiopia have had a two-fold impact on revolutionary processes in Ethiopia: first, they became a very particular model for interpreting the social problems the student movement aimed to address; and secondly, they produced a body of literature on the Ethiopian revolution that intervened beyond scholarly debate and shaped revolutionary processes as they unfolded. Given this dramatic history, my concern is not to prove whether members of the Ethiopian student movement were good or bad social scientists but to demonstrate how a certain idea of what it means to practice the social sciences shaped the outcomes of revolutionary Ethiopia. I seek to identify how writers and scholars understood themselves to be producing social scientific knowledge. Of course, constitutive of the history of the social sciences are various attempts to establish disciplinary protocols around how we investigate, map and describe social relations and their concomitant social institutions. In particular, positivism has had a particularly long-lasting impact on the way social science is practised in Ethiopia. One of the aims of this book is to think about the political and intellectual impact of this legacy.

In telling the dramatic story of the social sciences in Ethiopia, if I were to situate myself as holding better, more universally ascertainable facts than those who came before me, this would repeat the problems of positivist social science that I want to address. Instead, I propose that to think about the problem of the social sciences in Ethiopia is to search for an alternative method for practising the social sciences in Ethiopia. In this book, the search for that method is primarily explored by setting the critical theory of Marx and the Frankfurt School against the traditions of empiricism and positivism usually associated with mainstream social science practices. Mobilising the critical tradition in this way has allowed me to develop a notion of knowledge production as situated and relative, while also holding on to a notion of social progress as immanent to human activity.

For some readers of Ethiopian history, returning to the Marxist tradition as an alternative to mainstream social science in Ethiopia might seem counterintuitive, since so much of the positivism inherent to the Ethiopian student movement was exercised in the name of Marxist historiography. But my aim is to understand the limitations of the student movement through the very intellectual tools they set out for themselves. If the resources mobilised by the student movement contained certain questions or answers that were glossed over, evaded, or missed during the process of making revolutionary change, this has much to tell us about the limitations internal to that student movement.

3 Fieldwork

Over the past decade I have returned to Addis Ababa to conduct research trips nearly every year. On different occasions I have stayed in the field for periods as long as one year and as short as two months. When I began this project I intended to conduct consultations with public intellectuals and academics who had made a significant contribution to the development of the Ethiopian student movement or Ethiopian social policy. I never intended to use these consultations in this book except as anecdotal evidence, but expected that they would give me a deeper feel for the issues I wished to address. As well, these consultations would help direct me to the kinds of government documents and other literature that I would need to build my case study.

Over time, I did manage to talk with nearly all of the scholars and stakeholders discussed in the pages of this book. However, while many people were willing to talk to me informally, I was reluctant to ask them to do formal interviews. I felt awkward objectifying their answers as evidence leading towards a factual account of my research problematic. The more I had conversations with people, the more I became convinced that the truth of what I was seeking out did not lie in the evidence produced by any one participant in the Ethiopian student movement or any one participant in Ethiopian politics. This taught me that the truth I sought lay in an amalgamation of crisscrossing discourses, policy choices, and even military strategy. It was up to me to erect signposts from the past by returning to the texts produced by the Ethiopian student movement, reading minutes of meetings, listening to the popular songs of the day, etc. All my interview subjects could do was give me hints as to where fragments of those signposts might lie. The work of this book lay in weaving together a narrative from fragmentary archival and oral evidence. Many of my consultations consisted of discussions over lunch or spontaneous conversations in the hallway after a seminar. Some of these were arranged, while others were the result of being in the right place at the right time. All were open-ended, with the aim of allowing me to engage in a process of hypothesis-building rather than hypothesis-testing. By spending extensive time in Ethiopia, in addition to gathering archival data, I was able to exchange and discuss my research with those most affected by it. It is thus not clear where data collection ends and anecdotal evidence begins. After all, I am not a disinterested participant in Ethiopian social life. Members of my extended family have been involved in all aspects of Ethiopian politics and state-building. A lifetime of eavesdropping also forms a large part of the archive that I am digging into. As I discuss in Chapter 1, it might be that this book is closer to the genre of memoir than the traditions of the social sciences.

4   Structure of the Book

This book is organised in two parts. The first section, from Chapter 1 to Chapter 5, is entitled 'Knowledge Production and Social Change in Revolutionary Ethiopia'. The second section is entitled 'Theory as Memoir: The Problem of the Social Sciences in Africa'; this section is a long essay concerned with building a theory of knowledge production for Africa based on the case of the Ethiopian student movement. The chapters in the first section of the book are primarily concerned with discovering the social science concepts and principles that shaped the debates of the Ethiopian student movement. I then link those debates to social policies taken up by the various regimes that followed in the wake of the 1974 revolution and into the post-cold war period after 1991. In these chapters I delve into the historical limits placed on the possibility of critique in Ethiopia by examining the ways in which the social sciences in that country have become a terrain of struggle through which politics is worked out.

I begin Chapter 1 with a bodily experience, a set of memories of personal loss and longing related to growing up in a family where Ethiopian politics was routinely discussed. I show that my experience is not reducible to a set of personal conundrums: it is instead the place where knowledge of the world begins for me. The circuitous paths I cut through the primary documents produced by the Ethiopian student movement, while also engaging debates on the nature of African social sciences, critical theory, and the history of capitalism, capture something of the transformation of personal and social being in revolutionary Ethiopia, and allow me to pose to myself the same questions I found in the literature of the Ethiopian student movement. Answering those questions in turn structures my interpretation of the literature of the student movement and connects Part 1 of this book with Part 2. This is the situated knowledge of an alternative social science practice rooted in an understanding of the body as the site of the sedimentation of multiple social and political histories.

Beginning in Chapter 2 I examine how the secondary social science literature on the Ethiopian revolution has shaped, and is also a product of, political outcomes in revolutionary Ethiopia. Chapter 3 considers the primary documents produced by the Ethiopian student movement of the 1960s and 1970s in order to discuss how the student movement understood its relationship to the social sciences. I focus mostly on reading through *Challenge*, the premier English-language journal of the Ethiopian student movement. I also discuss the impact of the ideas produced by the Ethiopian student movement by examining a number of key policy documents produced by the two regimes that have followed in the wake of the 1974 revolution. I show here how social science discourses filter down and shape political practice; and in Chapter 4 I further discuss the consequences of the student movement on society by showing how the ideas of the Ethiopian student movement were contested during the 2005 federal elections in Ethiopia. Ultimately, what links my inquiry into the 2005 elections with the Ethiopian student movement is the question of what is ideologically reproduced each time we practice the social sciences as a space of universal (and neutral) meaning-making. Chapter 4 links my case study back to the historical relevance of the applied and theoretical social sciences in Ethiopia at a particular moment in time, giving a clearer sense of the social sciences in Africa as a historical and philosophical, epistemological and ontological problem. This discussion continues in Chapter 5 of this book where I look at the ways in which the political contests of 2005 set the tone for how politics has played out in the following decade in Ethiopia (2005–16).

In Part 2 of the book I outline how my research journey led me to investigate the problem of the social sciences and their relation to Eurocentric thought. I trace an unfolding debate within both African studies and post-colonial studies that calls into question the relevance for both Africa and Asia of the applied and the theoretical social sciences. I consider Dipesh Chakrabarty's book *Provincializing Europe* as an exemplary text that brings together many of the threads in the debate about the role of the social sciences in the global south. I have been especially interested in the way Chakrabarty links his critique of the social sciences to the universalisation of capitalist social relations across the globe; therefore, I ask what it means to open up a historical and philosophical discussion about African political and social life that moves beyond a conception of bourgeois freedom as the space through which social science knowledge is produced, rethinking the relationship between critique and the varied historical transitions to capitalism that Africa has undergone.

While Part 2 of this book is primarily concerned with extending my engagement with Ethiopian social sciences into a broader treatment of debates on what the social sciences can and cannot do in Africa, this conversation begins in Chapter 3, where I show that within this debate Partha Chatterjee has linked the limits on social science research in the third world to the larger issue of the limits placed on anti-colonial nationalist thought. In Part 2, I discuss how Mahmood Mamdani has demonstrated that the limits to knowing Africa are linked to forms of governing Africa. Combining the positions of Chatterjee and Mamdani, I suggest that epistemological positions are always tethered to structures of power and forms of being. While the social sciences often pretend to be a trans-historical and universally accessible form of knowledge production, their origin can be linked to the social history of capitalist and colonial development. This universalising conceit of the social sciences then provides the overall epistemological framework for the claims made by both the Ethiopian student movement and Ethiopian civil society advocates in the 2005 elections. Both the Ethiopian student movement and latter-day civil society advocates in Ethiopia are pragmatically committed to a conception of bourgeois freedom that is spelled out as an ideal form of knowledge production.

This book is not a history of the Ethiopian student movement, nor is it an attempt to write a history of the Ethiopian revolution. Instead, I am interested in historicising methods of knowledge production in Ethiopia (and Africa), while simultaneously building my own method that can speak to the historical conundrums of my case study. My review of the literature that critiques the role of the social sciences in Africa is not meant to be exhaustive; rather, it is meant to show that despite this literature we still do not have a method to get at the historical dynamics at play between knowledge production and social practice in revolutionary Ethiopia. I am particularly concerned with the fact that while the social sciences in Ethiopia have been constitutive of the social conflict they attempt to describe they continue to masquerade as a neutral arbiter of social conflict. To think about the problem of the social sciences in Ethiopia must then also be to search for an alternative method for practising the social sciences. Even as I eschew a commitment to a social scientific positivism I try not to fall prey to a method that invites an endless play of meaning. Too much is at stake in the relation between social scientific knowledge production and social practice in revolutionary Ethiopia for such easy relativism.

PART 1

Knowledge Production and Social Change in Ethiopia

⁚

CHAPTER 1

The Children of the Revolution: Toward an Alternative Method

My interest in Ethiopian political life stems from a need developed early in life to understand 'the meeting of force and meaning'[1] in the various popular and academic narratives constructed around the Ethiopian revolution of 1974. If I had an intuition that meaning was always inextricably accompanied by a relation to force, this is because my own childhood experiences were profoundly shaped by the residue of sadness that permeated Ethiopian family life for those who emigrated from the country in the 1970s and 1980s. As I grew up in Canada, Guyana, and Barbados while also travelling between other major metropoles, I found that what framed any meaning I might construct out of being Ethiopian in these various geographies was an intense sense that the émigré adults around me had lost something that none could name explicitly. What bothered me most as a child – although some of this might be an exaggerated memory constructed in retrospect – was that nearly every Ethiopian social event I attended with my parents in the 1980s seemed to end with the burning of myrrh and a replaying of variations on a typical ballad taken from the Amharic songbook entitled Tizita (Memory). This song form, which has probably been re-recorded by every major contemporary Ethiopian singer worth their salt, was exemplified at the time of the revolution by Mahmoud Ahmed's stirring version, recorded one month after the revolution and running nearly 13 minutes. Directly addressing an absent lover and an absent memory, Mahmoud Ahmed's song laments:

> Tinan'tenan t'so, zaren tentereso
> Kenegem teweso, amna'nem adeso
> Yemetal tizita gwazun agbesbeso

> Outdoing yesterday, shouldering on today,
> Borrowing from tomorrow, renewing yesteryears,
> Comes tizita (memory) hauling possessions

---

1   Gordon 2008, p. xv.

Other typical Tizita song lyrics echo similar sentiments, such as:

> Tizita'ye antewneh, tizitam yelebgn
> Tizita'ye antewneh, tizitam yelebgn
> Emetalhu eyalk, eyekereh'ebgn

> My tizita [memory] is you, I don't have tizita [memory]
> My tizita is you, I don't have tizita
> You say you're coming, yet you never do.[2]

Dagmawi Woubshet has written that the word Tizita has three related meanings in Amharic: the first is memory and the act of memory, which some translators also associate with the English word nostalgia; the second meaning refers to a scale or mode of Ethiopian music; and the third meaning, Woubshet tells us, incorporates the first two meanings by referring to the type of song cited above.[3] As musical scale and popular song form, an actual Tizita song has the ability to capture the complex ways in which memory conveys both collective and individual experience; as a mode of music Tizita reminds us that memory always depends on a structuring principle if it is to be communicated and shared with others. At the same time, Tizita is a formal musical style 'which positions lack and longing as the song's spatial and temporal coordinates (lack is "here", longing is "then")'. This implies that the structure of memory can betray the present as much as the lover does, if not more: 'My tizita [memory] is you, I don't have tizita [memory]'. At the same time, as a popular idiom Tizita also shows us that lived memory has a way of usurping formalised styles. Thus, as we saw earlier: 'Outdoing yesterday, shouldering on today, / Borrowing from tomorrow, renewing yesteryears, Comes tizita (memory) hauling possessions'. The very definition of memory in Tizita is what Freud called the uncanny.[4]

---

2 For both of these verses I am relying on a translation of the song in Woubshet 2009. Woubshet points out that 'Amharic thrives on polysemy. Here the possessive *tizita'ye*, *my tizita*, refers to the singer's own melancholy memory, but also to the absent lover, since in Amharic the possessive is an ornament placed around certain nouns – "my" love, beauty, life, memory – to show affection in addressing a beloved. The second clause in the first two lines contains another generic trope – the singer's disavowal of all memory but that of love's loss – which positions lack and longing as the song's spatial and temporal coordinates (lack is "here", longing is "then"). The third line – the absent lover's empty promise of a return – reprises and affirms the longing stated ambiguously at first'.

3 Woubshet 2009, p. 629.

4 Freud defines the uncanny as the class of things which lead us back to the familiar but which had been forgotten by conscious memory: 'Our analysis of instances of the un-canny has led

If Tizita was a popular song form in the post-revolutionary period in Ethiopia this is because it not only conveys a profound sense of lost memories, but worse, it also conveys a sense that through loss of the object of love the very art of memory can also be lost. Not only does the song lament the loss of content, the very polysemy of the word and the song form laments the loss of a structure of feeling. Without the action of love, both form and content have the potential to disappear. In essence, then, Tizita conveys a feeling of time as being out of joint with itself: social life in transition.

> My tizita is you, I don't have tizita
> My tizita is you, I don't have tizita
> You say you're coming, yet you never do.

Thinking back to my childhood dislike of Tizita, what seems to have bothered me most was that the replaying of this melancholic scale felt like a way of adding salt to an open wound. In particular, the replaying of Mahmoud Ahmed's recording, with its insistent rhythm, became for me the embodiment of a communal effort to make knowable what was in fact an invisible presence; at the same time, this plea to make contemporaneous that which belonged to another country also felt like nothing less than an invitation to occult practices: the adults were collectively talking to ghosts. Of course, as a child of émigrés all too aware that the adults around her ought to assimilate into new proper modes of behaviour, I felt ashamed of those who in their weakness seemed to be something other than responsible. Instead, I wanted to cure the adults of their commitment to nostalgia. Even as a child I sought to reconstruct the past that I thought belonged to the adults around me in as forceful and present a way as possible, so that they would feel obliged to let go of their longing for an absent memory. In other words, I felt compelled to sketch notes towards an account of the socially determinative forces of social change, loss and apathy that allowed the adults around me to recognise each other through a structure of feeling that spanned across multiple borders. Here, then, were the childhood seeds of the research practice that has led to this book.

---

us back to the old, animistic conception of the universe, which was characterized by the idea that the world was peopled with the spirits of human beings ... It would seem as though each one of us has been through a phase of individual development corresponding to that animistic stage in primitive men, that none of us has traversed it without preserving certain traces of it which can be re-activated, and that everything which now strikes us as "uncanny" fulfills the condition of stirring those vestiges of animistic mental activity within us and bringing them to expression'. Freud 1955, pp. 217–56.

Ironically, if this account is at all true, I wanted to excavate the past through a living dialogue with what had haunted my childhood as a series of invisible ghosts. Albeit intuitively, I wanted to develop a research practice as an active method to confront what was invisible in my childhood but still shaped it as a bubbling, 'seething presence'.[5] Rather than taking silence and the invisible as a sign that nothing had happened, I ended up treating ghosts as the ineffable fact of something that had yet to be expressed in the certitude of given language.[6] In trying to escape the structure of feeling embodied in Tizita I adopted its methodology – I too longed for an absent memory and struggled to find a form that would allow me to conjure ghosts into a visible entity. Lack is here, longing is then.

In using the term 'structure of feeling' to describe the Tizita form, I harken back to Raymond William's discussion of the term in his book *Marxism and Literature*. His concern for practical consciousness as something different from official consciousness strikes me as relevant to my research practice. Williams writes:

> Social forms are evidently more recognizable when they are articulate and explicit … Many are formed and deliberate, and some are quite fixed. But when they have all been identified they are not a whole inventory even of social consciousness in its simplest sense. For they become social consciousness only when they are lived, actively, in real relationships, and moreover relationships which are more than systematic exchanges between fixed units. Indeed just because all consciousness is social, its processes occur not only between but within the relationship and the related. And this practical consciousness is always more than a handling of fixed forms and units. There's frequent tension between the received interpretation and practical experience. Where this tension can be made direct and explicit, or where some alternative interpretation is available, we are still within a dimension of relatively fixed forms. But this tension is as often an unease, a stress, a displacement, a latency: the moment of conscious comparison not yet come, often not even coming … There are the experiences to which the fixed forms do not speak at all, which indeed they do not recognize.[7]

---

5   Gordon 2008, p. 17.
6   To describe this experience of language I take my cue from Gordon, who writes: 'The ghost, as I understand it, is not the invisible or some ineffable excess. The whole essence … of a ghost is that it has a real presence and demands its due'. Gordon 2008, p. xvi.
7   Williams 1977, p. 130.

For Williams, what is called the social is usually made recognisable by subsuming the everyday flow of life into formal concepts and structures that belong to the past. A structure of feeling, on the other hand, is less than an ideology or an established worldview; instead it attempts to show how emergent forms of life are part of social processes that cannot be fixed. Articulating something as a structure of feeling shows how affective elements of experience are a part of social relationships.[8] Here the vernacular and the mundane are no longer reduced to the personal, nor are they seen as the secondary outcome of larger historical processes. At the methodological level, a 'structure of feeling' requires the critical analyst to recognise elements in the world that connect practical life with institutional forces that are in turn shaped by the everyday 'in a living and inter-relating continuity'.[9] This, it seems to me, is the temporal space of what I want to call the methodology of Tizita: longing and loss, social life in transition. Tizita, for me, became a way to convey the apprehension of a social experience that was neither a mere personal experience nor some epiphenomena, but at the same time could not be named in the usual ways since its telos remained an open question.[10] It would then become the method through which I could finally move beyond the empiricism and positivism that has come to dominate so much of Ethiopian studies.

1   I Don't Have Tizita

The Tizita method came to me affectively long before I could theorise it. In my attempt to understand what it is, I have been helped by the approach of other scholars interested in the archives of revolt, loss, and failure. In the following section I discuss a number of these authors in order to begin to delineate how Tizita became an alternative method that guided my research practice throughout the writing of this book, in contrast to mainstream Ethiopian and African studies.

In *Conscripts of Modernity*, David Scott proposes that historical criticism always exists within a problem-space delineated by a horizon of struggle in the present. For Scott, the past is always strategically constructed as a usable memory for those with the power to control the manner in which stories are told. He argues that there are moments of social transition where the telos

---

8   Williams 1977, p. 132.
9   Ibid.
10   Williams 1977, p. 31.

of time can suddenly appear to be out of joint with itself precisely because 'the old languages of moral-political vision and hope are no longer in sync with the world they were meant to describe'.[11] The synchronic unfolding of events becomes less transparent, resulting in the loss of hope for 'an acceptable future'.[12] Such moments are also tragic, as they highlight the ways in which the human being is always vulnerable to forces outside of rational control.[13] For Scott, tragedy often becomes a popular and necessary mode of expression during times of great historical upheaval because at its best it aims to capture the contradiction of differing social forces that individuals in a historical moment come to embody.[14] Tragedy is a form of historical criticism that can be contrasted with romance, since this latter form either seeks to posit past choices as an inevitable step toward our present moment, or makes the present become a vindication of past hardships. In contrast, tragedy allows us to take a measure of the past through the discontent of the present, as it shows that although vindication might be strived for, it is chancy, it might fail.[15] The discontent of the present as such becomes visible because the present is shown to have been produced by someone else's future hope. Past, present and future have, for Scott, their own specificity, rather than being moments of inevitability.

The story of the self-emancipation of slaves in eighteenth-century Haiti, as written by C.L.R. James in the second edition of *The Black Jacobins*, is for Scott an example of a great work of tragedy. James mobilises a memory of resistance to racist rule to show us that history is a contradictory process, framed by a set of over-arching structures and an open-ended telos that can diverge from intentions. Even if Toussaint L'Ouverture can heroically construct a problem-space in which to act, he is at the same time unable to calculate for all the contingencies set out before him. In the end, Toussaint is overwhelmed by an irreconcilable set of social forces such that, whatever choices he makes, he is doomed to failure – a matter both of personal failure and the fact that Toussaint was conscripted to a set of circumstances that cannot be controlled by a voluntaristic willing. After all, 'men make history but not in circumstances of their choosing'. Knowing this, Scott argues that James's 1963 narrative is written out of fidelity to James's own present, so that in seeking to reconstruct the frame-

---

11   Scott 2004, p. 2.
12   Scott 2004, p. 210. The idea of 'the loss of an acceptable future' has been lifted by Scott
      from Raymond William's work on modern tragedy. See Williams 1979.
13   Scott 2004, p. 13.
14   Scott 2004, p. 166.
15   Scott 2004, p. 15.

works that compelled Toussaint into both action and failure James draws out the ways in which Toussaint is indeed a conscript of his own historical period. Thus, for Scott, James's emplotment of the tragic hero posits Toussaint's future as our past:

> not as a path towards necessary vindication but as a way to measure the difference between then and now including the difference in our frameworks of memory. In turn this allows 'a horizon for what was at stake [in our present moment] to come into view'.[16]

For Scott, C.L.R. James's writing style is instructive for the offspring of the post-colonial state because his tragic voice had the creative courage to write from the position of present discontent.[17] On the other hand, the problem of post-colonial theory as it exists today is the common assumption that the questions posed about our post-colonial present share the same problem-space as the anti-colonial movements that fought to create the post-colonial state in the first place. Scott then is at pains to show that the post-colonial state is the end result of the determination to answer questions posed during the anti-colonial struggle. He writes: 'The view I wish to commend is that it is not the anti-colonial nationalist's answers that have needed changing so much as the post-colonial theorist's questions that need dissolving'.[18] In conflating anti-colonial answers with post-colonial questions we remain blind to the structures of feeling that make our present moment what it is. More importantly, we remain blind to the call to find new questions and new answers that are rooted in our present.

Scott's focus on the relation between artifice and contrivance as the generative space through which memory is mobilised is not without its problems, however. He creates a sharp separation between past, present and future, limiting our access to the past as a mere recourse to possible generative statements within a discourse. Memory as such becomes mere rocks piled up by the discursive forces of the day. In an article called 'Archaeologies of Black Memory', written as an introduction to an issue of the journal *Small Axe*, Scott is quite dismissive of the turn to the study of memory and haunting that dominated the humanities in the late twentieth century. Scott sees this work as romantic, conservative and ideological, since for him it asserts individual memory as a

---

16   Scott 2004, p. 4.
17   Scott 2004, p. 22.
18   Scott 2004, p. 6.

privileged 'lieu de memoire', different from social memory. For Scott, this kind of work is methodologically anti-archaeological.[19]

But what if, as Avery Gordon asserts, haunting is social? It seems to me that if we are all conscripts of the structuring antagonisms that constitute modernity – white vs. Black, exchange value vs. use value, free labour vs. bonded labour, etc. – it must also be the case that these antagonisms do not lodge themselves in the body as 'a mere sequence of instantaneous experiences which leave no trace'.[20] Rather, they also lodge themselves as a series of cracks in sedimented barriers. The body is a heritage that reaches out beyond itself. As Gordon argues, the legacy of unresolved social violence is also one that struggles to make itself known even as it is repressed – *borrowing from tomorrow, renewing yesteryears, comes tizita (memory) hauling possessions*. In this sense, then, past and present overlap in unexpected ways so that the key to understanding both submerged and emerging structures of feeling is to remain attuned to the cracks in the sequence of power's appropriation of our bodies. Thus, I want to take what Paul Gilroy in a different context has called an anti-anti-essentialist position with regards to the specificity of the structuring antagonism of modernity.[21] I remain committed to a notion that, in some sense, modernity posits a 'changing-same' in relation to the dynamics of race and class that are yet to be overcome.[22] If we are all conscripts of modernity then we must share some of the same conditions of living as the generations that came before us.

Scott's primary concern in *Conscripts of Modernity* is producing new hope by historicising old hopes, but he also shows that this endeavour is necessarily linked to a concern about narrative form. Scott asks what forms of remembering close down the possibility of remaking a usable past for the present. I, too, am concerned with how different narrative forms shape a relation to past, present and future, and following Scott I want to move away from romantic narratives that desire to vindicate the present through a return to a golden moment in the past. Instead, I stay within the key of tragedy, acknowledging that even if the colonial subject was forcefully conscripted to modernity, there is still no necessarily transparent end goal that could reverse that tragic moment. In this vein, I contend that the ghosts of the past I seek to play with are not the same as the ones that faced the generation of Ethiopians who were both producers and direct victims of the 1974 revolution. In order to make this distinction, I seek to temporalise the answers that were offered in response to Haile-Selassie's

19   Scott 2008, p. ix.
20   Gordon 2007, p. 20.
21   For a discussion of this term see especially the Preface in Gilroy 2000.
22   Ibid.

regime by asking what horizon is at stake in revisiting the story of the Ethiopian revolution more than forty years later. I posit the Ethiopian revolution as the creative product of a group of people who were able to mobilise the past and so construct a problem-space that posed questions in a particular direction. As Scott suggests, this means recognising that the beginning of my longing starts where a previous generation set up answers. I have not lost the lovers that my parents lost, even if we contend with many of the same structuring antagonisms.

But how do other children of the revolution remember this turbulent time in Ethiopian history, and what is at stake for them when they recall the revolution? Although the Soviet-style military junta (the Derg) that governed Ethiopia from 1974 until 1991 dominated the representation of the revolution during its period of rule, its own self-generated narrative of the revolution has become a ruined and submerged narrative.[23] Today in Addis Ababa one can visit the Red Terror Martyrs Museum and mourn the victims of the Derg regime (many of whom are former members of the EPRP) without much context for thinking about the revolution as a broader social and military process.[24] Yet the interviews I conducted for my MA thesis (which looked at memories of transition in post-cold war Addis Ababa) confirmed that even as the Derg has become part of a submerged narrative in the country it once ruled, it forms one thread in a tapestry of stories about a revolution that is made up of many other narrative threads that share crisscrossing transnational affinities. In thinking about the stories people tell about the revolution I find myself less interested in how we might distinguish each story from the others, however important that might be, than in how we can understand the present as the shared aftermath of intertwining and intersecting narrative threads. In so doing we can contrast our present – the tapestry of the past – with the conditions of its cultural transmission. To put it another way, we can open up homogenous empty time to the heterogeneous possibilities that might be resurrected in each tiny layer of history that makes our present: spatialising history.[25] Three dominant narrative threads that I have

---

23   For a fuller description of this see Zeleke 2010.
24   The EPRP is that branch of the student movement that was crushed and defeated when the Derg military took power in 1974.
25   The idea of spatialising history first came to me through David McNally's reading of Walter Benjamin's work on German tragic drama. McNally argues that Benjamin strove to develop a method to de-mythologise historical experience with its movement towards an inevitable telos by transforming distinct temporal moments into a stage where the fragments of experience can show our inherent alienation from ourselves and nature. The aim here is to bring history to a standstill so that we can reclaim it as our own: 'The rubble of our historical experience – the petrified objects, the smashed and broken things, the

picked up on while reading through, viewing, and listening to representations of the Ethiopian revolution frame my work; these make up the tapestry of stories people tell about the revolution. Together they show what is at stake in connecting historical hauntings to the question of knowledge production.

The first thread emerges from the writings of former members or supporters of the Ethiopian student movement. These include Gebru Tareke, John Markakis, Kiflu Tadesse, Andreas Eshete and Hiwot Teferra, important intellectuals of the revolution who were living in Ethiopia prior to 1974, went into exile soon after, and returned either to live or to visit Ethiopia in the post-1991 period.[26] Some, including John Markakis and Andreas Eshete, have also actively participated in the affairs of the current EPRDF government in the post-Derg era. All of these writers and thinkers share an ambivalence towards the social meaning of revolutionary violence, and all view the fall of feudalism as ushering in a socially progressive transformation, even as they attempt to bear witness to the brutality of the military regime (the Derg). This ambivalence has parallels with the sentiments expressed towards the Derg regime in documents produced by the current ruling party, the EPRDF, whose founding roots lie in the rural insurgency against Soviet-style socialism that some of the students built in the period after 1974. In turn, one can trace the ambivalence of the EPRDF towards revolutionary violence to their need to both celebrate their own conditions of possibility – which lie in the break with the feudal regime of Haile-Selassie – and to separate themselves from the military regime that ruled Ethiopia from 1974–91.

The second narrative thread typifies the work of the first generation of cultural producers, who were young adults at the time of the 1974 revolution. Some of them were tangential participants in the student movement and its political

---

piles of corpses – still speak a mute language of broken hopes'. See McNally 2001, p. 176. Benjamin himself wrote in Thesis 14 of his 'Theses on the Philosophy of History': 'History is the subject of a structure whose site is not homogenous, empty time, but time filled by the presence of the now. Thus, to Robespierre ancient Rome was a past charged with the time of the now which he blasted out of the continuum of history. The French Revolution viewed itself as Rome incarnate. It evoked ancient Rome the way fashion evokes costumes of the past. Fashion has a flair for the topical, no matter where it stirs in the thickets of long ago; it is a tiger's leap into the past. This jump, however, takes place in an arena where the ruling class give the commands. The same leap in the open air of history is the dialectical one, which is how Marx understood the revolution'. Benjamin 1968, p. 261.

26 On Andreas Eshete's role within the ESM, see Woubshet 2010. Although not Ethiopian, John Markakis has always been a partisan supporter of the EPRP. See Markakis and Ayele 1977; Markakis 1981. On Kifle Tadesse, see note 5 above. Hiwot Teffera was a former participant in the EPRP, and recently published a memoir of her experience of the revolution in Teferra 2012.

parties, but now produce work from a standpoint of reflection rather than as participants in an organisation. Here I am thinking of writers such as Paulus Milkias and Messay Kebede,[27] who have written critical histories of the student movement, and film-makers such as Salem Mukria and Haile Garima, who have made critical film works about the revolution.[28]

Despite the ideological or philosophical differences these cultural producers might claim, they share a tendency to see the revolution as rooted in the street demonstrations organised by the Ethiopian student movement in the early 70s, while also positing it as having corrupted the students' innocence by taking a demand for reform and turning it into a total demand for regime change. These writers, thinkers, and film-makers picture the students as a newly formed modernising elite, who lived a fairly sheltered middle-class existence in Addis Ababa but were moved to a call for justice as they matured into an awareness of the poverty that existed in the rural areas of the country. They understand the students' quest for justice as right-minded though naïve, and this naïveté is often conflated with the innocence of a country on the brink of modernisation. The students' lack of sophistication is understood as a double failure on their part to take up their rightful vocation as a modernising elite. They are blamed for their inability to use their education for the purpose of offering a practical programme of economic and social modernisation, while at the same time this lack is seen to be at the root of the country's vulnerability to the military junta that took over after the initial student-led revolt of 1974. Consequently, in this narrative, the schools that were founded through the modernising foresight of Haile-Selassie and fostered student excellence are seen as the paradoxical foundation of all that brought his regime to an end. This amounts to framing the revolution as the product of the folly of youth, unable to make meaning out of their own demands and instead unleashing a torrent of unexplainable violence, senseless loss of life, civil war and rising ethnic tensions, pitting families and friends against one another.

The third narrative thread sees the events of 1974 as a catastrophic break from the tradition of indigenous Christian rule that is said to have dominated social life in the Abyssinian highlands since the 4th century AD. This thread permeates a diverse array of writers, social movements and artistic forms,

---

27   Milkias 2006; Kebede 2008.
28   Both filmmakers have made critically acclaimed films about the revolution. Selam
      Mekuria's film *Ye Wonz Maibel: Deluge* (1997) is a personal investigation of family tragedy
      amidst revolutionary change, while Haile Gerima's two films on the revolution, *Imperfect
      Journey* (1994) and *Teza* (2008), both pose the question of unspeakable violence as the
      aftermath of revolutionary change.

including the relatively well-known cultural productions of the Rastafarian movement who revere Haile-Selassie as the leader of an independent African country; it is also the story told by former members of Haile-Selassie's regime. For the Rastas, chronicling ancient African traditions enables the construction of a usable past for the revolutionary goal of overcoming white-supremacist rule in the New World. Paradoxically, however, the goal of black vindication is married to the celebration of a feudal social structure. Thus, despite the goals of total social revolution shared by the EPRDF and the Rasta movement, the meeting of these two social movements can only be framed by what Brent Hayes Edwards describes as 'decalage': that generative gap in time and space that so often frames the meeting of different sections of the African Diaspora.[29] Indeed, the sentiments of the Rasta movement have had their uses for former members of Haile-Selassie's regime, some of whom organised a pro-monarchy political party under the banner of the Ethiopian Democratic Union, which receives accolades from many sections of the African diaspora.[30]

A new generation of cultural producers born in Ethiopia during the early days of the revolution, but now mostly working in the US, Canada, and other popular destinations for émigrés, are beginning to fold the second and the last narrative into one, so that the Pan-Africanism of Haile-Selassie becomes a way to bemoan the gap between present mores and lost meanings. In the lead-up to the tumultuous 2005 federal elections in Ethiopia, a number of US-diaspora-based websites and blogs shaped their condemnation of the current Ethiopian regime through a strange mix of pan-African pride and a longing for the Ethiopia embodied in persons such as Haile-Selassie.[31] Two recent novels that reflect this new trend in diaspora writing that speaks back to the home country are Maaza Mengiste's *Beneath the Lion's Gaze* and Dinaw Mengestu's novel *How to Read the Air*.[32]

---

29 Brent Hayes Edwards' book *The Practice of Diaspora* makes a point of showing that diaspora discourses are constituted through 'necessary misrecognitions', a term he borrows from Kenneth Warren's work on African American literature, so that attempts at creating an early twentieth-century black international must be viewed as necessarily skewed by the various boundaries that the international is attempting to overcome. The point for Edwards is that national boundaries become the archive, or 'generative space', that shape what can or cannot be said about black culture even as attempts at transcending national boundaries are made (Edwards 2003, p. 7).

30 MacLeod 2014.

31 The following blogs represent a cross section of popular debates on the 2005 Ethiopian election. See: Weichqugud http://weichegud.blogspot.com/, Ethio-Zagol: The State of Ethiopia, http://seminawork.blogspot.com/, Ethiopundit, http://ethiopundit.blogspot.com, Enset: http://www.enset.org and Ethiomedia, http://ethiomedia.com.

32 Mengiste 2010; Mengestu 2011.

THE CHILDREN OF THE REVOLUTION: TOWARD AN ALTERNATIVE METHOD   31

A reading of these two novels will provide an example of how the present understanding of the Ethiopian revolution is a tapestry of narrative threads. These novels' treatment of history involve historical, political, social, and epistemological questions that will concern us throughout this book. Through them, we can discern the ghosts that haunt the shared conditions of life for those of us who are the children of the revolution.

Maaza Mengiste's novel *Beneath the Lion's Gaze* maps fact onto fiction by recounting the events of the 1974 revolution through the eyes of Dawit, a young history student who attends Haile-Selassie I University and is moved by a visceral sense of injustice to protest the feudal land tenure system that had dominated the country. Through Dawit, Maaza is able to give her readers a chronological, nearly documentary-style account of the 1974 revolution, and to recount the events that eventually forced her to leave the country. In contrast, Dinaw Mengestu's *How to Read the Air* is less bold in its attempt to tell the truth about the revolution. Instead, Dinaw takes up the plight of the Ethiopian émigré whose failure to assimilate into the US is attributed to the violence he experienced before arriving in America. The past, for Dinaw's characters, is always the site of a recurring trauma; Ethiopian subjectivity is imagined as a shattered whole unable to repair itself in a new context. Despite differences in style, both Maaza and Dinaw deal with the Ethiopian revolution as the twin story of a break from the past and an initiation into senseless violence. Both authors frame pre-revolutionary Ethiopia as a stand-in for a pre-modern Ethiopia untarnished by the fragmentary violence of modernity. Maaza's novel then offers her characters redemption by reasserting the existence of 3,000 years of courage and dignity in the body of Ethiopians, saying 'the body has to move when the heart doesn't think it can'.[33]

Beneath the Lion's Gaze begins by following Dawit as he grows from a naïve student into a full-blown guerrilla fighter, mapping his personal growth onto the chronology of events that led to revolutionary change. We follow Dawit from the time of the student demonstrations to the overthrow of Haile-Selassie's regime, the installation of the Marxist junta, and the summoning of a civil war against the junta by the Ethiopian People's Revolutionary Party (EPRP). Early in the novel Dawit is pictured as a handsome young man who sports an American-style Afro, bell-bottoms and a liberated girlfriend. Rather than being influenced by socialist ideology (which in this novel is entirely associated with the USSR and Cuba), it is suggested that what Dawit really craves is American-style liberty. His radicalism is seen as the consequence of a modern,

---

33   Mengiste 2010, p. 10.
33   Mengiste 2010, p. 10.

rational and well-educated background; he is the son of a doctor who was himself trained through a scholarship offered by Haile-Selassie. In the end, Dawit comes to understand the folly and authoritarianism behind the revolutionary regime, and, coming to his senses, becomes an active member of a rebel group committed to challenging the military's rule.

This group, called the Patriotic Lions in Maaza's novel, closely resembles the Ethiopian People's Revolutionary Party (the EPRP), who waged urban guerrilla warfare against the post-1974 regime known as the Derg. However, the association of Dawit's group with the name Lions also draws other parallels: with Haile-Selassie's pet lions, which play a prominent role in the book as augurs of a lost bravery, and the Black Lions, an Ethiopian anti-colonial guerrilla force that fought during the Italian occupation from 1935–41. The overlapping associations of the word lion allow the reader to connect post-revolutionary Ethiopia with an image of lost bravery and lost sovereignty. In this way, Maaza instructs her readers to feel empathy for Dawit while at the same time limiting identification with the social movements he belongs to.

What is mourned here is the loss of a 3,000-year-old telos; what is emphasised is the fragile afterlife of a vanishing bravery. Transformed into memory, the Revolution and the resistance to it lose their specificity and become dissolved into myth; its ghosts become mere avatars of a generalised loss. Historical difference is reduced to a homogeneity that does not befit its tragic core. Maaza Mengiste has constructed what David Scott would call a romantic novel: the present is vindicated through a return to a golden moment in the past.

On the other hand, Dinaw Mengestu's *How to Read the Air* is explicitly aware of its own intervention in history. It begins from the premise that '[R]egardless, history sometimes deserves a little revision, if not for the sake of the dead then at least for ourselves'.[34] Yet the novel ultimately eschews this notion in order to show how personal relationships and history persist in each other's bodies in complicated ways. For Dinaw the loss of homeland is irreparable; he offers instead the persistence of personal intimacy as a shelter and source of recovery from social evils. We might say that Dinaw's novel offers the kind of conservative 'lieu de memoire' that Scott warned us against; despite this, in the novel the invention of history as imagined narrative becomes the space of social healing.

How to Read the Air is the story of three intersecting journeys. First, the protagonist Jonas recounts his Ethiopian émigré parents' drive across the American mid-west soon after his mother's arrival in America. Jonas conjectures that his father intended the trip to be a kind of honeymoon that would reconsti-

---

34   Mengestu 2011, p. 69.

tute marital love in new surroundings, but for Jonas the journey's true meaning is that America exacerbates trauma by insisting on the 'ability to unwind whatever ties supposedly bind you to the past and to invent new ones as you went along'.[35] Trauma is repeated in unexpected ways, precisely because, in the attempt to make a new life, America fosters estrangement between people who were otherwise quite intimate.

As readers we are never sure whether Jonas's parents actually took the trip he describes. But Jonas reconstructs the trip by travelling along the same route he imagined his parents took thirty years before as a way to create signposts in the land that was the condition of possibility for the breakdown of their marriage. By inventing an archive of his parents' relationship Jonas is able to conjure the forces of the past that continue to persist in him. Through imagining a past for himself and his parents, Jonas posits a past that, whether or not it happened, is most certainly true for him.

If Jonas's parents are unable to connect with each other in America, Jonas suggests that this is because his father's journey to America broke him in ways that, for Jonas, become the absent figure of all of his relationships in America. The third journey that dominates *How to Read the Air* is Jonas's father's journey out of Ethiopia, through Sudan and eventually to America; this time, the story is told through prompting from Jonas's students at a small private school in New York City, where he teaches English. Jonas begins to tell his father's story because his students are curious about his blackness. He believes that his father's story will give them access to something both real and exotic. While the story Jonas tells seems plausible at first, it becomes clear that he exaggerates its plot lines in an attempt to hold his students' attention, meeting their expectations of what an exotic African story might sound like – tales of cruelty and arbitrary violence. At the same time, Jonas needs to exaggerate and invent this story in order to create a memory of what his father might have gone through, and in so doing give a context to the domestic violence that his father wreaked on Jonas and his mother during their journey in America.

As readers, we become invested in these invented, possibly false narratives. But, as with the students' expectations of Jonas, offering readers a series of false stories raises the question of what kind of expectations we bring to our reading of Dinaw's novel. It also makes clear that while narrative is always a matter of invention, it can also function as a tool for both deception and truth-seeking. Speaking of his job working with refugees, Jonas says: 'if I didn't know for certain when they (the refugees) entered, I assigned them the narrative that

35   Mengestu 2011, p. 98.

I thought they deserved'.[36] Jonas uses his gift of story-telling to render the lived experiences of the refugees into something legible and understandable. He says that this is really what it means to pull off 'narrative effect': 'I quickly discovered as well that what could not be researched could just as easily be invented based on common assumptions that most of us shared when it came to the poor and distant, foreign countries'.[37] Narrative effect allows Jonas to both find a way to connect to people and avoid conflict through meeting people's expectations of the stories he should tell. But this only lasts for so long. Eventually his stories come to be seen as implausible, and the violence he has repressed through narrative effect bubbles up as a seething presence. Dinaw shows that the need to repress this bubbling presence compels the protagonist of his novel to tell more stories, over and over again. This is the paradox of narrative for Dinaw Mengestu: it is both a lie and an avenue towards freedom.

Despite trying to control his own story, narration escapes Dinaw Mengestu's protagonist. At the beginning of the novel the quest for some kind of ability to narrate the past combines with the American 'ability to unwind whatever ties supposedly bind you to the past'. Jonas is constantly changing the stories around the circumstances of his life so as to learn how to live in the world – carrying off narrative effect. But this only makes him a liar, more concerned with how to live up to the expectations of his listeners than learning how to stay true to his own story of what persists in him. The process of telling stories can never really help contain the violence repressed within Jonas. That violence eventually erupts through the uncanny dissolution of whatever connections he might have made with people. Jonas is unable to sustain relationships. In the novel Jonas loses everything: friends, family, lovers, and any kind of human interaction are undermined.

If Jonas feels compelled to reconstruct his parents' journey by traversing the ground that made them possible, this is because it allows him to conjure the unnameable ghosts that haunt him as a force-field in which the past, and its transmission over time, play themselves out. In the end, Jonas and the reader both must allow lack and longing to confront each other so that the present mode of existence can no longer be a part of natural history (an inescapable given): narrative effect dissolves and the present becomes an object with ethical prescience. Reaching the conclusion of the novel, we are invested as readers in a confrontation with ghosts; more importantly, we become invested in the task of writing around a present absence without effacing absence itself. We

---

36   Mengestu 2011, p. 23.
37   Mengestu 2011, p. 24.

are guided in this when Jonas tells us that the domestic violence in his house was not just about fighting over sugar or misplaced materials but was actually a fight about 'the right to exist, to live and breathe god's clean air'.[38] Each fight brought about a ghostly visitation. Jonas says: 'ghosts are common to the life of any child: mine just happen to come to dinner more often than most'.[39] It is only after discovering the ethical presence of ghostly absence that Dinaw Mengestu's protagonist can live a life beyond narrative effect. Before then, he has an amoral but compulsive relationship to story-telling.

In the end we come to see that Jonas's compulsion for story-telling has always been about trying to narrate absence, to narrate ghosts; while this requires imagination, Dinaw also suggests that there is both an honest and a dishonest way to confront a ghost. One way further invisibilises the ghost while the other makes a seething presence knowable; the search for a method to make a seething presence knowable is the book's central theme. Jonas needs to confront ghosts, but in trying to do so he always ends up deceiving himself and those around him by telling stories, compulsively repeating the damage of the past rather than resolving it.

It seems that Dinaw Mengestu is trying to tell us that this is what traumatised people do. We see this in particular with Angela, the girlfriend of the protagonist, who is an African-American woman from a poor background and a victim of sexual assault. She also has a tendency to tell stories that are not quite true and that change from time to time.[40] Angela has trouble keeping track of her own story, but in trying to love her the protagonist does not judge her for lying. Instead he says, 'I tried to detect a pattern in the stories, one that would say more about who Angela was and what she had gone through, but obfuscation was too great, all I could see were her hints of an injury that she had yet to let go of'.[41] This is instructive for reading Jonas's compulsive lying/story-telling, suggesting how both the reader and Jonas can develop an ethical relationship to story-telling. The air that the novel's title instructs us to read is the air that vibrates and becomes suddenly charged between two people preceding an unforeseen violent act.[42] Obsessed with reading the air for auguries, Jonas fails to see what already bears down on him as a bond. To tell a lie in the process of story-telling is to be like Jonas and to step outside oneself in order to be fully at

---

38   Mengestu 2011, p. 9.
39   Ibid.
40   Mengestu 2011, p. 48.
41   Mengestu 2011, p. 47.
42   Mengestu 2011, p. 66.

ease with narrative effect and the repression of a seething presence.[43] Truth-telling, on the other hand, knows that if the body has its own language this is because limbs and lungs are also a repository for events long forgotten by conscious memory. Peel away the walls of the body and you are bound to remove the placeholders that keep the past from spilling out towards you. Yet the walls of the body are not mere ethical relationships, as the novel proposes, but political and economic structures. The force-field of the body is the sedimentation of world-historical conflict. By rubbing the time of longing against the lack that is here we create a counter-history capable of de-naturalising the air that we breathe. This is the work of the children of the revolution. This is our search for a method to re-read the meaning of the 1974 revolution and its aftermath.

Once I had completed the majority of writing for this book, it struck me that not only had I employed the methodology of Tizita to listen to 'memories that were hauling possessions', but so had Jonas. In a strange way, I had modelled this book after *How to Read the Air*. As the narrator of this book, I am also Jonas, erecting possible signposts to help me in my interpretation of the past, but my discussion of the limits of Jonas's engagements with ghosts also teaches us how to read my book beyond simply writing the kind of 'useful past' David Scott describes. Indeed, because I am somewhat weary of a notion of a 'useful past' and instead favour thinking about 'seething presents', I offer no easy punch lines. Instead, I take seriously Walter Benjamin's idea that the future is a bit like a medusa – we cannot have an open future if we try to stare into it. It is better to spatialise history: explode the sediments (or here, the tapestry) of the past.

It is an odd habit of thought to want to read the present or the past from the point of view of the future, a job best left to fortune-tellers and peddlers of false hope. For the social scientist, fortune-telling comes easily, since we have all become used to modelling the future as path-dependent. In our day-to-day existence psychoanalysis teaches us that there is another way to confront the drudgery of the present. The task is not to predict the future based on an experience of the past, but to re-open the future through confronting in theory and practice the unresolved contradictions of the past as it shapes the present. The appearance of the linear continuum of the past into our present and our future can only be assured by force. How else can power guarantee the passivity of human agents in the face of historical contingencies? But passivity is also the neurotic's attitude to the past, stuck in the process of repetition compulsion. The work of the analyst is not to write history from the point of view of force,

---

43   Mengestu 2011, p. 97.

but to find those moments where the transition of the past into the present is a false resolution of social contradiction. Theory as memoir – how the dust settles is not exactly predetermined.

The method of Tizita operates at multiple valances. It poses the question of what it means to live today by pointing out how the present is structured by an inheritance from the past, and yet that present is always experienced as an ambivalent tension created by the possible loss of a structure of feeling and the emergence of new modes for making memory possible. This book is attentive to all three of these valances as the author's own but also as an alternative approach to reading against the grain of the present. It allows me to think structure, inheritance, the loss of inheritance, the loss of memory and renewal – *borrowing from tomorrow, renewing yesteryears, comes tizita (memory) hauling possessions.*

CHAPTER 2

Social Science Is a Battlefield: Rethinking the Historiography of the Ethiopian Revolution

In his essay 'Battling with the Past', Alessandro Triulzi examines how historiographical trends that originated in western scientific institutions have come to dominate the writing of the Ethiopian past.[1] In particular, Triulzi attempts to capture the origins and consequences of using the disciplinary tools of 'modern history' to frame historical narratives about Ethiopia. He observes that the first wave of modern historical studies about Ethiopia coincided with the growth of nationalist conviction and the intensification of state-building projects within both Africa and Ethiopia. Methodologically, this meant that twentieth-century histories of Ethiopia often followed a pattern of combining readings of European archival documents with readings of documents from the Ethiopian Orthodox church, Ethiopian royal chronicles, and Ethiopian land grants (often recorded by the church). Given that the Ethiopian documents were usually written in Ge'ez or Amharic, the centrality and exceptionalism of Ethiopia's literary traditions were foregrounded. Since Ethiopian literacy itself was associated with the Amharic- and Tigrinya-speaking regions of what is also called Abyssinia, this inevitably meant that modern historical studies on Ethiopia were concerned with extolling the centralising power of the states associated with the Amharic-speaking regions of Ethiopia at the cost of marginalising the stories of non-Christian, non-highland, non-literate, and non-cultivating groups that exist within the current boundaries of Ethiopia.

Many of the historians associated with the initial establishment of this state-centred historiographical style were trained at the School of Oriental and African Studies (SOAS) under the auspices of Roland Oliver, one of the foremost figures in shaping twentieth-century African studies. In particular, many of the first Ethiopian scholars to write in the style of modern academic history, and who were later housed in the History Department at Haile-Selassie I University College (later Addis Ababa University), were trained under Roland Oliver.[2] These include well-known persons such as Tadesse Tamrat, who in 1972

---

1 Triulzi 2002.
2 Triulzi 2002.

published *Church and State in Ethiopia*; Merid Wolde Aregay, who throughout the 1970s and 1980s wrote extensively about medieval Christian Ethiopia; Bahru Zewde, who has made significant contributions to our understanding of twentieth-century Ethiopian history; and Mohammed Hassan, who was one of the first persons to write a 'professional' history of the Oromos – a numerically large but socially marginalised ethnic group in Ethiopia. Hassan's book, *The Oromo of Ethiopia: A History 1570–1860*, is often understood as having started a new trend towards examining the history of non-Abyssinian Ethiopians. But Triulzi counters this claim by stating that it is in fact the literature produced by the Ethiopian student movement that marks the first major break from Abyssinian state-centred histories, even while using the tools and methods of modern historical studies. Astutely, Triulzi observes:

> The student movement readily acknowledged the inequalities between the different regional and ethnic components of the [Ethiopian] Empire, but after a heated and divisive debate consigned the national question to revolutionary change and regional autonomy to be achieved within the reformed State of the future.[3]

This implies that historiography and political practice have been explicitly connected since the 1960s in Ethiopia. Of course, all history is written from the perspective of the ethnographic present, but the concern is that in Ethiopia present modes of expressing ethnic or national identity are often read back into the historical past as primordial and unchanging. Scholarly interventions in relation to any given primordial identity are thus encouraged, and then read as decisive action in the contemporary political field, a pattern that can be read back into the founding moment of modern Ethiopian Studies and its association with the central state apparatus. Ethiopian historiography, then, is meant to decide not only who the losers, winners, and heroes of the past are, but also the losers, winners and heroes of the future. Historiography becomes interest-driven in an extremely instrumental fashion.[4] A publicly committed history

---

3   Triulzi 2002, p. 278.

4   In *Peasants and Nationalism in Eritrea: A Critique of Ethiopian Studies*, Jordan Gebre-Medhin attributes the 'idealized reading of Ethiopia as an ancient empire unified by the existence of a great cultural tradition' to the work of the social anthropologist Donald Levine. The School for Oriental and African Studies is certainly not the only source that has helped foster the Orientalist approach to Ethiopian Studies, but this should not distract us from Triulzi's wider point, that the Orientalist approach can be tied to a wider state-building project in Ethiopia. Levine's work has been profoundly influential in Ethiopia Studies and he himself has not shied away from using his work to intervene in public policy debates. Indeed, after the 2005 elec-

instrumentalised to perform a specific political duty turns out to be equally as problematic as the supposedly academically-driven Orientalist histories of the mid-twentieth century. Triulzi puts it this way:

> [T]he reading of the past in Ethiopia appears to be coercively linked to the different expectations each group is advancing for its own imagined self in the country's future.[5]

An outcome of this dynamic is that historiography on Ethiopia has been strongly shaped through a centre/periphery paradigm that posits the Amhara region of Ethiopia as the country's centre, while all the other societies and communities that were included within the boundaries of Ethiopia in the late nineteenth and early twentieth century are conceived of as the Ethiopian periphery. In fact, Jean-Nicolas Bach has argued that the centre-periphery model has become a 'great tradition' within Ethiopian Studies, in so much as the field has become primarily concerned with either extolling the virtues of the centralising state or pointing out the existence of other nationalities within the borders of Ethiopia, sometimes going further by accusing the modern Ethiopian state of being a colonial power in the borderland regions.[6] The problem is that this paradigm takes the central state at its word and, instead of mining the archive or oral histories to show the active participation of non-Amhara peoples and groups in the process of making the modern Ethiopian nation-state, ends up 'legitimising the dominant positions claimed by agents of the centre'. What is lost is the role of 'diverse social networks' in the process of nation-state formation.[7]

One consequence of this is that the historiography of the revolution has tended to assume the centre/periphery model as a model of interpretation, but failed to theorise it as a political practice that constitutes the literature itself. Many researchers do acknowledge that the present-day Ethiopian nation-state only came into existence in the late nineteenth century, but the dominance of the centre/periphery model means that the nation-state form is under-theorised in Ethiopia, seen as either having a nearly static centre with continuity from the ancient to the modern era; a stage in the telos of human history

---

tion Levine played a mediator's role between the ruling party and jailed opposition members, and in 2009 he was invited to explain Ethiopian culture at the World Bank. See Gebre-Medhin 1989, p. 7. Also see Levine 1974.

5 Triulzi 2002, p. 281.
6 Bach 2015.
7 Bach 2015, pp. 281–2.

(led by the centre); or a modular adaptation of an original developed in Europe (again led by an advancing centre).[8] While the literature on the Ethiopian revolution does acknowledge the effect of the central state on borderland communities within a changing global context, very little work has considered how global processes helped to remake the social and political forces of the central state. The relationship of the centre to the periphery is read as the intensification of age-old tendencies within the Abyssinian state, when it was more likely the result of the activation of new social processes within a global context. This historiography takes for granted the description of the centre offered by the centre rather than subjecting it to a broader sociological or historical examination. A crucial question is missed: how are forms of consciousness linked to political practice? The literature has inadvertently and sometimes purposefully become part of the process of state-making and the political battlefield; intellectuals and the social sciences have become linked in a complex and sometimes surprising nexus.

In order to think beyond the centre/periphery model, we need to examine the formation of the modern Ethiopian nation-state from a point of view that asks not only what a state is, but *why the nation-state now?* Partha Chatterjee asks this question when trying to delineate the contradiction between the problematic and the thematic of anti-colonial nationalist thought in his book *Nationalist Thought and the Colonial World*.[9] He argues that while anti-colonial nationalist thought takes as its adversary a counter-discourse – the discourse of colonialism – it is the theory and practice of European colonialism that sets up the frame of the questions and therefore the answers that structure nationalist thought in the first place.[10]

Attempting to illuminate the paradox of anti-colonial nationalist thought, Chatterjee separates out and focuses on the relationship between what he calls *the problematic* and *the thematic* of nationalist thought by defining the problematic as the common thrust and ensemble of issues that can be described

---

8   Later sections of this chapter addresses these issues: For understanding the Ethiopian state as a static centre, see the discussion of the work of Messay Kebede, Christopher Clapham and Donald Donham; for theorists who posit the Ethiopian State as a stage of human history, see my discussion of Fred Halliday and the Ottaways; and for writers who posit the Ethiopian state as a modular adaptation of an original, see my discussion of the work of John Markakis.

9   This is the same question Jeffrey Herbst asks in his survey of pre-colonial African states. He argues that shared and overlapping sovereignty was a common feature of the pre-colonial African state. See Herbst 2014.

10   Chatterjee 1999.

under nationalism, as well as the historical possibilities and practical or programmatic resolutions of those issues. On the other hand, the thematic of
nationalist thought is defined as the rules of inference that govern the construction of an argument, as well as the logic used to relate a statement of evidence
to the structure of an argument – or, in other words, the epistemological and
ethical principles that are rooted in social practice and that are appealed to in
order to justify anti-colonial nationalist problematics.

The writing on the Ethiopian revolution presents a confrontation of the
problematic of anti-colonial nationalist thought with the limits embedded in
the thematic of anti-colonial nationalist thought. Even as anti-colonial nationalist thought seeks to repudiate western imperialism and its institutions (this
is the problematic of nationalist thought), social practices that organise global
capitalist relations place limits on the epistemological principles that can be
appealed to in order to overcome western imperialism (this is the thematic of
nationalist thought). The question of how to manage a transition to capitalism,
coupled with the fundamental economic and cultural problem of what to do
with 'backward' farmers and peasants in the context of a transition to modern capitalism, means that any effort to coordinate efforts for state-building in
the third world will take on the dichotomy between tradition and modernity
as its arena of action. As such, the anti-colonial state takes on the form of 'the
nation-state as theorised and executed by Europeans'.[11] Even in its attempt to
overcome western modernity, the sociological determinism of a certain idea of
modernity becomes the taken-for-granted horizon through which anti-colonial
nationalist thought plays out. This horizon allows the historiography of the
Ethiopian revolution to become mired in questions of coevality and the stages
of world history. Rather than seeing this as inevitable we need to theorise historiography as part of social struggle. The contingencies associated with the
emergence of a *nation-state system* are the arena through which third world
politics takes shape. In the case of Ethiopia, in the late nineteenth century
the nation-state became the site of unique, creative and unpredictable social
struggle. I am not trying to discount the dimension of the state that attempts
to manage relations of exploitation; even if there was a certain kind of inevitability to the nation-state, the new social relationships that it gestured towards
remained very much in flux. What the Ethiopian nation-state would become
was not exactly a given.

Let us take a brief step back in history in order to understand this. In the
Horn of Africa since the late nineteenth century the entire region was reshaped

11   Ibid.

into what were supposed to be socially homogenous nation-states. But this forging of national identities happened in a context where social life was already organised through a complex variety of language systems and religious practices that overlapped with peasant-based and pastoral economic arrangements. This raises the question of what forces led to the nation-state becoming the only form of governance available to indigenous groups in the Horn of Africa in the late nineteenth century. Specifically, why and how did one local prince named Minilik, who ruled over Shoa (in the present-day Amhara region of Ethiopia), end up building a modern nation-state that extends to the contemporary boundaries of Ethiopia? After all, he was not the only one trying to incorporate the diverse areas of the Horn of Africa into a nation-state project.

The building of the Ethiopian nation-state project was a response not only to European incursion, but to a regional scramble to engage the nation-state project. Once Mohammed Ali's very modern and intentionally capitalist dynasty in Egypt conquered the Fung dynasty in Sudan, Egypt was presented as the main rival to a number of competing leaders in the Horn of Africa, some of whom were in fact early nation-state builders in their own right. One of the most instructive battles for Teodros (who is usually considered the initiator of the building of a modern nation-state in Ethiopia) was against the Egyptians in the late 1840s. Bahru Zewde reports that the Battle of Dabarqi was where Teodros first understood that he needed to free himself from military coalitions with other sovereign rulers by establishing a standing army.[12] Similarly, the Mahdist State in Sudan also rose as a response to the Anglo-Egyptian colonisation of Sudan, but was emboldened to establish authority over a wide swath of people so as to participate in both capital accumulation and the brutalities of forging national boundaries. The Mahdists also attempted to incorporate parts of what is now north-western Ethiopia into their rule, and by the late 1880s this forced Yohannes, a feudal prince in what is now northern Ethiopia, to battle them to his death. The Mahdist victories were short-lived, however; the British, led by Gordon, eventually defeated them militarily, leading to the establishment of Anglo-Egypt Sudan, which would last from 1898 until the rise of Nasser in the early 1950s. Meanwhile, the vacuum left by Yohannes' death was filled by Minilik's march north, where he demanded submission to his rule. Since Yohannes had busied himself with affairs to the northwest, Minilik had the time and energy to both conquer and incorporate many independent social formations in what is now southern Ethiopia. Finally, the process of forming

---

12   Herbst 2014.

Ethiopia's modern borders was completed in the Battle of Adwa in 1896, when Minilik decisively repelled Italian claims to sovereignty in the areas south of the Merab river.

This is not to say that Minilik would have always used the language of the nation-state to describe his own anti-colonial political project. More probable is that even as his claim to national sovereignty vis-a-vis the Italians in Eritrea invoked the modern nation-state, the language of empire also allowed him to conquer and make Christian large parts of present-day southern Ethiopia. Still, the limits that the scramble for Africa placed on Minilik's activities show that an emerging nation-state system was a determining force in shaping his notion of empire. The limits on the boundaries of the modern nation of Ethiopia are not a coincidence. Similarly, even if recent historiography on Mohammed Ali frames him as someone seeking to remake Cairo into a centre of the Otto-man empire, in the end his imperial project was brought to a halt through local resistance on the ground coupled with new dynamics brought about by the European presence in Asia and Africa. All this is part of the long story of how the nation-state became the only form available to non-Europeans in the process of claiming sovereignty. To me, then, it does not seem useful to theorize Minilik as shaped more by local notions of empire than by a burgeoning nation-state system: both models co-constituted and limited each other, but one system was also more dominant.

Across a diversity of ethnic groups, princes, sheiks, laymen, chiefs and kings all participated in the scramble for Africa by attempting to claim sovereignty in an international arena where the apparatus of the nation-state was the only mechanism through which this could be done. The process of nation-state building in Ethiopia inevitably marginalised other leaders in the region, including aristocracies within the traditional orbit of the Abyssinian state. The Ethiopian nation-state was not born out of the problem of competing ethnic groups, but out of the process through which regional hierarchies of power were reconstituted by the forces of global history.

Still, the outcome was not given. The problem with so much of the public his-toriography on Ethiopia that Triulzi has discussed is that it posits both Minilik and Haile-Selassie as traditional Abyssinian leaders, when in fact the process of state centralisation led by both marginalised large parts of the regions that the literature associates with centralised Abyssinian rule (including Gondar, Gojam, and Tigray north and south of the Merab river). The nation-state pro-cess also mobilised so-called peripheral leaders into coalitions with Minilik in order to secure the borders of modern Ethiopia. Nonetheless, the ideological justification of the burgeoning nation-state did rely on projecting the Amhara region as seamlessly connected to older Christian empires in the Horn of Africa.

A national ideology was developed through updating semi-feudal notions of church and state, while at the same time it subordinated relatively autonomous kingdoms and lineage-based societies into a frequently brutalising state apparatus.[13]

The Italian occupation of Ethiopia from 1936 to 1941 signified the failure of Haile-Selassie's regime to mobilise resources for this project. In 1936 Haile-Selassie was unable to pull off what Minilik did in the Battle of Adwa – regional leaders did not unite in the fight against European imperialism, nor was he able to marshal international law to protect his sovereignty. Neither guns, land, nor political allies could be found in large enough quantity to buttress the burgeoning Ethiopian nation-state. Italian rule marked the moment when indirect rule became formalized as policy practice. During this period, regional identities opposed to the central state continued to blossom and were increasingly willing to make political alliances outside the ambit of Haile-Selassie's reach. It was only once the English declared war on the Italians during World War II that Haile-Selassie was able to rely on British military initiative and policy implements to return from exile in England to become the head of state in Ethiopia.[14] Many of the policy reforms we associate with a centralising state in Ethiopia were actually established during the British occupation of Ethiopia (1941–4). These include new tax laws that undermined the base through which regional leaders could extract tribute from peasants; the establishment of a police force; and, importantly, the military suppression of regional rebellions through British force of arms. Moreover, the British exercise of authority was made possible between 1941 and 1944 because the British subordinated Haile-Selassie's decision-making capacities to the British East African Authorities.

The rise of a civilian left in Ethiopia can be seen as part of the continued effort to creatively articulate the shape of the Ethiopian nation-state. By the 1960s regional problems (sometimes expressed as the nationalities question) were pushing the country into a political and military crisis (at least in Eritrea, Bali, and the Somali territories). On top of that, a rising petty bourgeoisie was unable to find a place for itself in the political economy set up by Haile-Selassie's state. This is why the main agenda items of the student movement were how to expand membership within the Ethiopian state; how to reorganise the state to address regional inequalities; and how to build an economy where the newly forming petty bourgeoisie could have a role. Even if the colonial state in modern Ethiopia had a sporadic existence, the social and political dynamics

13　See Donham, Donald and Wendy James (eds.) 1986.
14　See Cumming 1953; Sterling 2010.

of the scramble for Africa set the stage for the entire series of actions pursued in the name of state formation from the time of Minilik onwards. The consequence of this constantly contested state formation was that a centralised national identity in formation was continually confronted with other forms of collective identity that, ironically, began to explain themselves through the homogenising language of nationalism and ethnicity. This is the social and political context that the student movement of the 1960s and 1970s aimed to address.

The secondary literature on the revolution has failed to investigate the ways in which social being (practical consciousness) is constituted by the conditions it wishes to explain. It takes for granted the very terms through which the civilian left in Ethiopia has chosen to explain and describe social reality. Sometimes this is an intentional blindness; but because the social conditions being explained reproduce the dichotomies of centre vs. periphery or modernity vs. tradition, often the secondary literature does so as well. The instrumentalisation of knowledge echoes the discourses of (an ever-changing) centre even as it attempts to resist that centre.

1   Early Histories of the Revolution and the International Left

Two of the earliest academic accounts to shape the discourse on the Ethiopian revolution were *Class and Revolution in Ethiopia* (1978), written by John Markakis and Nega Ayele, and *Ethiopia: Empire in Revolution* (1978), written by David and Marina Ottaway.[15] It is important to note when reading the arguments in *Class and Revolution in Ethiopia* that Markakis' co-author, Nega Ayele, disappeared during the period when their book was being composed, presumably killed by the post-1974 military regime. Markakis has as a result become associated with those writers and intellectuals who, from the very onset of the fall of Haile-Selassie's regime, condemned the intervention of the military in the revolutionary process.

On the other hand, even though *Ethiopia: Empire in Revolution* was published in 1978, the Ottaways take a clear stance in support of the military takeover of the Ethiopian state.[16] Even though the Ottaways acknowledge that the year 1974 in Ethiopia was marked by a significant increase in social protest, they are highly dismissive of the Ethiopian student movement and the civil-

---

15   Markakis and Ayele 1986; Ottaway and Ottaway 1978.
16   Ottaway and Ottaway 1978, p. 112.

ian left as 'corporatist, individualistic, and libertarian'.[17] For them, the student movement was vocal on campus but docile off campus, and neither taxi drivers protesting fuel prices or teachers protesting education sector reforms had a well-defined idea of what political institutions should be created to consolidate the emerging socialist system. For these reasons the Ottaways end up describing the revolutionary process itself as an accident of fate, sparked by a power vacuum created on the one hand by the fact that Haile-Selassie was aging, and on the other by the fact that succession to power was blocked by infighting amongst different parts of the aristocracy and its liberal detractors. If the military was the primary mover of the revolutionary process, this was because there was no opposition or underground movement in Ethiopia with a clearly articulated political programme.[18]

The Ottaways read the in-fighting in Haile-Selassie's regime as a symptom of a broader context, fitting it into the post-war attempt to modernise and centralise the Ethiopian state. For them, Haile-Selassie's regime signifies the structural failure both to address the loss of a political base in the rural areas, a consequence of state centralisation, and to build a political base within the newly created urban educated class. In this sense, the Ottaways read Haile-Selassie's regime as unable to bring stability to a state that needed to enter the modern era. For them, the revolution exposed the weakness of the regime, while the merit of the military lay in its ability to address concrete and feasible goals, such as finding practical solutions to economic problems, suppressing the feudal opposition, and dealing with secessionist movements.[19] Seemingly approving of these aims, they write:

> The civilian opposition had in mind an abstract model of a socialist political system, but it was too doctrinaire in its intellectual and emotional hatred of the military to accept the fact that this model did not fit the main political reality of the Ethiopian situation. Revolution without the military was impossible.[20]

The Ottaways are also confident enough to claim that the Ethiopian revolution was not merely a nationalist revolution, nor even a plot engineered from above; rather, for them the Ethiopian revolution should be compared to the European bourgeois revolutions of the eighteenth and nineteenth centuries, albeit occur-

---

17   Ottaway and Ottaway 1978, p. 64.
18   Ottaway and Ottaway 1978, p. 25.
19   Ottaway and Ottaway 1978, p. 63.
20   Ottaway and Ottaway 1978, p. 112.

ring in a truncated time period. They have no problem claiming that while the
Ethiopian revolution was horrific, it was no bloodier than the famine of 1973.[21]
By saying this the Ottaways not only diminish the politics involved in organising violence, they also present the deaths during the revolution as something
akin to a natural disaster.

The stakes were violent at the time when Markakis and the Ottaways wrote
about the student movement and civilian left: these writers were not addressing a vague and amorphous group of positions, as the latter insinuated, but
specific political parties operating under particular mandates and shaped by
precise tactics and strategies. At the time it was published, Markakis and Ayele's
work would have had to be associated with the position of the Ethiopian
People's Revolutionary Party (EPRP). Founded in 1972, the EPRP was an offshoot
of one branch of the Ethiopian student movement and became well known
for launching an urban guerrilla military campaign against the Derg regime.
At the time, its organ *Democracia* was the most widely circulated newspaper
in Ethiopia. Thus, when Markakis and the Ottaways take decisive positions in
relation to one group or another, it raises the question of what is being said in
the guise of social science neutrality. At the very least, given Nega Ayele's death,
one senses that the relationship of power, violence and intellectual activity in
these writings is less than clear.

The Ottaways' biography is nearly as interesting as Nega Ayele's and can also
help us understand what is at stake in their writing on the Ethiopian revolution. The Ottaways lived in Ethiopia prior to the outbreak of the revolution and
remained there until the end of 1977. While living in Ethiopia, David Ottaway
was employed as a journalist for the *Washington Post* while Marina Ottaway was
a lecturer at the University of Addis Ababa. Later, Marina Ottaway would make
a career for herself as a social science researcher in a number of Washington
D.C.-based think tanks, including the Carnegie Endowment for International
Peace. She is presently employed as a senior expert on social conflict in North
Africa, the Middle East and Ethiopia at the Woodrow Wilson Centre, an arm's
length research institution chartered by the US congress with the aim of providing policy advice on global issues. Her employment history is interesting, given
that we know the success of the Ethiopian revolution can partly be attributed
to the fact that, early on, the US government did not object to the fall of Haile-
Selassie's regime.[22] Much of the Ottaways' book seems congruent with this US
position, as either explanation or justification.

<hr />

21   Ottaway and Ottaway 1978, p. vi.
22   Gebre-Medhin 1989.

On the other hand, in Ayele and Markakis' book the military's participation in the revolution is understood as blocking popular aspirations towards the making of a democratic socialist state. They insist that we understand the Ethiopian revolution as a three-cornered conflict between the military, which claimed control of the state; the civilian opposition, which forcefully contested the soldiers' claims for the state; and the various national liberation movements that were striving to detach themselves from the state. Therefore, Markakis and Ayele begin their narrative with the feudal class system in Ethiopia and its relationship to the organisation of the Ethiopian state. Haile-Selassie's regime was not so much characterised by its being a feudal regime, but the early twentieth-century incorporation of Southern territories under Ethiopian sovereignty dramatically reshaped state-society relations, with the throne itself transformed into a centralising power.[23] For Markakis and Ayele, Haile-Selassie's regime marked the historical stage whereby an indigenous feudal system was linked with incipient capitalist forces.[24] The structure of Haile-Selassie's regime was not coincident with the era in which it existed, but was instead a traditional regime, giving 'shelter' to emerging foreign capital but fundamentally rooted in an older mode of production.[25] For this reason, the social contradictions of 1974 exploded along both class and national (ethnic) cleavages, and the feudal regime was no longer able to foster the complacency towards social hierarchy that it had grown used to relying on in order to prop up its existence. Ultimately, this meant that the Ethiopian revolution was the result of the evolving relationship between various social classes under what had become an increasingly anachronistic social system.[26]

Two key concepts are important in Markakis and Nega's theorisation of Haile-Selassie's regime. The first is the *bureaucratic-military bourgeoisie*, and the second is the *salitariat*.[27] These two terms are to some degree interchangeable, as they are meant to capture the specific defects of the Ethiopian bourgeoisie under peripheral capitalism. The term *salitariat* describes a non-productive class created in the post-war period, who were dependent on a salary from the state in order to sustain their livelihood. This class did not generate surplus wealth through investing in productive activity but did so through investment in urban real estate, buying shares in foreign-owned companies and acquiring land through patronage grants. It did not have a secure foothold in an

---

23   Markakis and Ayele 1986, p. 44.
24   Markakis and Ayele 1986, p. 16.
25   Markakis and Ayele 1986, p. 30.
26   Markakis and Ayele 1986, p. 16.
27   Markakis and Ayele 1986, p. 48.

economy that remained agrarian and continued to be dominated by small-hold farmers. The *bureaucratic-military bourgeoisie* can be differentiated from the *salitariat* in that they represented the first cohort of students coached within a modern educational system and specifically trained to take over the process of modernising and centralising the state apparatus.[28] The difference between the *bureaucratic-military bourgeoisie* and the *salitariat* is that by the 1960s the state apparatus became clogged, and upon leaving school students were no longer able to attain the social horizons they had come to expect from participating in the modern economy. As a result, the *bureaucratic-military bourgeoisie* came to be seen as mere retainers of the regime, while at the same time blocking the younger and better-educated *salitariat* from finding prestigious jobs within a state that they understood as in need of reform.[29] The younger and better-educated *salitariat* began to see the *bureaucratic-military bourgeoisie* as an obstacle to progress more generally, and thus to turn to radicalism.[30] Markakis and Ayele go on to argue that this newly emerging *salitariat* had a sense of a corporate or group identity that tied them together with workers, southern peasants, soldiers and the petty bourgeoisie. This shared class interest eventually brought all these groups together in a spontaneous, unorganised, and leaderless convergence against the regime. The very spontaneity of the popular movements of 1974 also meant that the various groups involved were not able to develop their own organisation and political leadership before the soldiers pushed forward to monopolise power. And yet, in order to gain support from the civilian left, the military regime was responsive to popular aspirations, adopting a number of proposals for social and economic reform that gave it the veneer of being a leftist government, while also causing much confusion amongst leftists at home and abroad about which group was merely claiming to be socialist and which one was actually setting the stage for a socialist state. Markakis and Ayele are unequivocal that one ought not be fooled into mistaking the Derg regime for anything less than a military junta.[31]

This is in contrast to yet another early intervention in the historiography of the Ethiopian revolution by the well-known British leftist Fred Halliday, who collaborated with his marital partner Maxine Molyneux to publish a take on the Ethiopian revolution that is exceptionally dismissive of the EPRP, who they

---

28   Markakis and Ayele 1986, p. 34.
29   Markakis and Ayele 1986, p. 50.
30   Markakis and Ayele 1986, p. 72.
31   Markakis and Ayele 1986, p. 17.

blame for escalating a reckless terrorist campaign from which the Derg regime was unable to climb down.[32] Halliday and Molyneux's analysis of the Ethiopian revolution purports to synthesise revolutionary theory with the practical history of the Ethiopian revolution. As a result, much of their discussion of the revolution is concerned with a detailed description of the 'clamorous coalition of urban opposition groups' that had already initiated a confrontation with Haile-Selassie's regime.[33] These groups are posited as having 'a prior, instigatory role that pushed the military's turn to politics'.[34] The logic of presenting the historical evidence in this way is to show that revolution from above is not so much an alternative to revolution from below as an extension or fulfilment of a mass movement from below. The rise of the military ought to be interpreted as the consolidation of the achievements of the mass movements from below.[35] Halliday and Molyneux also claim that by definition civilian forces that shape the context for a military coup will feel that they have been robbed of a victory they helped produce, but claims by such groups should not be taken at their word.[36] Instead, they write: '[revolutions] are not voluntaristic enterprises capable of yielding a wide variety of outcomes'.[37] For them, it is a mistake to describe the revolution as a series of betrayals.[38] Becoming too concerned with the failures of the military leadership in Ethiopia leads to missing the broader structural transformations that have occurred in the country since the Derg came to power. These changes include the destruction of an entrenched ruling dynasty; a land reform process that enfeebled those who held social and economic power in the rural areas; and the shattering of a long-established pattern of Amhara ethnic domination.

Echoing the Ottaways, Halliday and Molyneux are dismissive of the Ethiopian civilian left, while claiming that a significant social revolution was carried through by the military. Indeed, for them, the Ethiopian revolution is actually a vindication of Ellen Kay Trimberger's sociological model, which posits that an autonomous section of the state apparatus, such as the military, can bring about a revolution from above. One gets the impression that Halliday and Molyneux are speaking directly to both Markakis and the larger international left which had taken a position against the Derg.

---

32   Halliday and Molyneux 1982, p. 112.
33   Halliday and Molyneux 1982, p. 15.
34   Halliday and Molyneux 1982, p. 30.
35   Halliday and Molyneux 1982, p. 31.
36   Halliday and Molyneux 1982, p. 35.
37   Halliday and Molyneux 1982, p. 13.
38   Halliday and Molyneux 1982, p. 29.

Even though Halliday and Molyneux dismiss views like Markakis's as voluntarist, they justify their use of the Trimberger model by claiming that 'the theorists of structural crises might have gone too far in devaluing the role of conscious political action by revolutionary agents'.[39] For them, historical contingency plays a role, in that the military represents purposive action that might otherwise not have led to a revolution.[40] Halliday and Molyneux's descriptions of the problems of peripheral capitalism do not diverge in any large measure from the social crises identified by Markakis and Ayele or the Ottaways. Crucially, for them, Haile-Selassie was unable to manage a non-revolutionary transition to capitalism precisely because an antiquated state maintained by western imperial powers was managing an exogenously driven transition to capitalism. The structural crises in Ethiopia can therefore be summed up as an incomplete transition to capitalism that weakened the traditional ruling class and allowed for the rise of an urban-based civilian opposition embedded in the state apparatus but detached from a social base.[41] This being the case, when Halliday and Molyneux offer cautious support to the Ethiopian revolution one wonders: what allows them to choose the military as the centre of purposeful action over and above the civilian left?

It seems to me that part of the answer to this question has to do with Halliday and Molyneux's understanding of political will as linked to the historical time period in which action occurs. Theoretically, Halliday and Molyneux place the Ethiopian revolution within a historical time period that is not coeval with the western world. They write: '[the Ethiopian revolution] belongs to the time of European absolutism prior to anti-colonial revolutions and it simultaneously belongs to another time, one posterior to the latter'.[42] What the Ethiopian revolution is meant to achieve is then a stage in human history, even if, paradoxically, the Ethiopian state has not developed the social capacity to carry through the transition to capitalism, because it has had an exogenously driven transition without developing a true bourgeoisie. One can only surmise, given that the civilian left is not a true bourgeoisie, that the force of the military is preferred as a force of progress. One suspects that for all of Halliday and Molyneux's openness to human action, historiographical and social science models quickly become prescriptive determinants of what is correct political behaviour.

---

39   Halliday and Molyneux 1982, p. 13.
40   Halliday and Molyneux 1982, p. 15.
41   Halliday and Molyneux 1982, p. 17.
42   Halliday and Molyneux 1982, p. 18.

As mentioned earlier, Fred Halliday was a prominent member of the British Left, and from the mid-1970s until the mid-1980s was also a member of the editorial board running the journal *New Left Review*. I do not think it is a stretch to connect his writing on Ethiopia to both the history of the journal and the history of the New Left in Britain. In an essay that looks at Isaac Deutscher's effect on the British left, Neil Davidson points out that many of the editors and contributors of the *New Left Review*, including Fred Halliday, saw the USSR as a harbinger of human progress even while distancing themselves from Stalinism. But by the end of the cold war, instead of viewing socialism as a democratic project that belonged to the popular masses, Halliday actually repudiated his position on the USSR.[43] In an interview he gave in 1990, Halliday claimed that if 'the socialist experiment of the revolutionary kind failed and failed badly, it failed necessarily and not contingently'.[44] While this statement may seem inconsistent with Halliday's earlier position on Ethiopia, epistemologically it is symmetrical with his denunciation of the capacities of the Ethiopian civilian left. It is not that Halliday was no longer committed to communist values; it is that the passage of time had proved that the required stages of world history could not be bypassed in the journey towards socialism. He confirms this position himself when he writes:

> The greatest mistake of Marxist and socialist thinking was not the underestimation of nationalism nor the overestimation of socialism and its potential but rather the underestimation of capitalism itself, both in terms of its potential for continued expansion and in terms of its not having within it a catastrophist teleology: in the apt words of Bill Warren, '"Late capitalism", late for what?'[45]

---

43   Neil Davidson writes: 'For those, like Fred Halliday, who had essentially seen the Soviet bloc as the bearer of socialist progress, the debacle [of the cold war] "means nothing less than the defeat of the communist project as it had been known in the 20th century and the triumph of the capitalist". Incredibly, some writers who had previously accepted *International Socialism*'s position on the nature of Stalinism began to endorse a Deutscherist position *after* the USSR had collapsed. It would be going too far to say that every Deutscherist has now switched sides to support the US, capitalist globalisation, "liberal values" and the invasion of awkward Third World states. For every Halliday or Hitchens there is a Davis or an Ali. Nevertheless, Deutscherism made it easy, for those who had no countervailing belief in the ability of the working class to sustain them, to transfer their allegiance from Moscow to Washington'. Davidson 2015.

44   See Postel 2015.

45   Halliday 1990, p. 11.

The echoes of the Ottaways that we sensed earlier in Halliday and Molyneux's writing on the Ethiopian revolution may have been more congruent with Washington, D.C. than we might have initially thought. I find that if I am to take any of these authors seriously, it will be in order to think about how social science models become tools for doing politics, including the politics of mobilising the military field. If Halliday and Molyneux's position on Ethiopia can be linked to a tendency of the British (and western) left, it is important also to ask who on the British left they were writing against. While it seems to me that Halliday and Molyneux were taking a position against Markakis and Ayele, given that Markakis' position came to be associated with the *Review of African Political Economy* (ROAPE), Halliday can also be seen as writing in conversation with ROAPE and the Ethiopian social movements and political parties that over time came to be associated with that journal, especially in relation to the civil wars in the Horn of Africa in the 1970s, 80s and early 90s.

Halliday's reference to Bill Warren in the passage quoted above seems a touch uncanny in this light, given that Warren renounced ROAPE soon after the journal published its first editorial in 1974. Warren is well-known for advocating the idea that colonialism and capitalism brought development to Africa and needed to run their course. What Warren would have objected to in the 1974 ROAPE editorial was the explicit attempt to challenge modernisation theory through a dependency framework that linked the causes of African poverty to colonial history and the structures of international markets. As early as its first editorial, ROAPE posited itself as more than just an academic journal, imploring future contributors to produce actionable research through a clearly defined method and approach:

> Though we do not have at hand a completely worked out analysis we do have a common starting point. We are not neutral about the kind of method that offers the best chance of coming to terms with the realities of African underdevelopment. The perspective of the Review will be in this sense Marxist – not in offering a blueprint for some future society, nor in supporting a particular type of regime, as popular usage mistakenly might indicate, but in using a method which analyses a situation in order to change it.[46]

In a 1985 retrospective assessment of where this approach had led ROAPE, the Editorial Working Group compares itself with other major journals on the west-

---

46   ROAPE Editorial Board 1974.

ern (international) left, including the *New Left Review, Monthly Review,* and *Class and Science*.[47] Two things stand out in the 1985 assessment: the first is that, unlike many of the other journals on the left, the editorial working group at ROAPE claims that it is run as a collective and without a cult of personality dominating editorial decisions. Secondly, the journal claims to be informed by a 'politics of disillusionment' towards post-colonial Africa and, as such, sees it fit to deepen its commitments to social transformation though 'opening the [its] pages towards authentic expressions of socialist alternatives … We are seeking much more than Nkrumah's political kingdom'.[48] This is written without a hint of irony as to what a sentence like that might mean to someone reading it in Africa, especially since that reader would have an appreciation for the fact that the editorial team was based in the United Kingdom. At the same time, the mere fact that the editorial working group felt the need to use this same editorial space to remind readers that the journal was neither a political party nor involved in direct organising is testament enough to the measure of importance the editorial working group attributed to itself. The disavowal of being a mere organ of persuasion is also a declaration that persuasion in itself is quite a task, and that ROAPE was so good at what it did that people often mistook the journal for more than it actually was. The Editorial Working Group writes:

> All of us sought to make the journal relevant to political struggles in Africa – rather than simply doing solidarity work in the UK (not, incidentally, the major area where the journal circulates). The 'extramural leftism' and other experiences in popular and party educational programmes have to some extent helped us to reach a readership beyond the confines of academia, though the same tradition has also limited our political practice. This strange mix of elements has combined to produce what is in terms of circulation and viability at least, a 'successful' journal.[49]

One of the things that has always surprised me about the historiography of the Ethiopian revolution is that many of the debates first articulated in the journals of the Ethiopian student movement were transferred to the pages of the *Review of African Political Economy* without much change in tone or clarity of concepts. Over the years many primary documents, such as party manifestos and position papers from the Ethiopian People's Revolutionary Party, the Eritrean People's Liberation Front, and the Tigray People's Liberation Front also

---

47   ROAPE Editorial Board 1985.
48   ROAPE Editorial Board 1985, p. 99.
49   Ibid.

came to be published in ROAPE. It is also striking that the journal published no pro-Derg documents. It is clear is that many political organisations in the Horn of Africa were aware of ROAPE and deliberately sent documents to the journal, while various editors at ROAPE sought to make the journal a principal venue for the publication of these organisations' documents. Much of this may have to do with the fact Abdul-Mejid Hussein, a prominent member of the EPRP, was also a member of the Editorial Working Group at ROAPE in the 1970s. During the post-Derg transition, Abdul-Mejid Hussein would become a cabinet minister and ambassador to the UN. Moreover, in 1998, as chairman of the Somali People's Democratic Party Central Committee, he would foster an agreement between various Ethiopian Somali insurgent groups so as to bring a sizable section of these dissidents into a coalition partnership with the EPRDF.[50] Hussein's journey from EPRP member to social science practitioner to member of government is interesting if we recall that the nationalities policy supported by the EPRP was one of respecting ethnic (national) autonomy within a regional context. It was this policy that in no small way differentiated the EPRP from the Derg regime and was also responsible for creating major divisions within the Ethiopian student movement. Although the TPLF took an even more strident position on the nationalities question than the EPRP,[51] during the post-1991 transition period the EPRDF resolved the problem of the nationalities question in ways that closely resembled the position articulated by the EPRP in the early 1970s. In this sense, Hussein's rise to government power can also be seen as the fruition of work that allowed him and the politics he supported to cross from the classroom to the battlefield to the seat of the state. After all, Hussein's move from EPRP member to editor of ROAPE to state minister is also coincident with the fact that, from very early on, ROAPE published numerous documents from the various secessionist groups operating in Eritrea and Ethiopia, as well as those of the EPRP.

An examination of the publication record of ROAPE reveals that as early as 1975 the journal issued a small pamphlet by Addis Hiwet entitled *Ethiopia: From Autocracy to Revolution*.[52] Addis's pamphlet also proved to be one of the most important early interpretations of the Ethiopian revolution, widely read among Ethiopians who had recently been exiled by the Derg regime. Even though Addis' work is highly researched and was issued by an academic publishing house, the more general academic literature on the revolution hardly

---

50   See Cliffe 2004. For a fuller biography of Abdulmejid Hussein, see also G 2002.
51   This may have led to a number of military skirmishes between the two groups in the early period of the Ethiopian civil war.
52   Hiwet 1975.

takes up his work except in a very cursory fashion. His popularity amongst Ethiopian exile readers can be accounted for by the fact that they would have known that Addis Hiwet was a pen name for a member of the Ethiopian student movement who was most likely also living in exile (the name translates to New Life). Although Addis Hiwet's biographical details remain sketchy, a few things are clear from his text: first, he is opposed to the Derg on the grounds that it was in danger of entering a Bonapartist moment and, second, he was interested in building a revolution in Ethiopia based on what he calls the 'popular democratic upsurge' of 1974. Equally important in his definition of this upsurge are the urban-based civilian left and the various national secessionist movements and rural rebellions that had built up ground in the years prior to 1974. While Addis Hiwet's work cannot be directly linked with any one political party, his essay certainly took a position on the debates that had torn the Ethiopian student movement apart and would eventually tear apart the larger civilian left that remained in Ethiopia. That Addis' work was published by ROAPE must have had something to do with the deep ties that the editorial working group had with members of mass movements and political parties in Ethiopia. Thus, whether intentionally or not, the social science perspective offered by ROAPE collapsed into a politically expedient description of social reality. Would a reader of ROAPE have the critical tools to distinguish between the two? Did the larger editorial working group make this distinction? I do not think the proposition that all knowledge production is biased can satisfactorily explain the way social science and politics come together when examining the historiography of the Ethiopian revolution. Instead one has to be attentive to the movement of ideas and persons between various organisations and institutions and across numerous national borders, some of which is made clear and some of which can never be easily apparent – not even to those transporting the ideas from one location to the other.

Over time, the ROAPE stance regarding the Horn of Africa seems to have deepened along a particular political line. In the 1977 editorial on the Horn of Africa, Mustafa Khogali asks 'which, if any of the parties in the Horn disputes is acting consistently with any Marxist and Leninist principles regarding the national question and proletarian internationalism?'[53] While the editorial asks this question, the primary documents published in that issue of ROAPE are only from the Eritrean People's Liberation Front.[54] By the time we arrive at the 1984 ROAPE special issue on the Horn of Africa, edited by John Markakis

---

53   Khogali 1977, p. 7.
54   Khogali 1977.

and Lionel Cliffe, there is no longer any attempt to grapple with the meaning of
the revolution beyond supporting the various nationalist movements such as
the Eritrean People's Liberation Front and the Tigray People's Liberation Front.
This is especially striking given that Markakis and Cliffe include a new article
from Addis Hiwet, who cautions readers to make a distinction between the
Ethiopian revolution and the present regime. Addis goes on to say that since
the beginning of the revolution there have been numerous regimes, not just
one. In their editorial Cliffe and Markakis reduce Addis' admonishment to an
abstraction, and ask instead: 'what would it mean in terms of political practice
to defend a revolution but oppose the military dictatorship and its policies?'[55]
According to them, Addis' statement is too harsh since it could too easily result in the charge of being counter-revolutionary from those opposed to the
Derg regime. Markakis and Cliffe's oblique reply to Addis is that 'socialists must
not be so bemused by the complexities in the analysis that they simply retreat
into an apathetic fence-sitting in the face of the enormity of the suffering and
the historical importance of the events being played out there [in the Horn of
Africa]'.[56] Markakis and Cliffe then go on to equate the conditions that gave
rise to African nationalism in the 'anti-colonial stage' with the conditions that
gave rise to the secessionist movements in the Horn of Africa. For them, the
opposite of apathy naturally means support for the EPLF and the TPLF, as well
as the secessionist movements operating in South Sudan. Curiously, Markakis
and Cliffe do not specify what the conditions for African nationalism might
be beyond a general claim that what unites these movements is 'a common
perception of material deprivation and social discrimination, sustained and
compounded by political oppression'.[57] In this iteration of anti-colonialism the
Amhara ethnic group in Ethiopia and the Arabs of Khartoum are to be equated
with the colonial powers in Europe.

In the 1984 ROAPE editorial on the Horn of Africa, not only do Markakis and
Cliffe decry the 'socialist pretensions' of the Derg regime, they also claim that
the TPLF and EPLF are putting socialist tenets into practice in the liberated
zones that they operate. Markakis and Cliffe encourage their readers to believe
that the struggles and sacrifices of the rebel groups will bring tangible socialist
benefits to those who are presently engaged in a military struggle against the
Derg regime. In the post-civil war period, both Cliffe and Markakis would actively participate in the new regimes in Eritrea and Ethiopia, with Cliffe advising
the Eritrean land commission on government land reform while Markakis,

55   Markakis and Cliffe 1984, p. 7.
56   Markakis and Cliffe 1984, p. 2.
57   Ibid.

among other things, was invited to Gojjam province in Northern Ethiopia to celebrate the twenty-fifth anniversary of the Amhara National Democratic Movement (part of the current ruling EPRDF, but also a remnant of the former EPRP).[58]

In 1996, in the context of the EPRDF/TPLF transition to power in Ethiopia, Markakis wrote a ROAPE editorial update on the Horn of Africa that takes a much more optimistic tone. Given that the EPRDF had implemented a federal system that devolves authority to ethnic groups, Markakis now believes that the EPRDF has solved the problem of national integration by drawing a 'distinction between national identity and citizenship'.[59] One also gets the sense that Markakis is celebrating a victory that was a long time in the making, since ethnic (national) self-determination was one of the goals articulated by the civilian left in the early days of the revolution. At no point in the editorial does Markakis problematise the manner through which the new federal arrangement in Ethiopia collapses culture and language groups into political and national entities. Instead, he merely wonders if the central government will uphold the constitutional proclamations towards decentralisation.[60] Markakis' critique remains at the level of questioning policy implementation and does not question the connection between the concepts embedded in policy and the ground, or how the two might reconstitute each other in a dialectical play.

In 1998, Giles Mohan, then editor of ROAPE, wrote an editorial that examined the history of ROAPE and its relevance to radical political movements in Africa. Although not directly writing about the Ethiopian civil wars of 1975–91, there is no better description of what ROAPE became for many Ethiopian and Eritrean organisations during that period than when Mohan writes:

> [F]or our colleagues in Africa, authoritarian governments have often attempted to silence critical academics so that scholarship is a key site of political struggle. Indeed, in this regard, the fact that the Review of African Political Economy is not based on the continent is a source of political power, enabling a level of critical debate that would be difficult in many of these countries.[61]

---

58 For a more in-depth description of Lionel Cliffe's intellectual legacy in Eritrea see Tesfai 2003. For a description of Markakis' participation at the ANDM celebration see Alemu n.d.
59 Markakis 1996, p. 471.
60 Markakis and Ayele 1986, p. 471.
61 Mohan 1997, p. 264.

I do not think it is a stretch to see ROAPE as part of the strategy of building an international profile for political movements in the Horn of Africa. The
venues through which an international profile was sought exerted an inadvert-
ent effect on the concepts and ideas used to build up an appealing international profile. As Mohan himself admits, the relationship of ROAPE to political
struggle involves vexed questions about how political movements build political power. ROAPE was an important site that linked intellectuals, the social
sciences, and the battlefield in a complex and surprising nexus.

2   Historiography of the Liberated Zones

The political and intellectual lines drawn by ROAPE in relation to the Horn of
Africa also shaped a wider body of literature produced by a younger generation of scholars and journalists giving ethnographic accounts of the liberated
zones operated by the EPLF and TPLF in the 1980s. Though the lines that draw
this literature back towards ROAPE are not always explicit, these works share
the assumptions of Cliffe and Markakis' basic propositions in their 1984 ROAPE
editorial on the Horn of Africa. Cliffe and Markakis' editorial can be taken as a
summation of an intellectual consensus that had become established in the
western left with regards to the civil wars in the Horn of Africa. The works
that I group into this body of literature were also responsible for bringing the
wars in the Horn of Africa to the attention of a very broad popular audience,
and while many of the authors associated with this body of literature went
on to develop book-length accounts of the insurgent movements, ROAPE often
provided the first venue for their early work. These authors include David Poole,
who wrote one of the first academic accounts of the Eritrean-Ethiopian war,
Eritrea: Africa's Longest War (1982); Dan Connell, who is well-known for his
many journalistic accounts of the EPLF; John Young, who in 1997 published
a history of the TPLF entitled *Peasant Revolution in Ethiopia*; and Jenny Hammond, whose 1990 *Sweeter Than Honey: Ethiopian Women and Revolution: Testi-
monies of Tigrayan Women* helped secure an image of the TPLF as a highly
progressive organisation sensitive in part to issues of gender equity.[62]

There is a consistency in all of these works in terms of the themes addressed.
Frequently emphasized is the capacity of the TPLF and EPLF to launch a
people's war based on the principle of organising liberated zones through a

---

62   Poole 1980, which later became Poole 1982; Cowan 1983; Hammond 1990; Gebre-Mehdin
       1983; Bennet 1983; Connell 1982, 1993; Young 1996, later developed into Young 1997.

policy of economic self-reliance, land reform, and gender equality. These war-time institutions are always read as the basis of a new society that will come after the war. The testimonials and ethnographic accounts are often centred on a redemptive narrative structure, where the suffering of today is posited as payment for a just society tomorrow. Reading through these works, which are often based on interviews that elicit descriptions of experience in the war zone, what becomes unsettling is not the attempt to muster support for the insurgent movements, but that the authors take the insurgents' promises at their word. What is often taken for granted is the history of how people come to feel that they belong to a particular ethnic or national group and its attendant political struggle. The process of how an ethnic identity is forged into an oppositional political identity is also left unquestioned. In John Young's account of the TPLF, or example, the author feels no obligation to investigate the actual social processes that led to the TPLF revolution, but instead spends most of his book showing that the TPLF victory can be attributed to a combination of political leadership, Derg regime stimulus to revolt, and an inherent sense of nationalism within the Tigray people.[63] Interestingly, this actually goes against the newer histories of the TPLF produced by the Tigrayan scholar Gebru Tareke, who points out that one would be hard pressed to show that a coherent ethnic or national Tigrayan identity existed prior to intellectuals shaping and articulating local grievances in a particular direction. Gebru's major contribution to the historiography of the Ethiopian revolution is to argue that 'ethno-nationalism was nurtured in the heart of the revolutionary wars'.[64] He has also shown that the revolutionary wars launched by the TPLF were the result of 'the organized will of a few radical urban intellectuals' primarily coming out of the Ethiopian student movement.[65] The challenge for a historian of the TPLF's victory over the Derg is then to explain the TPLF's capacity to connect the political ambitions of an urban middle class with the frustrations of a rural peasantry. Coercion and persuasion must have been involved in mobilising peasants for warfare, given that the TPLF was not created out of the grievances of the agrarian population.[66] Thus Gebru says that the authoritarian aspects of the present regime could have been predicted from the way the people's war was organised.[67] But even as he says this, Gebru is not dismissive of the element of social justice embedded in the civil wars. For him, regional

63   Young 1997 p. 36.
64   Tareke 2009, p. 81.
65   Tareke 2009, p. 8.
66   Tareke, 2009, p. 81.
67   Tareke, 2009, p. 53.

disparities and unequal development were the real result of a modernising, autocratic regime. Tigrayan urban middle-class students faced severe structural limits in terms of regional and individual economic prospects, as well as cultural alienation at the centre. Similar to the other urban middle-class students in Addis Ababa, Tigrayan students were part of an emerging class that occupied a contradictory social position within a changing nation-state system.[68] The founding of the TPLF can be seen as one path towards resolving the structural limits placed on this social group. The TPLF was always only one pole in a set of myriad possible responses to these structural issues. From this perspective, Young's work mistakes a project driven by young urban intellectuals as a necessary ethnic or nationalist problem. On the other hand, Gebru suggests that ethno-nationalism was a highly creative theory and practice that attempted to address intransigent social problems. Insisting on the inventive and creative aspects of the TPLF and the EPLF does not imply that the insurgents were deceitful, but that the relationship between the language of political mobilisation, the practice of political organising, coercion, and leadership will always be more complicated than what can be elicited by ethnographic techniques. In particular, because Young is unable to place the TPLF within a broader historical framework, the role that ethnographic interviews play in his book is to simply replicate the discourses of cadres and party officials rather than reveal the contradictory social content within the TPLF political project. This is why, in the post-civil war period, Young and many of his intellectual cohort could only express dismay or disappointment when the TPLF or EPLF governed on the side of authoritarianism. This sense of disappointment expresses a moral outrage that places politics in the Horn of Africa into an overly voluntarist framework, echoing some of Halliday's concerns with the political position associated with ROAPE.[69]

---

68   Tareke 2009, p. 81.

69   Our survey of the contribution of the international left to the historiography of the Ethiopian revolution would be incomplete if we did not mention René Lefort's important text *Ethiopia: A Heretical Revolution*, which was originally published in French. I have chosen not to include a discussion of the book in the main body of this chapter as I believe that its argument does not differ in any substantial way from Fred Halliday and Maxine Molineux's thesis that the Derg regime represented a revolution from above. Epistemologically, Lefort's work faces the same historicist problems as Halliday in so much as Lefort reads the Ethiopian revolution as simultaneously telescoping 1789, 1917, the Chinese revolution and the western left of 1968. Lefort's main aim in his book is to demonstrate why the international left should take the Ethiopian revolution more seriously. See Lefort 1983. Interestingly, Lefort continues to comment on contemporary Ethiopian affairs and, not unlike Halliday, more recently has been interested in demonstrating that the Ethiopian peasant lacks the capacity to participate in liberal democratic processes. Thus, as in Hal-

3   Historical Contiguity

Let us now turn to two more important strands that have contributed to the historiography of the Ethiopian revolution. These are the work of Donald Donham and Christopher Clapham, two thinkers whose work can be seen in many ways as diametrically opposed both to each other and to the previous histories of the Ethiopian revolution we have examined in this chapter.

In his book *Transformation and Continuity in Revolutionary Ethiopia* (1988), Christopher Clapham provides an appraisal of the institutional changes that have occurred within the Ethiopian state in the post-revolutionary period. Clapham is primarily concerned with showing that the Derg regime is a continuation of the great tradition of state-building that has dominated Ethiopian political life for millennia.[70] In this sense Clapham's work fits into what Triulzi identified as the state-centred historiographical trend that has dominated Ethiopian Studies since its inception. Donham, on the other hand, is probably best known for his edited volume *The Southern Marches of Imperial Ethiopia* (1986), which seeks to show the multiple, often violent processes of subjugation that led to the late nineteenth-century unification of the Abyssinian state.[71] Donham's work is particularly associated with attempts to re-centre Ethiopia's southern 'periphery' as a vantage point through which to disentangle Ethiopian state mythology from actual lived history. His book *Marxist Modern* (1999) is an ethnography of the Ethiopian revolution as it played out amongst the Maale people, a small ethnic group located in Southwestern Ethiopia. The main aim of the book is to convey Ethiopian narratives of the revolutionary process, and at the same time to discover the myriad spatial and temporal references through which local narratives of the revolution are constructed. Donham does not take the ethnic group he is studying to be a homogenous group, nor does he attempt to reproduce their 'thought'. Instead, his approach is to use multiple conflicting narratives to create a genealogy of the revolution as it played out in Maale. He is able to show that even as the revolutionary state penetrates the local, the local rewrites the centre through social cleavages that have a specific

---

liday, the vexed question of the coevality of the Ethiopian populace with the rest of the world continues to be an underlying conceptual tool that informs his analysis of the telos of Ethiopian politics. However, like Christopher Clapham, whose work we will now look at, Lefort argues that democratic centralism provides an excellent mechanism to both allow mass participation and tightly control the state decision-making process, keeping it in the hands of a small group of people. For Lefort this explains the success of the Derg regime and the present EPRDF regime. See Lefort 2007.

70   Clapham 1990.
71   Donham and James 1986.

history for the Maale people, often applying revolutionary discourses to non-revolutionary pursuits. One of the merits of this style of ethnography is that, in contrast to the work we have surveyed in relation to ROAPE, Donham is able to show that what is taken to be primitive is coeval with what are taken to be the most modern forms of life. To this end, Donham coins the term vernacular modernism to describe the narratives of revolution that he reproduces in his book.[72]

Earlier in this chapter we contrasted state-centred histories of Ethiopia with accounts of Ethiopia that seek to convey the history of non-dominant ethnic groups; the contrast between Clapham and Donham falls on this fault line. Yet their works also contain many hidden similarities. By working through Clapham and Donham's contributions we can ask whether and in what ways these texts elucidate the undercurrents which have shaped the Ethiopian revolution. Or do these texts also collapse into easy narratives of villains, victims and heroes?

According to Christopher Clapham, the 1974 revolution in Ethiopia was both genuine and marked by fundamental and irreversible change in the organisation of society. Clapham's most significant contribution to the literature is to argue that the success of the Ethiopian revolution can be linked to Ethiopia's previous experience with state rule. Contrasting the Ethiopian revolution with other anti-colonial revolutions, Clapham claims that the success of the Derg regime lay in its capacity to build both a party and a state that continued to link elites to the most basic units of society, although in this case this was achieved through mass-based organisations such as peasant and urban dwellers' associations.[73] Precisely because the revolutionary state in Ethiopia did not exist sui generis, it was able to mobilise an already established national identity to produce a sense of patriotic duty to the state. For Clapham, the war with Somalia and the campaign against the rural insurgencies played a decisive role in fostering this national feeling. Nonetheless, Clapham takes for granted a congruence between an Ethiopian state and a certain felt nationalism within the population, and thus does not find it necessary to periodise the last one hundred years of the pre-revolutionary Ethiopian state except in terms of its continued expansion, centralisation and growth.[74]

Clapham asserts that there is 'no necessary connection between revolution and structural conditions'.[75] Rather, for him, it was Ethiopia's relative

---

72   Donham 1999, p. 1.
73   Clapham 1990, p. 9.
74   Clapham 1990, p. 27.
75   Clapham 1990, p. 9.

lack of incorporation into the world economy that allowed state power to be contested in the first place. While Clapham links the centralising tendency of the Ethiopian state to its mid-nineteenth-century contact with European imperialism, the story of the centralisation of the Ethiopian state is told as a mostly internal affair. The boundaries of present-day Ethiopia are never really explained. Left out of this story are the myriad ways that capitalism and imperialism have shaped the Ethiopian state without producing western-looking development. Clapham can then fit the Ethiopian revolution into Theda Skocpol's description of the Russian, French and Chinese revolutions, claiming that what the Ethiopian revolution shares with those revolutions is that it occurred in an agrarian society governed by an absolutist monarchy.[76] Moreover, Clapham explains that Ethiopia's ability to rebuild an effective state apparatus has something to do with a capacity built into its culture and religion. That is to say, for Clapham, the Leninist party closely resembled the authoritarian and esoteric aspects of Orthodox Christianity. If the Ethiopian people easily accepted a revolutionary vanguard, this is because the vanguard felt to them like the esoteric priests of the church.[77] One suspects that this is the reason Clapham attempts to classify Ethiopia with the great historical revolutions in Russia and China. Built into their cultural DNA, according to some accounts, is also a tendency to accept the structure of authoritarian rule.

Skocpol's model of revolutionary change allows Clapham to divide the Ethiopian revolution into two periods: (a) one in which state power is contested and (b) one consisting in the consolidation of state institutions. Even though Clapham published his book in 1988, this division allows him to take the Derg regime as a fact established on the ground. Perhaps this is why he shows little interest in the rural insurgencies that were the concern of the authors associated with ROAPE. He writes instead: 'Eritrea and Tigray have been the battlefield of major insurgencies ... without seriously threatening the stability or survival of the state'.[78] This misses Gebru's point that, in terms of both persons and ideas, there were clear continuities between the rural insurgencies and the urban civilian left that contested the shape of the state in the 1970s. For Gebru, the rural insurgencies are revolutionary wars. This means, at the very least, that the Derg does not belong to Skocpol's period of institutional consolidation; perhaps, instead, the time of revolutionary consolidation belongs to the post-1991 era.

---

76   Clapham 1990, p. 16.
77   Clapham 1990, p. 79.
78   Clapham 1990, p. 206.

In Clapham's rendering of the Ethiopian revolution the role of ideology is also easily dismissed as the 'mere rationalization of the interests of its proponents'.[79] But this proposition seems to neglect the fact that to win over certain sections of the left *and* to shape policy outcomes, the military appropriated the language and ideas of the civilian left. Logically, the course of events should lead one to ask: if some ideas promote liberal democracy while other ideas establish peasant associations, then surely the choice to organise society using the tools of one ideology over another is more than the 'prudential adaptation to a new rhetorical style'?[80] It must be that some ideas produce different policy outcomes and different social practices. Moreover, even if ideas are expressed for purely rhetorical effect, the relationship between ideas and their users is not unidirectional. Tools change their users as much as they shape specific goals in the world (even if that goal is domination of the population). The relationship between language, political mobilisation and the shaping of reality is more complicated than simply saying that language can be instrumentalised.

This is Donald Donham's point when he says that vernacular modernism is constituted through what he calls *cross talk*: a process which can be defined as the dialectical shaping of local discourses through the global circulation of stories that we tell about one another.[81] Donham seeks to show how the metanarrative of modernity is internalised as a story of having to catch up with the 'advanced' world, and is simultaneously a story that motivates local discourses towards a particular aim. Cross talk shapes local actors' perception of themselves to the degree that they also understand their actions as being made on a world stage. Taking the urban intelligentsia in Ethiopia as a prime example of how cross talk works, Donham is keen to show how stories of the Chinese and Russian revolutions shaped perceptions of what had to be done in Ethiopia. According to Donham, educated Ethiopians understood socialism and capitalism as two competing narratives of modernisation, but socialism allowed Ethiopians to define themselves in opposition to westerners and also in relation to their own backwardness.[82] In other words, Ethiopians used Marxism as a tool to position themselves in the modern world.[83] This proves, for Donham, that to think about the Ethiopian revolution is to think about how stories get layered on top of each other in order to motivate social action.[84] The merit of

---

79   Clapham 1990, p. 9.
80   Ibid.
81   Donham 1999, p. 2.
82   Donham 1999, p. 25.
83   Donham 1999, p. 131.
84   Donham 1999, p. 8.

describing the Ethiopian revolution in this way is to show that narrative representations allow different social groups to interact, clash and sometimes transform each other. It also allows him to discover how the relationship between an urban vanguard and a social class is fostered without simply presuming their identity to be coincident.

One of the first ways in which Donham disentangles the relationship between an urban vanguard and the rural population in Maale is to show that revolutionary discourse initially inspired a coalition of socially disaffected persons to bring a court case against the local Maale king. Donham shows that the grievances expressed in this court case had their roots in the colonial impact of Minilik's state on local traditions of governance. Thus, what is ironic about these early revolutionary protests is that the disaffected Maale used the discourses of the revolution to demand the restoration of an order that preceded Maale's incorporation into the Ethiopian state.[85] This early revolutionary initiative was later opposed by the urban youth who had been sent into the rural areas through the Zemecha campaign (also known as the Development and Co-operation Campaign). These youth were meant to implement the Derg's land reform proclamation and the governance structure that accompanied the legislation. However, the youth sent to Maale were inevitably anti-feudal and anti-tradition, and this often translated into opposition to the restoration of a Maale past. Instead they were inspired by a forward-looking modernist discourse that had little to do with questions of fairness or justness as they specifically arose in Maale. Donham claims that during the Ethiopian revolution the Amhara political centre continued to be the venue through which 'the metanarrative of modernity' was concentrated and then 'mapped onto different ethnic differences'.[86] Donham, quite ironically, contrasts this with Haile-Selassie's state, whose main aim was to centralise authority in a modernising state. One of the unique contributions of his work from an ethnographic standpoint is to show that little substantial difference existed between the programme of the revolutionary state and Haile-Selassie's regime.[87] After all, the word Zemecha is also associated with the military campaign responsible for incorporating southern Ethiopian ethnic groups into the Ethiopian nation-state. When the revolutionary state attempted to institutionalise itself in Maale, it sought to control the population through peasant associations that were further sub-divided into youth groups and women's groups. One of the consequences of this was that

---

85   Donham 1999, p. 39.
86   Donham 1999, p. 128.
87   Donham 1999, p. xix.

life was no longer organised through a ritualised hierarchy of tradition. Donham argues that this demanded a sense of personhood as free and equal with all those who were members of the mass associations. Donham discovered through his ethnographic study that those people who were most adaptable to such transformations in political subjectivity were not the poorest peasants in Maale, but evangelical Christian converts. This is because interactions with the missionaries from the Sudan Interior Mission had produced an experience of personhood as both highly individuated and organised through a higher central authority (the church) that also broke down into women's and youth groups.[88] Another irony of the Ethiopian revolution in Maale is that the anti-modernist discourses of Canadian missionaries is what prepared some Maale residents for participation in the hyper-modernist project of Marxist revolution.

Donham's primary project is to track the stories that modernists, anti-modernists and traditionalists tell about each other. In so doing he uncovers not only the way social meaning gets layered through a recurrent dialectic between different social stances, but also how those layered meanings shape social action.[89] By contrasting the different temporalisations of history offered by groups of people who often appear to have very different social positions, Donham ends up illustrating how different concepts and storylines build on each other to make sense of the world. In this way he is able to show the contingent connections between different narratives (and different narrative projects). Irony becomes the major literary device through which Donham constructs a paradoxical reflexivity that positions the analyst as the master storyteller in relation to the stories of the actors he studies.

Given all this irony, one might be forgiven for thinking that there was something a little glib in Donham's positioning of himself in relation to the stories he is telling. After all, like Ottaway and Halliday before him, Donham insists that there were no organised radical groups in Ethiopia prior to the revolution, and while he creates a contrast between competing narratives of modernity, he seems to discount the whole history of the student movement and its impact on the formation of a civilian left in Ethiopia.[90] This means that he must reduce the revolution to a creeping coup and, on the other hand, view competing discourses of progress as having lost touch with reality: 'modernist discourse quickly lost contact with qualifying reality, and its binary logic took on an unhindered life of its own. All grays became shades of black and

---

88   Donham 1999, p. 62.
89   Donham 1999, p. 8.
90   Donham 1999, p. 15.

white'.[91] What is not considered here is the possibility that political struggles could have an outer form that is expressed in narratives that are not coincident with their inner social content. Certainly, Donham does not conduct a historical sociology of class formation in Ethiopia, and while he is concerned with the impact of modernity on the imagination, he tends to define the modern as a discursive project rather than an economic structure that produces new patterns of migration, cash cropping, subsistence farming, and slave raiding. In his book Donham does not explore the relationship between changing economic structures and the structures of the imagination: how does economic and social activity motivate new stories, and how do they dialectically reconstitute each other? As such, his work does not really move us beyond the initial dichotomies that have shaped the historiography of the revolution and that are best represented by the opposition between ROAPE on the one side and Halliday on the other.

4   The Student Movement Grows Up

In the past few years a number of new works have been published by academics who were also former members of the Ethiopian student movement during the 1960s and 1970s. Major texts that can be included in this group are Messay Kebede's *Radicalism and Cultural Dislocation in Ethiopia: 1960–1974* (2008), Gebru Tareke's *The Ethiopian Revolution* (2009), and Bahru Zewde's important 2014 publication *The Quest for Socialist Utopia*.[92] Collectively, these works help us rethink the social roots of the Ethiopian revolution by demonstrating the impact of the student movement on both policy outcomes and state formation in the period following the 1974 revolution. Even more striking is that each author's reinterpretation of the Ethiopian revolution can also be understood as a retrospective analysis of a political project launched by his or her cohort of student colleagues.

In the end, Messay Kebede rejects the legacy of the student movement in the name of the restoration of an authentic national culture, which he takes to be the Christian culture of north-central Ethiopia and Eritrea. Kebede's main theoretical concern is to offer a speculative account of why Ethiopian students in the 1970s preferred Marxism to the path of reforming the central state. Bahru Zewde and Gebru Tareke's books have in common an attempt to

---

91   Donham 1999, p. 26.
92   Kebede 2008; Tareke 2009; Zewde 2014.

use new archival material to shed light on well-known events. Bahru Zewde's book stands out as a carefully researched work written within the empiricist tradition, which shows that the outcome of the 1974 revolution was the culmination of a series of organisational machinations within student groups that stretch back to at least 1965. Bahru is able to show this by mobilising the copious amount of material written by the Ethiopian student movements as the book's main archival source. However, precisely because Bahru's book is committed to merely showing the events as they happened, he only offers a limited interpretation of events. Similar to Messay, Bahru also sees the members of the Ethiopian student movement as belonging to an elite class of students engaged in adolescent rebellion and with a penchant towards a cult of violence. This cult of violence then becomes an explanation for the fissures between the various groups within the student movement and later between the various political parties in the post-revolutionary period. Bahru's work fails to grapple with the question of the social content that might be buried inside the political narratives expressed within the Ethiopian revolution. However, he does return us to the literature produced by the student movement, and provides us with a useful timeline that tracks the relationship between the student movement and political developments in Ethiopia. As such, the tools and theoretical repertoire that belonged to the student movement become part of the tools used to rethink the origins and consequences of the Ethiopian revolution. Similarly, Gebru Tareke examines the archives of the Ethiopian Ministry of Defence in order to show that there are clear continuities between the student movements that organised in the urban areas prior to 1974 and the rural insurgencies that dominated Ethiopia in the 1980s. He then posits that the post-1991 regime must be seen as the continuation of the revolution of 1974.

In light of this, I also think it possible to link Bahru and Gebru back to a tradition of writing that was perhaps first initiated by Addis Hiwet, an author discussed earlier in relation to ROAPE publications. This tradition aims at self-critique of the revolution by means of the goals and theoretical tools that were established by the student movement itself. As discussed earlier, Addis Hiwet argued that a distinction can be made between the Ethiopian revolution and the Derg regime. Similarly, Gebru states that one of the goals of his book is to 'use historical memory of collective resistance to mold a more egalitarian society'.[93] This differs from Messay's work, whose aim is to restore what has been lost in Ethiopia by rejecting the legacy of the student movement. This raises the question of whether a narrative project that is tied to a normative

---

93   Tareke 2009, p. xii.

goal as outlined by Gebru or Messay must inevitably instrumentalise knowledge on behalf of a particular group or set of institutions. In Chapter 1 I have tried to deal with this problem by disentangling critique from the writing of mainstream social sciences, suggesting that critique is connected to history's own possibility through the revelation of the contradictions of past human struggle and its redemption through self-conscious struggle in the present. As I have suggested, my intellectual project is to open up the future by seeking contradiction in 'the air that we breathe'. As a result, I think it would be useful to close this chapter with an examination of the work of Gebru Tareke and Addis Hiwet, and to compare their claims to Messay's speculations. I suggest that Gebru and Addis Hiwet get us closer to examining the contradictions of the Ethiopian revolution, while Messay keeps us mired in a narrow nationalism that is based in counter-factual conjecture. In the following chapter, I use Bahru Zewde's work on the student movement to further interpret the movement's literature and its link to post-revolutionary policy documents. In this way, we will be able to draw out how theory and practice have been linked in writing on the Ethiopian revolution. The goal for the rest of this chapter is to show that what Messay, Bahru, Gebru, and Addis Hiwet have in common is that they push the historiography of the revolution in a new direction by allowing us to pose the question of how different groups of people cohere into a social group that comes to have interests expressed in political struggle. This will helps us to move beyond the centre/periphery model of state formation in order to begin to uncover its contingent processes.

The main concern of Messay's study is the failure of the Ethiopian education system to promote a national culture that would establish continuity between past traditions and the modern era. Messay never actually defines what he means by modernity except to suggest that what marks a prosperous and politically stable country today is that it has been able to manage a successful transition from tradition to modernity through centring that transition on a time-honoured cultural identity. Examples of countries where Messay believes this transition has occurred are Japan, India and Nepal.[94] Nonetheless, he draws a distinction between westernisation and modernisation, and thus a corollary concern of his book is that the transition to modernity in Ethiopia has been built on an education system that fostered westernisation, or what he alternatively calls cultural alienation.

Given his initial assessment of the problem of cultural alienation, Messay's book also comes to be concerned with why Ethiopian elites have not had the

---

94   Kebede 2008, p. 33.

creative wherewithal to use the repository of rich cultural traditions that exist in the country to lead such a positive transition to modernity. In the case of Ethiopia, Messay suggests that, despite the presence of Islam, the country has a common cultural identity that is rooted in Orthodox Christianity and the Kebre Negast and, given this, he is bewildered by the fact that elites have been unable to use this identity to rebuild a modern national project (RCD 50). Messay defines liberalism as necessarily positing a relationship of continuity between past and present, while Marxism assumes it can create a tabula rasa that will rebuild society from scratch.[95] The implication here is that the Ethiopian student movement failed in its duty to lead the country in so much as it chose the path of Marxism and cut off Ethiopia's ties with its past. Thus another part of Messay's project is to ask why the Ethiopian student movement did not turn to liberal ideas of change in order to promote a transition to modernity; this is where he links the problem of cultural alienation to the problem of elite leadership. For him, the education system in Ethiopia is responsible for cultivating a kind of colonial self-hate that turned the student movement towards tabula rasa politics and to Marxism in particular.

The scorn that Messay directs towards much of what he calls the Ethiopian elite is particularly focused in his discussion of Haile-Selassie, who he sees as the progenitor of the modern Ethiopian state but also blames for divesting Ethiopian elites of the confidence to build a modern country through the cultural pillars of historic Abyssinia.[96] For Messay, Haile-Selassie's historic failing is grounded in the fact that the military defeat of the coloniser convinced Ethiopians that they were not colonised. This allowed Haile-Selassie to try to centralise the modern state through a system of credentialisation rooted in an education system that was set up by foreigners and that treated previous systems of Ethiopian knowledge production as irrelevant to the new mode of being. Instead of linking past and present, Haile-Selassie's regime positioned newly educated elites as vanguards of a new beginning and as 'rectifiers of a civilizing mission perverted by racism'.[97] If the students of the 1960s chose Marxism it is because in many ways they were taking Haile-Selassie's project to its final conclusion: creating the clean slate that Haile-Selassie tried but failed to set up. For Messay, this also means that Ethiopia's main challenge since entering the modern era has not been socio-economic crises but the institutionalisation of a cultural malaise that in turn is unable to address the socio-economic problems of the country. Poverty is as such a symptom of bad

---

95   Kebede 2008, p. 35.
96   Kebede 2008, p. 50.
97   Kebede 2008, p. 45.

cultural politics, not its result. To be more precise, for Messay, Haile-Selassie had produced an elite class that addressed questions of poverty and inequality by seeking their cause in politics instead of rooting them in their own cultural ineptitude.[98] While Messay's main intellectual project is to demonstrate the need to decolonise the Ethiopian mind, here decolonisation means reviving lost traditions through a transition to modernity within a liberal political framework.

This brings us to the other major claim of Messay's work, which is that because intellectuals were the leaders of the revolution, the revolution must not have had economic demands as its primary motive.[99] Messay simply equates members of the Ethiopian student movement with what he calls an elite class, without theorising the historical formation of the students beyond what he takes to be a self-evident categorisation. Thus he can claim that the class identity of the revolution's leaders is further evidence as to why an economic-structural argument cannot explain the roots of the revolution. For Messay nothing about the Ethiopian economic situation required a turn to Marxism. Instead the students' dedication to radicalism merely reflected a perception of Marx as the latest stage in a western philosophical tradition to which the students felt they belonged as Christians. If the students rejected liberalism it was not because liberalism was inappropriate, but because they treated Marxism as one might treat any *a priori* commitment to a religious doctrine. They were zealous and ideological. For Messay, this made Ethiopian students both eccentric and isolated from society. Unfortunately, this also allowed the students to abuse their power as elites and to use a genuine social crisis to frame the grievances of ordinary people 'in terms of their own cultural eccentricity'.[100] Taking a page from Clapham, Messay understands radicalism and Leninism as highly useful tools that allow new elites to enthrone themselves within the hallways of power without having to be accountable to past traditions and ways of doing things.

Cultural alienation, liberalism, radicalism and modernity operate as key heuristic devices in Messay's interpretation of twentieth-century Ethiopian events. Yet in his book he offers very little discussion of the social and political history of these controversial terms. Reading his book, one might even be forgiven for not knowing that these terms are burdened with a history that implicates them in a variety of political battles elsewhere on the globe. Unable

---

98 Kebede 2008, p. 5.
99 Kebede 2008, p. 3.
100 Kebede 208, p. 32.

to locate them within a broader context, Messay Kebede ends up describing Ethiopian history through his highly idiosyncratic understanding of these terms. For this reason, it becomes very difficult to systematically follow his explanation of radicalism in Ethiopia. One is often at a loss to know what to do with the way a lack of conceptual clarity moves the text along. For instance, is there any serious history of liberalism that could support Messay's general claim that liberalism is simply based on continuity with the past? Can radicalism only be associated with the Marxist tradition? Does radicalism not have a history within the making of bourgeois revolutions? Moreover, is it possible to have a meaningful discussion of modernity without linking the modern project to broader economic and social processes?

Another difficulty with Messay's approach is that his book is concerned with reconstructing an idea of an Ethiopia that could have been created if the students had chosen liberalism as a path towards modernisation. But whether his conjectures might have come true cannot be proven except through a fantastical reconstruction of the past. This strategy does not open history up to explanation but keeps it bogged down in what cannot be proved. In this chapter I have been suggesting that it is possible to approach history with a much simpler task. How did members of the Ethiopian student movement come to choose Marxism as their guiding ideology, and what does that tell us about the limited choices available to them? The point here is to show that the resolutions of past contradictions shape our present. Where we do have agency is in our ability to pry open the resolution of these past contradictions as they exist for us today so that the future can have its own possibilities given back to it.[101]

Although Messay Kebede acknowledges his own participation in the Ethiopian student movement, he began his career as an academic when he joined the Department of Philosophy at Addis Ababa University in 1976. In 1996, after a twenty-year tenure, he was dismissed from his job along with forty other professors who were associated with the former Derg regime. The reasons for this collective dismissal have been speculated about in numerous blog posts and newspaper articles, and are not something I can address here. However, it is well known that in the mid-1980s Kebede chaired the AAU discussions of the Derg constitution that was implemented in 1987. It was not until 1998 when Messay joined the Philosophy Faculty at the University of Ohio (Dayton) that he became an advocate for conservative and nationalist values. This has

---

101   In terms of helping me clarify the problem with Messay's counter-factual method, I am
        indebted to Evans 2014.

tied Messay's intellectual work to a broader Ethiopian diaspora-based political movement that claims that the ethno-nationalist policies of the incumbent regime are anti-patriotic and chauvinist. In Chapter 4, I examine how the discourses of this movement partially shaped the outcome of the 2005 elections in Ethiopia. In that chapter I return to Messay's work and reframe it as part of the lasting impact of the Ethiopian student movement in terms of shaping current political discourses on Ethiopia.

In many ways, Gebru Tareke's work can also be understood as part of the ongoing attempt to rethink how contemporary issues of state governance in Ethiopia are shaped by the lasting legacy of the Ethiopian student movement. However, rather than present the past as something that could have happened differently, Gebru is more concerned with discovering how politics, military strategy and various emancipatory visions were linked in the Ethiopian civil wars of 1974 to 1991. Later, he asks how this has determined the shape of the Ethiopian state today.

Gebru periodises the Ethiopian revolution as a twofold process. In the first phase, the common goal of dismantling Haile-Selassie's autocracy united the opposition, while the second phase, which began as early as 1975, can be characterised by the fragmentation of the left into a number of groups with important ideological differences. At a general level, Gebru sees this fragmentation happening in two directions: on the one hand, there were groups such as the TPLF and EPLF who led a rural insurgency, and who Gebru calls Maoist; on the other hand, there were the urban-based parties that either coalesced into the Derg regime or were eliminated by the urban warfare of 1975–8. Gebru calls these urban parties Leninist and associates them with a top-down, state-driven, authoritarian socialism. The year 1975 in Ethiopia, for Gebru, was marked by the simultaneous launch of two revolutions: one that was based in the city and that relied on force and physical compulsion to be institutionalised, and a second revolution that was both regional and ethno-nationalist in nature, but that also mobilised a large segment of the rural population through a people's war guided by insurgent intellectuals. For this reason, Gebru concludes that the civil wars of the 70s and 80s were in fact *revolutionary wars*.

Earlier in this chapter I used Gebru Tareke's writing on the Ethiopian revolution to critically engage John Young's research on the history of the TPLF. I emphasised that Gebru had argued that prior to the launching of the TPLF, Tigrayans who were peasants would have had little concept of either a social identity or collective destiny beyond their rural communities.[102] Gebru Tareke

---

102   Tareke 2009, p. 88.

has also argued that the process of participating in war-making is what was responsible for producing a national Tigrayan identity where none existed before.[103] He argued that when the TPLF resolved the question of 'unequal development, social repression and cultural alienation' through a policy of ethno-national autonomy, 'the TPLF put into practice what a section of the Ethiopian student movement had demanded'.[104]

The TPLF was founded by eleven urbanites (many of them former students at Addis Ababa University) as well as an elder named Sihul who was a popular and well-known social bandit operating in the area where the TPLF first set up its base operation. The elder Sihul acted as a credible mediator between the local community and the TPLF and secured permission for the TPLF to reside in the village. In this founding story of the TPLF we can see that there was never an easy correspondence between the demands of the rebels and the needs of the villagers. Part of what Gebru shows is that peasant reaction to both the central government and the TPLF depended on which military force could guarantee security of livelihood, which would also include protection from the other's raids.[105] For Gebru, in the end what determined victory for both the TPLF and EPLF is that they understood the vulnerability of the peasant population and were able to incorporate the political and social organisation of peasant life into their overall military strategy; this is why he says that the TPLF and EPLF fought a people's war.

Here we should bear in mind that the organisational patterns of the Derg regime were often mimicked by both the TPLF and EPLF. Both fronts set up a quasi-state system structured through democratic centralism, which penetrated the local level through peasant associations as well as women's and youth associations. The peasant associations were also responsible for instituting redistributive land reforms, while the mass-based associations organised programmes of gender equality and political education. Music shows and dramas were organised by these groups to inculcate new socialist values amongst the mass of the people. The TPLF and EPLF also operated a school for cadres that trained participants in military strategy and Marxist theory. Lastly, individual behaviour was often brought into line with the political and military goals of the TPLF through criticism and self-criticism sessions at the village level.

All of this gave the population a sense of participation in the formation of a new apparatus for governing daily life, while at the same time curtailing the

---

103   Tareke 2009, p. 81.
104   Tareke 2009, p. 327.
105   Tareke 2009, p. 90.

available options for action. The people's war was what Gebru terms a system of 'guided democracy' in which non-cooperation on the part of the population often resulted in systematic harassment, social ostracism and loss of property or even life.[106] The deep penetration of the quasi-state apparatus into daily life meant that psychological intimidation often disciplined participants into compliance.[107] In the end, Gebru claims that the success of both the EPLF and the TPLF must be found in their ability to create a political identity that linked the ambitions of a few radical urban intellectuals with the frustrations of ordinary people.[108] This links back to the main argument of his book, which is that the 'politics of organizing violence' shaped the outcome of the twin revolutionary process and the subsequent state(s).[109]

This also means that when the TPLF launched a war against the central government it linked the grievances of the local population to larger social and political processes.[110] In many ways, those processes were the same conditions that had shaped the urban-based student protest movement of the 1960s and 1970s. The TPLF was only one of many responses in the country to the material and social contradictions created by Haile-Selassie's regime. For Gebru, the urban-based students from Tigray were also part of that social group that Markakis has labelled the salitariat: a newly formed petit bourgeois group who were excluded from jobs within the bureaucratic-military bourgeoisie but lacked socio-economic opportunities beyond the central state apparatus. That the TPLF chose to describe this structural-economic conundrum as a regional and ethnic contradiction was part of what split the Ethiopian left into various positions. What links the rural insurgencies with the Ethiopian student movement is the fact that they were both a response to the same social processes. At the same time, it must be conceded that the rural insurgents won a military victory over those who described the problem of Ethiopian politics differently. This has had a dramatic impact on the shape of the state. Ethiopia today is a federal republic organized around ethno-nationalist groups and, much to the chagrin of theorists such as Messay Kebede, the current constitution now recognises the right to self-determination up to secession for any nation, nationality or people within the federation. What tied each of the various factions of the student movement together was the demand to resolve the contradictions of Haile-Selassie's regime by including the masses in politics. However,

---

106   Tareke 2009, p. 68.
107   Tareke 2009, p. 90.
108   Tareke 2009, p. 82.
109   Tareke 2009, p. xiv.
110   Tareke 2009, p. 81.

what tore the student movement apart was its participants' lack of agreement on the methods that might be used to get there, as well as the type of political system needed to realise such a goal.[111]

This brings us back to our initial concerns about the relationship between the social sciences and politics, including the politics of the battlefield. As Gebru has shown us, the ideas of the student movement shaped the battle lines that were drawn in the Ethiopian civil wars of 1974–91. Our reading of the historiography of the revolution has also shown us that these battle lines are often redrawn within the literature as moral or political positions, without any sense of their origins within an earlier intellectual debate. The twin processes of the Ethiopian revolution can be linked back to debates about strategies and tactics within revolutionary movements, and yet the literature is more or less blind to this fact. This can be attributed to the tendency in the literature to connect the Derg with the revolution, while relegating the story of the rural insurgencies to a different historical process. As a result, the stabilisation of the Derg regime after 1978 is read as the moment when the student movement of the 1960s/70s drops out altogether from the scene of Ethiopian history. What this forgets is the dual relationship of the student movement to both the rural insurgencies and the institutions and policies of the Derg regime. Messay, who grasps this complex relationship, attempts to skirt any critical engagement with the student movement by simply declaring it invalid. The virtue of Gebru's work is that he understands the student movement to also have been an intellectual movement that dramatically shaped the revolutionary process in Ethiopia. When Gebru posits the Ethiopian revolution as a twofold process that produced both a rural insurgency and an urban uprising, he is also suggesting that the impact of the student movement can be seen in the victory of the rural insurgencies over the Derg regime and the establishment of the 1995 constitution. Similarly, when Gebru disentangles the historical formation of a national Tigrayan identity from any sense that it might be rooted in a primordial community, he is also demonstrating that the structural pressures that produce nationalist movements are unique to a particular historical period. In this way, he is able to move us away from the less than fruitful discussion of what constitutes an authentic identity, and towards one where we consider how questions of equality and justice raised by the era of nationalism were dealt with during the rise of ethno-nationalist movements in Ethiopia.

For me, paying attention to the student movement and the subsequent revolution is not so much about whether or not the students got their Marxism

---

111   Tareke 2009, p. 25.

right, but how they understood the nation-state project and how they attempted to transform it. Discussion of the national question (i.e. Eritrea, Tigray, southern nationalities, etc) is about how a new class of people produced by a new and developing nation-state grapple with the particularities of their social formation. The students were largely from non-aristocratic families; they were a new social group produced by the newly modernising state, but this does not make them elites. Rather, what is interesting is how they made sense of their social position *vis-a-vis* the history of global forces that created this regional nation-state in the nineteenth century. It was not a given what the students did, nor how they envisioned their role. Yet a large part of the historiography of the region reads everything this new social group does as either an analogy of something else (Halliday, Ottaway), or as having a completely internal logic (Clapham, Messay). What I find interesting is not whether Ethiopia is like France or Russia, but that this new social group theorised its own crises and made sense of itself using tools and language taken from all over the place. It produced its own literature and political theory, not in isolation from the world but in conversation. Were they good scientists or even good Marxists? For me, this is a bad question. The task at hand is to link consciousness back to the social conditions that it relates to. Revolutionary processes in Ethiopia are part of a longer story about the creativity involved in nation-state building. Viewed this way, we can draw out the practical ways in which theory transformed practice, but also how practice changed theory on the ground. This is the terrain on which we must engage the whole of the Ethiopian revolution.

Perhaps this is why Addis Hiwet preferred to use the term 'popular democratic upsurge' to collectively refer to the strikes, rebellions and insurgencies that preceded the 1974 revolution. Rather than spending his time predicting the outcome of this democratic upsurge, in the bulk of his book Addis Hiwet looks backwards, placing the events of 1974/75 into a historical context. A crucial part of his argument is that the 1974 rebellion must be understood as a revolt against the contradictions of the modern Ethiopian state, whose history he says does not extend into a limitless past but can be firmly established as beginning in the 1890s when Minilik's empire-state was finally recognised as a sovereign reality. While Addis Hiwet characterises Minilik's state as military-feudal-centralism, he also distinguishes it from the pre-capitalist empire we might associate with the name Abyssinia, because the dynamics of international capitalist-imperialism were decisive in determining the shape of the newly formed empire-state.[112] The forces that created the Gold Coast, the Ivory

---

112 Hiwet 1975, p. 52.

Coast, the Sudan, and Kenya were the same forces that shaped the creation of modern Ethiopia.[113] He also argues that we must pay attention to the specific ways that those broader historical pressures 'activated internal social-political forces'.[114] Crucially, for Hiwet, the wars of the nineteenth century simply mark the process of establishing the modern state in the first place.[115] The fundamental questions of Haile-Selassie's regime revolved around the relationship of the provincial rulers to the central state. For instance, the modern state now had to ask: how would tithe and tribute be collected in the newly incorporated regions of the empire-state? How would the central state mediate relations between local traders and international markets? More specifically, how would the state restructure class relations as well as labour and land tenure regimes in the various regions that supplied international markets with coffee and slaves? Lastly, how would this affect local trade and transportation circuits? In the end, Addis Hiwet argues that it was to Haile-Selassie's great detriment that he was unable to address these socio-economic questions to any satisfactory degree. Hiwet writes:

> The popular democratic upsurge marks a new chapter in Ethiopian history. It is a revolt against the societal conditions of the 1890s, 1900, 1940s, and 1960s, as much as it is a revolt against societal conditions in 1974. It is the result of a fundamental historical contradiction – land tenure, feudal absolutism, the nature of the relationship of social and class forces – as they developed during the last 80 or so years. The popular democratic upsurge is actually a watershed between the present and the future.[116]

Given this complex history, we can agree with Donald Donham that globalised cross talk shapes local actors' perception of themselves to the degree that they also understand their actions as being made on a world stage. Yet since Donham's narration of the revolution in Maale makes a caricature of the encounter between the periphery and what he perceives to be the centre of power in Ethiopia, he has only scratched the surface of the archaeology of stories that need to be uncovered to understand what is at stake in the Ethiopian revolution. Donham is not alone in this; as we have seen, it also characterises much of the research on rural insurgencies in Ethiopia associated with ROAPE. Much

---

113   Hiwet 1975, p. 2.
114   Ibid.
115   Hiwet 1975, p. 52.
116   Hiwet 1975, p. 3.

of that work can be juxtaposed with the attempt by former members of the Ethiopian student movement to think though their own historical legacy in the society they attempted to change. In their work, there is at least an attempt to creatively think through the limitations placed on the Ethiopian centre as it relates to global economic systems, and an attempt to see these structural pressures as dialectically constitutive of social relations in rural Ethiopia. I agree with Addis Hiwet that the questions posed by the student movement are quintessentially related to the scramble for Africa; but their answers, too, are a story about African political thought on the world stage. Part of what the Ethiopian student movement was theorising was the fact that both Minilik and Haile-Selassie led Ethiopia's bourgeois revolution from above. This again raises the question of what stage of history the student movement represents.

Such a question can only arise in a context where the problem of nationalist thought is seen as a mechanical representation of a pre-determined sociological problem common to modern life everywhere. But in thinking that, we lose sight of the fact that constitutive of how politics is organised in the non-western world are the institutional processes that must be put into place in order to allow different social groups to be included in the nation-state. These institutional processes respond creatively to initiatives from below and from above and are shaped through social struggle. Social inclusion within the nation-state cannot be described as an issue of having to overcome obstacles to modern life that are embedded in 'traditional' forms of organising life; rather, the struggle over the form and content of inclusion/exclusion are constitutive of what political life is within the colonial world. And yet even the counter-discourse of localism falls victim to sociological determinism when it sets up the dichotomy of local versus global. It too describes the problem of modernity as a confrontation between different cultures and stages of history rather than a problem of social tensions that are produced by political processes (even if those processes also manifest as a problem of cultural expression). This is at the root of why the historiography of the Ethiopian revolution can so easily be instrumentalised: overall this body of literature fails to take seriously the very conditions that produce the dichotomies it wishes to address – modernity vs. tradition, reason vs. tradition, poverty vs. wealth creation, and so on. Instead it aligns itself with the story of modernity as a clash of cultures and attempts to delineate the winners and losers in that clash.

This reproduces the problem of what Partha Chatterjee has pointed out: at the level of the thematic, anti-colonial nationalist thought accepts the dichotomy between east and west, tradition and modernity, rationalism and mythology that has been created by the structure of power that nationalist thought seeks to repudiate.[117] Even though anti-colonial thought aims to produce a different discourse, it takes on this representational structure, resolving the structure's problems by assuming it as its own space of autonomy.[118] Chatterjee writes:

> [T]he 'object' of nationalist thought is still the Oriental, who retains the essentialist character depicted in Orientalist discourse. Only, he is not passive, non-participating. He is seen to possess a subjectivity which he can himself 'make'. In other words, while his relationship to himself and to others have been posed, understood, and defined by others, i.e by an objective scientific consciousness, by Knowledge, by Reason, those relationships are not acted upon by others. His subjectivity, he thinks, is active, autonomous and sovereign.[119]

For Chatterjee, this problem is reproduced in the debate about the rationality of African systems of thought within the academic field now known as African Philosophy. The debate about African systems of thought was initiated by thinkers such as Robin Horton and Peter Winch; Chatterjee reminds us of the major questions asked in this debate: how do we interpret the fact that large numbers of people (those who are other than European) hold beliefs that are false? Should we in fact say that their beliefs are false? If we do so, do we then also ask why these beliefs are held as true, or is that in fact an ethnocentric project? Is it better that we simply apply the principle of charity in our study of the other and assume that for the way of life of the other their beliefs remain true? Or should we ask whether it is possible to find areas of agreement between the anthropologist and the other, opening up cultural beliefs to wide interpretation in terms of specific social circumstances and processes?[120]

These questions show that in this debate intelligence is sought through the functionalist reading of cultural practices. For Chatterjee, this functionalist reading of culture reveals the spurious philosophical grounds of the entire debate around rationality vs. relativism, precisely because it is clear that large classes of beliefs will not submit to a true or false paradigm.[121] Indeed, most meaningful conversations cannot be subjected to a simple criterion of truth vs. falsehood. Nor can the cognitive boundaries between cultures be so easily

---

117   Chatterjee 1999, p. 38.
118   Chatterjee 1999, p. 42.
119   Chatterjee 1999, p. 38.
120   Chatterjee 1999, pp. 16–17.
121   Chatterjee 1999, p. 14.

defined, and even within the natural sciences criteria for judgment have their own historicity. If in the sciences we claim to strive for scientific objectivity, questions of power, culture and ethnicity must also come into play. For Chatterjee, the insistence that the west is rational must mean something other than what it first appears to mean; its meaning must be wrapped up in debates that are bounded in time and space. The essentialism that Chatterjee wants us to worry about is that the 'sciences of nature' become the paradigm of all rational knowledge: where the principal characteristic of these sciences as they are now conceived is their relation to an entirely new idea of man's *control* over nature – a progressive and ceaseless process of the appropriation of nature to serve human 'interests'.[122] The subject-object relation between man and nature also becomes a way of describing the relation between man and his interests. In this sense then, the sciences of man become the knowledge of the self and other's interests, as well as a means of power of the self over man.[123] If this is so, what we mean by rationality must be a certain way of looking at properties of nature, ordering knowledge, and having an advantage over our objects: 'rationality becomes the normative principle of a certain way of life ... science'.[124] This takes us back to the question of a particular culture, but now, rather than focusing on whether the rationalists or the relativists are correct, the question becomes how 'changes in techno-economic conditions of production' have come to be associated with western culture as a whole. Following this conflation of technical and economic capacity with European culture, how is it that the whole of human history comes to be divided between dichotomies such as modernity vs. tradition, rationality vs. irrationality (tradition), secular vs. non-secular (tradition), scientific vs. mythological thought (tradition), etc.? This question, for Chatterjee, is central to getting at the contradiction between the thematic and problematic of anti-colonial nationalist thought. Because anti-colonial nationalists' texts assume the sociological determinism posited in the dichotomies listed above, even as nationalism challenges the colonial claim to political domination it also accepts the very intellectual premises of modernity on which European colonial domination was based.[125]

Of course, the intellectual premises of nationalist thought are not simply based on mere representational systems, but are actually connected to social processes in the world. The contradiction between the problematic and thematic of nationalism must be linked back to the very real limits of what the

---

122   Ibid.
123   Chatterjee 1999, p. 15.
124   Chatterjee 1999, p. 16.
125   Chatterjee 1999, p. 30.

anti-colonial struggles in most of the third world have been able to achieve. These include the weakness of local capitalist classes; the relation of political forces inside the country and their ability to coordinate efforts so that the corporate interests of one group can be subordinated to the broader interests of other classes; and the question of military force and whether a war of movement can be launched against colonial powers. Given that anti-colonial movements likely cannot set up rival military forces, these movements must instead mobilise the popular masses against the colonial state through a nationalist ideology and political programme. Because the popular masses are peasants, the question of mobilisation is intertwined with the fundamental economic and cultural problem of what to do with backward farmers and peasants. The European colonial state becomes folded into the preconditions for capitalist development and modernisation.[126] These historic limits demonstrate that the contradiction between the problematic and thematic of anti-colonial nationalism rests on the fact that 'passive revolution becomes the historical path by which a national development of capital can occur without surmounting those contradictions'.[127]

Passive revolution is a term Chatterjee borrows from Gramsci's work on the nature of bourgeois society in Italy. For Gramsci, what was remarkable in Italy was that the transition to a capitalist state was led from above, and depended on the simultaneous mobilisation and demobilisation of popular movements in order to push for molecular changes at the state level and to help coordinate the transition on behalf of capital. In the context of the third world, the idea of passive revolution suggests that anti-colonial struggles can be described as going through three stages of development. The first is the movement of departure, which Chatterjee describes as the moment local elites realise their backwardness and begin to develop a notion of modernity that is supposedly a combination of the superior moral qualities of the indigenous culture combined with the technology of the west (one cannot help but think of Senghor's negritude here). The second stage of the passive revolution is the moment of manoeuvre, where an elitist programme of upliftment, mobilisation and demobilisation of popular forces must occur at the same time; and the third stage is the moment of arrival, which for Chatterjee is the passive revolution 'writing its own life-history'.[128]

As a result of the passive revolution there is no dismantling of the institutional structures of colonial rational authority, neither in administrative or

---

126   Chatterjee 1999, p. 48.
127   Chatterjee 1999, p. 43.
128   Chatterjee 1999, p. 51.

economic institutions nor in the structure of education, science, research or cultural organisation. 'Indeed, the dominance of capital does not emanate from its hegemonic sway over civil society, but rather from the measure of control over the new state apparatus, which becomes the pre-condition for further capitalist development'.[129] If in his discussion of capitalist hegemony Gramsci is concerned with the connections between intellectual leadership and economic domination, Chatterjee is at pains to show that the structure of the post-colonial state is one that accepts a universal standard of progress, and thus institutionalises the thematics of the colonial state even as it repudiates colonial rule. Here the question becomes: 'Why is it that non-European colonial countries have no historical alternative but to try to approximate the given attributes of modernity when that very process of approximation means their continued subjection under a world order which only sets their task for them and over which they have no control'?[130]

One of the problems of the moment of arrival is that nationalism is rewritten as part of the teleological development of a backward people into modernity, with nationalism itself reduced to a sociological requirement of modern, industrial life. Questions of epistemology and cultural difference are reduced to the dichotomies between modernity and tradition, rationality and mythology – as we have seen in the debate about African Philosophy and systems of thought – when they should in fact be read as part of the process of doing politics within the ambit of the passive revolution: how are differences in language overcome? What kind of institutional power allows for some differences to be elided? How are various social groups included in the nation-state? These questions are of course relevant, since what is also common to the three stages of anti-colonial nationalism is that movement from the top (of gradualism, moderation and molecular change) in tandem with the movement of popular initiative from below is a struggle that is not pre-determined.[131] Here we can locate how the limits to intellectual life (including the social sciences) and the limits to social life become imbricated in contests for power, and the ways in which those contests connect back to a social base. In the case of the historiography of the Ethiopian revolution we can see how this created a complex nexus between intellectuals, nationalism, the war field and critique.

Nationalism in the context of the third world is not a modular adaptation of an already established process whose origin resides in the west, but rather

---

129   Chatterjee 1999, p. 49.
130   Chatterjee 1999, pp. 10–11.
131   Chatterjee 1999, p. 46.

an attempt to constitute a collective political subjectivity that could go beyond colonialism, but whose specific battles are fought out in the interstitial
spaces between the limits and possibilities of a paradoxical social situation.
Today in Ethiopia, we can say that the discourse of nationalism was a form
of creative anti-colonial state building even as it placed severe limits on how
collective grievances could be articulated. The Ethiopian student movement
attempted to go beyond the Haile-Selassie regime, while at the same time confronting various social interests contained within wider society. My reading
of the literature of the Ethiopian student movement in the following chapter
highlights how the form of argumentation adopted by authors of the student
movement relied on what Chatterjee calls the thematic of anti-colonial nationalist thought. I loosely organise the themes that emerge from the student movement literature around Chatterjee's three stages of anti-colonial thought (the
moments of departure, manoeuvre and arrival). It should be clear that I do not
perceive Chatterjee's three stages as necessarily linear, nor am I trying to map
the Ethiopian experience directly onto the Indian experience that Chatterjee is
concerned with. To do so would miss Chatterjee's point about the relative creativity and indeterminacy of anti-colonial nationalist politics. Rather, for me,
the three stages of anti-colonial nationalist thought become heuristic devices
that help connect the arguments of the student movement to shifting strategies
adopted by the student movement – strategies which aimed to address the
paradoxical social situation in which the students found themselves.

Challenge: Social Science in the Literature of the Ethiopian Student Movement

In the years between 1964 and 1974, Ethiopian post-secondary students studying at home, in Europe, and in North America organised themselves into a number of student unions. Shying away from making corporate demands on behalf of students, they instead articulated a new radical social agenda for the burgeoning Ethiopian nation-state. Each of these student unions produced journals that attempted to explore the relationship between social theory and social change as it might apply to the case of building a socialist Ethiopia. The titles of these journals include *Challenge*, *Struggle*, and *Combat*. What is most remarkable about these journals is that, collectively, they became the venues where the policy outcomes of the 1974 Ethiopian revolution were first articulated and argued over. In these journals we witness the development of the ideas and thoughts of much of the leadership that participated in the Ethiopian revolution after 1974, and can begin to understand the divisions that influenced the different political parties in the post-1974 period. In this chapter I focus primarily on one of these journals, *Challenge*, to track the development of ideas that influenced policy outcomes in revolutionary Ethiopia. Some of the key questions that I explore in this chapter are: Who were the major thinkers, and what were the major ideas that influenced debate within the Ethiopian student movement? How were ideas mobilised to meet political ends? What was the nature of the relationship between ideas, social sciences and policy that was nurtured through the efforts of the Ethiopian student movement? And lastly, how did these sets of relationships help pave the way for the circulation of intellectual persons from the world of letters to the world of governance, as well as to the world of military action and war-making?

Many of the political parties founded on the eve of the Ethiopian revolution later produced mass-based newspapers. For instance, the Ethiopian People's Revolutionary Party (EPRP), which was founded by Ethiopian students in exile in Algiers, the US, and Europe published *Democracia*, probably the most widely circulated newspaper in the immediate post-74 period, while the All Ethiopia Socialist Movement (commonly known by the acronym AESM or ME'ISON), a by-product of the Ethiopian Student Union Europe (ESUE), produced a paper called *Voice of the Masses*. However, the aim of these newspapers was to mobilise and organise the popular masses, while the journals produced by the Ethiopian student movement addressed a very specific and highly educated audience. I have therefore chosen to draw a distinction between these two types of writing platforms. One significant difference between the mass-based newspapers and the student union journals is that the former were written in Amharic, while the student journals were often written in English and focused on experimenting with different ways of applying concepts drawn from the university setting and the social sciences to the situation in Ethiopia. Because this chapter's central interest is the nexus between social science practice and political practice, I am largely concerned with how ideas debated in the theoretical journals produced by the Ethiopian student movement eventually travelled into political party platforms and national laws. I track this in the latter part of this chapter.

My reading of *Challenge* does not simply summarise the major debates of the student movement. Instead, I show how the students grappled with the question of how to include various social groups within a newly developing nation-state. The student movement represents both an attempt from the top to restructure state-society relations and a popular initiative by a newly educated class of students to reshape the state from the bottom. In rereading *Challenge*, my hope is to discover the limits and frontiers of intellectual life (including the social sciences) during this period, and to discover how the intellectual struggles of the student movement were connected to struggles for the Ethiopian state. In the end, my argument will be that the common themes that emerge from the articles in *Challenge* can guide us beyond the surface meanings of the texts in order to examine broader social meanings concerning the role of ideas in Ethiopian society and in shaping Ethiopian politics.

In Chapter 2 I argued that the territorial sovereignty established under Minilik (or the Mahdists) can be seen as one iteration of the creativity involved in anti-colonial nationalism, albeit with contradictory consequences for the populations of the Horn of Africa. In this chapter I show that the student movement represents yet another moment of creativity and contradiction that is not dissimilar from efforts made by various actors in the late nineteenth century in the region. My reading of *Challenge* highlights how the form of argumentation adopted by the authors of the journal relied on what Chatterjee calls the thematic of anti-colonial nationalist thought (see Chapter 2), even as a certain indeterminacy remained about how events might turn out.

Challenge was the organ of the Ethiopian Student Association of North America from 1960 until 1973, and at least one or two and sometimes three issues of the journal were produced each year.[1] The journal often reproduced

---

1   The group was also known as the Ethiopian Student Union North America after 1968.

resolutions and reports from a number of the major meetings convened by the Ethiopian student movement in North America, Europe, and Ethiopia. As a result, *Challenge* can be said to have both fostered and recorded many of the contentious debates that characterised the Ethiopian student movement in general. *Challenge* also provides us with a good record of the antagonistic debates around the nationalities question, a major issue that divided political parties in Ethiopia in the post-revolutionary period. As such, *Challenge* is uniquely positioned to give us a bird's eye view of the impact of the Ethiopian student movement on the development of Ethiopian politics.

There are two essays on the nationalities question not published in *Challenge* that are crucial to the overall debate in that journal and to the Ethiopian student movement more generally. The first essay, titled 'On the Nationalities Question in Ethiopia', was written by Wallelign Mekonnen and first published in the November 1969 issue of *Struggle*, a journal published by the student union at Haile-Selassie I University (HSIU) in Addis Ababa. The second is 'On the National Question ("Regionalism") in Ethiopia', written by Tilahun Takele. This essay was first published as a pamphlet distributed by a group of Ethiopian students based in Algiers, who received military training from the Algerian government.[2] It was discovered later that Tilahun Takele was a pen name and that the essay was either written by a number of members in the Algiers group or, more likely, by a leading member of that group, Berhane Meskel, who in 1972 would go on to found the Ethiopian People's Revolutionary Party (EPRP). Both Tilahun's and Wallelign's texts were also published in the March 1971 Newsletter of the New York Chapter of the Ethiopian Student Union of North America; my readings of these texts are based on this copy. Both texts served as bases for subsequent splits in the Ethiopian student movement and the Ethiopian left. As a result, I view both of them as important to the unfolding debates in *Challenge* and to the overall development of the student movement, and have included a discussion of these two essays as part of my overall discussion of *Challenge* in this chapter.

The history of *Challenge* can be periodised into four moments. First, from 1960 until 1964, *Challenge* was simply a scholarly journal of the Ethiopia Student Association North America (ESANA), which at the time conducted itself as a social club rather than as an organisation with political goals.[3] The second period of the journal's existence was shaped by the events of the twelfth congress of ESANA in 1964, where a new radical student executive was elected to

---

2 Zewde 2014, p. 253.
3 Zewde 2014, p. 99.

run ESANA and the association's journal, *Challenge*.[4] This new group believed that it was in their mandate to address social and economic issues in Ethiopia, including transforming the student journal into a tool for social change. In the issue of *Challenge* that immediately followed the twelfth congress we see a shift in the editorial content, which begins with the announcement that Ethiopian youth must break the vicious cycle of evil that comes from good men doing nothing.[5]

ESANA's transformation after 1964 also coincided with the election of a radical executive to the Ethiopia Student Union in Europe, as well as the announcement in *News and Views* (a student publication at Haile-Selassie I University in Addis Ababa) of the existence of the Crocodile group. According to the announcement in *News and Views*, the aim of the Crocodile group was to propagate Marxist ideas;[6] however, the group is also credited with organising much of the clandestine leftist pamphlets and study groups on the campuses of HSIU from 1965 until 1969. After 1964 the student movement in Ethiopia became more visible, and in 1965 it organised one of its most well-known demonstrations: the 'land to the tiller' march of 24 February 1965. Whether the increased radicalisation amongst the various student groups was fully synchronised or not, it is clear that the student associations were in communication with each other, and that after 1964 an increased spirit of radicalisation guided a unified and comradely student movement.

The unity that characterised the student movement from 1965–9 is distinct from the fissures that shaped the third period in the history of *Challenge*, which was centred on what came to be known as the nationalities question. The vocabulary of the nationalities question was first formally introduced into the Ethiopian student movement through a speech given by the student activist Wallelign Mekonnen on the campus of HSIU in October 1969. This is the speech that was later published as an essay in *Struggle* entitled 'On the Question of Nationalities in Ethiopia'. Both Wallelign's speech and the publication of the essay were the culmination of a year of intensified student activism that had also led to the arrest and jailing of a number of student activists, including Wallelign. The escalation of police intimidation against the student movement eventually led to the December 1969 assassination by an unknown gunman of the president of the University Students Union Addis Ababa (USUAA), student

---

4   See Alem Habtu's discussion of the early history of ESANA in Zewde 2010, p. 64.
5   This paraphrase of a well-known line from Edmond Burke is clearly taken out of the context of his generally conservative predilections. See Ayalew and Rahmato 1967, pp. 1–3.
6   See the description of the Crocodile group in Zewde 2014, p. 112.

activist Tilahun Gizaw.[7] The day after the assassination, students who were demonstrating at the University campus in solidarity with Tilahun were also subjected to more police intimidation, with three students being killed.[8] In the end, the student movement responded to increased state repression with a tactical decision to move student radicals out of the country.[9] Thus, students who later came to be associated with the leadership of EPRP either moved to Algiers (Berhane Meskel) or the USA (Mesfin Habtu). By the end of 1969 and into 1970 these recently exiled students began to confront the executives who had led ESANA and ESUE from 1965 until 1969. The nationalities question became the primary issue debated in this confrontation.

At the seventeenth congress of ESANA, in 1969, a series of resolutions were passed against separatist movements. In conjunction with the passing of these resolutions, the February 1970 issue of *Challenge* carried four articles from long-term ESANA activists specifically dedicated to describing the nationalities question as a problem of regionalism. One year later, in the July 1971 issue of *Challenge*, the nationalities question was again discussed, this time in a long-winded essay by Tumtu Lencho entitled 'The Question of Nationalities and Class Struggle in Ethiopia'. As it turns out, Tumtu Lencho was a pen name for Andreas Eshete, who had been a contributor to the February 1970 issue of *Challenge*, which focused on regionalism in Ethiopia.[10] By adopting the pen name Tumtu Lencho, Andreas appeared to be identifying with one of the oppressed nationalities in Ethiopia, the Oromo ethnic group.[11] Only one other article, entitled 'Mass Struggle vs. Focoism', appeared in the July 1971 issue of *Challenge*. This article was written by someone who had chosen the obvious pen name of Rejjim Gouzo (which in Amharic means Long Journey). Rejjim Gouzo's article served as a warning that the student movement was searching for shortcuts towards revolution by opting for vanguard-led guerrilla warfare, as opposed to engaging in long-term, bottom-up mass struggle.

Focoism is a theory of revolution that suggests that a vanguard of military cadres can provide a *focus* for popular discontent that will eventually lead a population to rebellion. The main point of focoist theory is that rather than waiting for the objective social conditions to ripen in order to instigate a population for insurrection, armed struggle in itself can provide the focus through

---

7 Zewde 2014, p. 173.
8 Zewde 2014, p. 175.
9 Yeraswerk Adamssie, Abdul Mohammed and Melaku Tegegn all claim this to have been the case in their oral history testimony in Zewde 2010.
10 Zewde 2010, p. 110.
11 Zewde 2010, p. 113.

which rebellion could be fostered. Focoism was first proposed by the French writer Regis Debray in his book *Revolution in the Revolution*, and took its inspiration from the Cuban revolution and in particular Che Guevara's attempts at guerrilla warfare in Latin America.[12] Abdul Mohamed, a participant in the student movement, has recalled that in 1969, two years before Rejiim Guozo's article was published, many of the student leaders (and soon-to-become political party leaders) spent time together in an Addis Ababa jail where they held reading and discussion groups. According to Abdul their reading list included the periodical *Monthly Review*, as well as thinkers such as Frantz Fanon, Paul Sweezy, E.H. Carr, and Bertolt Brecht, and also Regis Debray and Fidel Castro.[13] Abdul claims that by the end of 1969 student leaders referred to themselves as the vanguard of the revolution, 'until such a time that the working class and the peasantry attained the required level of consciousness'.[14] In the February 1971 issue of *Challenge* we can see an attempt by the older executive team within the student movement to stake out a position against new members who were raising questions of armed struggle, especially as it related to the struggle for Eritrean self-determination.

In July and August of 1971 Tilahun Takele's and Tumtu Lencho's articles became the basis for a debate on the nationalities question that dominated both the eleventh congress of ESUE and the nineteenth congress of the Ethiopian Student Union North America.[15] At the nineteenth congress ESUNA reversed its position on Eritrea and offered its support for the right to self-determination up to and including secession for all nations within the Ethiopian empire-state. The passage of these resolutions eventually led the president of ESUNA, Senay Likke, to lead a walk-out from the meeting, as he supported the resolutions from the seventeenth congress. Apparently, Senay also lamented the amount of time devoted to the nationalities question, and the fact that not enough time was spent on basic revolutionary science.[16] Later Senay Likke would return to Addis Ababa, where he would found the political party Labour League (also known as Woz League), a political party that in the early years of the Ethiopian revolution formed an alliance with the Derg regime. That alliance also included the AESM, but not the EPRP. The resolutions on the nationalities question passed at the nineteenth ESUNA congress and eleventh congress of

---

12   Debray 1967.
13   For Abdul Mohamed's comments see Zewde 2010, p. 98.
14   in Zewde 2010, p. 100.
15   See the participant testimony of Melaku Tegegn (pp. 69–76) and Abdul Mohammed (pp. 77–81), as well as the discussion on the nationalities question in Zewde 2010.
16   The exact quote from Senay Likke can be found in Zewde 2014, p. 214.

ESUE became the position of the AESM, EPRP and TPLF. As we shall see later in this chapter, the spirit if not the exact wording of resolutions of the nineteenth congress of ESANA were also enshrined in the 1995 constitution of the Federal Democratic Republic of Ethiopia.

In a recently compiled oral history of the Ethiopian student movement, a number of participants have recorded their retrospective analysis of the role the nationalities question played in dividing the student movement. Andreas Eshete remarked that he now believes that the gap between the various positions on the nationalities question was being deliberately exacerbated as part of a leadership struggle between the forces that evolved into the leadership of AESM and EPRP: '... both were convinced that the student movement was a source of power they must rally behind them. Both were fiercely competing to secure that support. In my view the national question was only a pretext'.[17]

On the other hand, Melaku Tegegn, Yeraswork Admassie, and Abdul Mohamed, whose views were also recorded in the same oral history project, suggest that after 1969 the differences in the ESM were over more than the nationalities question, involving organisational structure and the role of armed struggle. These two issues seemed to be particularly pressing, given the tactical decision to move the bulk of the student movement into exile after 1969. Similar to Andreas' views, other participants in the oral history project suggest that the nationalities question, while pertinent, was really used as an instrument of power to build organisational capacity. While it may be true, this view does not address the question of why the nationalities question was brought up in the first place. The nationalities question may have been reduced to a tool of power, but we still need to ask why this tool was used and not another.

In our discussion of the rise of the nation-state in the Horn of Africa in Chapter 2, I suggested that the student movement can be understood as the reaction of a new social group with a changing class status, produced by a new and developing nation-state. These students were grappling with the particularities of their social formation. I also posited that the rise of a civilian left in Ethiopia was part of the ongoing effort to creatively articulate the shape of the Ethiopian nation-state in the face of social and political contradictions introduced into the Horn of African since the rise of European imperialism in the region. This explains, to me, why the student movement was primarily concerned with how to address questions of the social inclusion of various nationalities, in addition to how to build an economy in which the newly edu-

---

17   Zewde 2010, p. 105.

cated class could play a role. The attempt to resolve the nationalities question in a particular direction must be read as one way to formulate and consolidate an answer to the larger historical context.

I mark the fourth period in the history of *Challenge* as beginning with the November 1971 issue of the journal. Here the nationalities question is raised yet again, but from the point of view of the resolutions adopted at the nineteenth congress. However, by the February 1973 issue of *Challenge* there seems to have been a reversal of the editorial position of the journal back to the positions of the seventeenth congress, while by the time we get to the August 1973 issue of *Challenge*, the journal has become an organ of the World Wide Federation of Ethiopian Students (WWFES), and again reflects support for the nineteenth ESANA congress.

The establishment of the WWFES reflects the final success of the attempt by the forces that came to be associated with the EPRP to take over some section of the student movement. The August 1973 issue of *Challenge* also represents the culmination of efforts by the EPRP to transform the student movement into an arm of the revolution. The final period of the existence of *Challenge* is marked by the effort to establish the World Wide Federation of Ethiopian Students in 1973. These efforts are marked by organisational acrimony and the final split of the student movement, with the ESUE leaving the federation to become an autonomous body. The split between the various sections of the student movement was replicated in the acrimony between various political parties in the revolutionary period in Ethiopia. While Berhane Meskel and the Algiers group were able to take over the organisational infrastructure of the WWFES, the federation itself became associated with the EPRP. At the same time, Haile Fida led the departure of the ESUE from the WWFES, which in turn became associated with the AESM. Upon the return of both groups to Ethiopia over the course of 1974 and into 1975, the acrimony turned into an urban civil war that is commonly referred to as Ethiopia's red terror. From my point of view, it is important that from the November 1971 issue until the final issue of *Challenge* in 1975, both the AESM and the EPRP targeted the student unions and the student movement in order to recruit members or to push forward their political positions, even if, as Melaku Tegegn says, 'most members of the student union were blissfully unaware of this'.[18]

For this reason, I leave off my analysis of *Challenge* with the August 1973 issue (Vol. xiii, Nos. 2), even though at least one issue of *Challenge* – the August 1975

---

18   Zewde 2010, p. 73.

issue entitled *Whither Ethiopia?* – was released after August 1973. In addition, after 1973 the journal *Combat* became the organ of ESUNA. It is unclear to me who was responsible for *Challenge* after 1973, and which sectarian issues the journal wished to promote or silence. By 1975 most of the student leaders who had moved abroad in the late 1960s and early 1970s had returned to Ethiopia to formally establish political parties and engage in the work of transforming the state. In this chapter I am tracking the contentious debate between student activists and the flow of those ideas into the politics of revolutionary Ethiopia, and it seems clear that by the end of 1974 the priority of the student movement had shifted from debating each other in the halls of the academy to shaping the outcome of the revolution through institution-building and war-making at home.

While the year 1973 in Ethiopia was marked by the revelation that the Ethiopian government had disguised the magnitude of a large-scale famine in the north of the country, 1974 began even more dramatically with a series of strikes, demonstrations, and army mutinies concerned with a number of issues, including changes to the school curriculum, increased food and fuel prices, and the declining work conditions of junior soldiers in the army. The demonstrations showed that the modern centralised state that Haile-Selassie had attempted to forge since coming to power in 1916 could no longer adequately respond to the growing protests, nor could it respond to the growing social contradictions within the country's diverse populations. In response, junior army officers elected by their colleagues formed a variety of division-based committees (the word for committee in Amharic is 'derg') that brought demands to both Haile-Selassie and to parliament. Simultaneously, members of parliament including Prime Minister Endalkachew attempted to use the different elected committees within the army to mobilise power around itself. Marina and David Ottaway have persuasively argued that the revolution in Ethiopia began in 1974 when different factions within the state, including the old aristocracy and the newly educated bureaucrats, attempted to shift the direction of the state to their interests. In turn, this combined to create a power vacuum within the state that prompted different social groups to both attempt to take over the already existing state, and to try to build an alternative state that could better manage the problems that the protests articulated.[19]

Looking back at the events of 1974 in Ethiopia, it might appear that the removal of Haile-Selassie from power and the turn to a Marxist revolution were part of an inevitable course of events. However, as Christopher Clapham has

---

19   Ottawa and Ottawa 1978.

argued, any explanation of the direction that the revolution took must be found
in the ways in which the urban areas were mobilised after 1974, meaning that
even if the committees set up within the army found themselves at the centre
of events, the framework within which they operated was established by events
outside of the army. Indeed, the major policies that changed the structure of the
Ethiopian state, such as land reform, nationalisation of urban housing, or the
arming of the peasant associations and urban cooperatives, all came from the
radical intellectuals who we can identify with the student movement. Because
of this, 'far from being imposed as part of a "revolution from above", many of the
measures which made the Ethiopian experience a revolutionary one appeared
to have been introduced as ad hoc responses to pressures from below'.[20]

Following the upheavals of 1974 many of the leaders of the Ethiopian Student
Union Europe and the Ethiopian Student Union North America returned to
Ethiopia and proceeded to formally establish their political parties there, which
included the All Ethiopia Socialist Movement (AESM), the Ethiopian People's
Revolutionary Party (EPRP), and the Woz League. As mentioned earlier, the
AESM and the Woz League aligned with the Derg (the military leadership), even
though both parties maintained their own autonomous organisations. According to both René Lefort and Andargachew Tiruneh, the AESM also played a
formidable role in persuading the military to adopt the policies on land reform,
urban housing, and the nationalisation of banks and large industry that the
Ethiopian revolution is best known for, as discussed later in this chapter. The
AESM also took over a number of ministerial positions and formed the core
of the Derg's political school, the Yekatit 12 School, in addition to forming and
dominating the Provisional Office of Mass Organisational Affairs (POMOA). The
former leader of the ESUE, Haile Fida, is also credited with having written the
Program of the National Democratic Revolution, which was issued in April 1976
and remained the major policy statement of the Derg regime until the dissolution of the provisional military regime and its replacement with a workers'
party in 1984.[21]

The debates that had plagued the student movement continued to haunt the
platforms and organisational structures of the ongoing revolutionary process
in Ethiopia, with the AESM and EPRP repeating the arguments of the student
movement in their respective newspapers, *Voice of the People* and *Democracia*.
In an effort to work with the left, between February and April 1976 the military regime allowed the various revolutionary parties to debate their policy

20   Clapham 1990, p. 43.
21   Tiruneh 2009, pp. 157–64.

differences in a forum called 'Abyot Forum' (Revolutionary Forum) in the only daily, state-owned Amharic newspaper, *Addis Zemen* (New Era). Andargachew reports that the debate was highly abstract, with little possibility for engagement except by those versed in Marxist theory.[22]

The EPRP's response to Haile Fida's *Program of the National Democratic Revolution* marks the final break between the EPRP, the military regime, and the left that supported the Derg regime. It also marks the final break between the various forces within the student movement that began to divide in the early 1970s. The basic differences between the EPRP and AESM remained the question of the self-determination of the nations and nationalities in Ethiopia, and the recognition of the Eritrean People's Liberation Front as the legal representative of the Eritrean people. The AESM believed that the EPRP misidentified the Derg as the principle enemy when, for them, the military was fighting feudal and imperialist reaction. The AESM believed that the military could be pushed to correctly transform the state, whereas the EPRP argued that the military had stolen the revolutionary initiative from the popular masses. The EPRP therefore called for the repeal of all laws curtailing democratic rights, and the enactment in their place of laws guaranteeing unlimited democratic rights for the supporters of the anti-feudal, anti-imperialist, and anti-bureaucratic revolution. The EPRP also called for the arming of workers and peasants so that they could lead a provisional people's government.[23]

By early 1976 this disagreement led to the targeted assassinations of AESM members by the EPRP. In response, the peasant associations and urban cooperatives that were formed in the early part of 1975 and were dominated by the AESM were authorised to establish revolutionary defence squads. Although the legislation that brought the peasant and urban associations into being stated that the primary purpose of the defence squads was to help in the process of redistributing expropriated property, many of the defence squads were ultimately used to carry out the AESM-led 'red terror' against the EPRP's 'white terror'.[24]

Perhaps the real tragedy of the Ethiopian student movement is that, despite the fact that it provided the governing ideology as well as the administrative structures that kept the Derg regime running until 1991, in the end the military regime found most of the student movement, including the AESM, to be too autonomous, and as such untrustworthy allies. By the end of 1977 the military regime was able to centralise authority around Mengistu Haile-Mariam, with

---

22   Tiruneh 2009, p. 143.
23   Tiruneh 2009, pp. 176–7.
24   Tiruneh 2009, p. 208.

violence itself becoming more bureaucratised.[25] As a result, many of the leaders of the student movement, including Haile Fida, Berhane Meskel and Senay Likke, were arrested or assassinated by the Derg regime. By the 1980s this left the Eritrean People's Liberation Front and the Tigray People's Liberation Front as the major forces fighting against the military regime, and in many ways the sole inheritors of one part of the legacy of the student movement.

We have seen that members of the Ethiopian student movement easily moved from student organising to mass-based politics, state-building, and civil war. Our question now is how did the ideas that travelled from the student movement to political parties and the military field shape the outcomes of the revolution. In particular, how did the students' sense that they were both practising and implementing ideas from the social sciences impact their desire to come up with formulas that they thought would solve social and political contradictions?

As I said in the previous chapter, I am not trying to prove that the students were good or bad social scientists; rather, I am taking seriously the students' own self-description of themselves as 'modern' and 'scientific' thinkers, applying scientific concepts and even scientific laws to their understanding of social problems in Ethiopia. But it is not clear to me what the students meant by the appellations 'modern' or 'science'. As we will see, sometimes the terms appear to mean that the students were applying universal laws of social development to further understand the situation in Ethiopia, while at other times science seems simply to imply a mode of judgment in relation to evidence, and at still other times it seems to merely mean rigorous thought or even simply to be a label of approval – I am modern or scientific, therefore I am right.

One thing that my reading of *Challenge* shows is that, despite their appeal to science, the reality that the students sought to describe was not an object with an independent existence separate from the questions they posed about reality. Rather, the questions they asked were clearly tied to the projects they sought to build. Once again, this is not because the students were bad scientists, though by their own definition they might be defined as such. Instead, what is important is that the distance between subject and object is rooted in history and our alienation from our own creativity, so that there are in fact no universal and ahistorical laws of human development. This does not make truth relative to an individual culture or person; rather, explanation is relative to the concrete set of social relations that make up our reality. The questions we ask about reality are always partial and yet tied to how we participate in constituting reality.

---

25   See Weibel 2015.

Critique, in my view, comes from accounting for the past as well as accounting for the partial ways through which we receive the past. In my inquiry into the literature of the student movement, a question that comes up immediately is whether the appeal to 'science' and the 'modern' excluded accounting for a concrete, historically given social situation. In turn, this raises the question of why the students turned to an appeal to science at this particular moment. Is there a link between the appeal to science and the attempt to grapple with nation-state formation? What does the pretence that reality can be independently conjured and analysed allow the thinker to do to reality? What kind of ontological license does it grant to the social science thinker and practitioner? To answer these questions, I turn to a closer examination of the writers and their words, while also providing a bit of biographical detail on some of the major contributors to *Challenge* in order to paint a wider picture of the institutional context that shaped their lives.

1   *Challenge* 1965–9: The Moment of Departure

Beginning in 1965, the journal *Challenge* was run by a small coterie of students, many of whom had been elected to the executive of the Ethiopian Student Association North America in 1964. These students, Melesse Ayalew, Hagos Gabre Yesus, Andreas Eshete, Dessalegn Rahmato, and Alem Habtu, often traded the roles of editor, assistant editor, and contributors of articles to the journal. Another 20 or so people sporadically contributed articles to *Challenge* in the years between 1965 and 1969.

Each of the six editors and assistant editors of *Challenge* were undergraduate students at some time between 1961 and 1967. Each of them attended well-known liberal arts colleges and universities in the US. Subsequently, each of the six also led highly successful careers as professors and teachers within a number of different university and college systems. For example, both Melesse Ayalew and Hagos Gabre Yesus began their university careers as undergraduate students at Brandeis University. Subsequently, Hagos also completed an M.A. at Brandeis and eventually pursued a teaching career at John Abbot College in Quebec. Melesse Ayalew completed a PhD in Political Science at Columbia University in 1975, in which he used the works of Frantz Fanon and Karl Marx to write about the problem of political revolutions in the third world. Melesse then returned to Ethiopia in the midst of revolutionary change in 1975.[26]

---

26   A record of Melesse's academic career can be found in African-American Institute 1976.

To get a sense of the atmosphere that Hagos and Melesse inhabited at Brandeis University, it might be useful to point out that Hebert Marcuse taught courses in political philosophy while they were students. In 1965 Marcuse had just published his book *One Dimensional Man*, a theoretical text that was one of the touchstones for the student movement both in the USA and globally. Angela Davis also attended Brandeis during this time, where she worked with Marcuse, among many others, to develop her own particular form of revolutionary activism and scholarship. Given that both Melesse and Hagos often placed the Ethiopian student movement within the broader global student movement, it seems certain that the campus atmosphere at Brandeis had more than a passing influence on them.

Andreas Eshete attended Williams College until 1966, after which he completed a PhD dissertation at Yale University in Philosophy, where he examined the topic of the social structure of freedom. Dessalegn Rahamto attended Anthioch College until 1967, and later completed an M.A. in Economics at Northeastern University, where he developed his expertise on the agrarian question. Finally, Alem Habtu attended Dickinson College during this period, and much later completed a PhD at the New School of Social Research.

In 1968, the six members of the editorial team of *Challenge* joined with Haile Fida and other participants of the Ethiopian Student Union Europe to found the All Ethiopia Socialist Movement. In 1970 Andreas returned to Ethiopia, where he began to participate in political agitation and mobilisation. Tamrat Kebede, a member of the ESANA and AESM who also returned to Ethiopia in 1969, has recently remarked that it is unclear whether his own agitation upon returning to Ethiopia was on behalf of the student movement or on behalf of the AESM. It seems that at the time it appeared to him that they were one and the same. During the early 1970s members of the various branches of the Ethiopian student movement shuttled between Ethiopia, Europe, and North America in order to agitate and organise amongst Ethiopian students wherever they might be.

At the time of writing this book, only Dessalegn, Andreas, and Alem continued to be active in the Ethiopian intellectual and political scene. As we shall see in Chapter 4, in the early 1990s Dessalegn co-founded, with Bahru Zewde and Zenebewerk Tadesse (all veterans of the student movement), the academic NGO Forum for Social Studies. Similarly, in the early 1990s Andreas and Tamrat Kebede, along with a number of other former members of the Ethiopian student movement, founded the academic think tank InterAfrica Group (IAG). From the early-to-mid-1990s IAG was well known for attempting to build consensus around the constitutional provisions of the soon-to-be-established Federal Democratic Republic of Ethiopia. In this capacity IAG was active in the Ethiopian public, as well as with international donors and actors.[27] Between 2001 and 2011 Andreas was also president of Addis Ababa University, and between 2011 and 2016 he was appointed as minister without portfolio and advisor to the Prime Minister's office. While Alem Habtu continued writing about Ethiopian politics and social affairs until his untimely death in 2016, he was primarily based in New York, where he held a position as professor of Political Science at Queens College.

While this group of students dominated the pages of *Challenge* between 1965 and 1969, many authors who were active in the movement and would become prominent members of the Ethiopian and Eritrean intellectual and political scene also contributed articles to *Challenge*. These include Haile Menkerios and Senay Likke. Haile Menkerios, who began his education at Brandeis in the mid-1960s and later completed an MA at Harvard, was a very active member of the Ethiopian student movement. He would eventually become well known as an Eritrean activist, spokesperson and leader. It is telling about both Haile Menkerios' career and the impact of the Ethiopian student movement that from 1991 until 2000 he was Eritrea's ambassador to both Ethiopia and the OAU (which is based in Addis Ababa). He presided over this position during the period when Eritrea became formally independent.

As for Senay Likke, he completed a Bachelors of Science degree at Lafeyette College in 1967, and then later completed a PhD in Chemical Engineering at the University of California, Berkley. His contribution to *Challenge* is based on his PhD research where he, in part, investigated methods for improving the efficiency of certain key traditional cottage industries in Ethiopia. As mentioned above, Senay Likke returned to Ethiopia in 1972, where he founded the political party Labour (Woz) League. During this period, Senay was also known for conducting political education workshops amongst soldiers in the Air Force barracks in the town of Debre Zeit (later Bishoftu).

Melesse Ayalew, Andreas Eshete, Dessalegn Rahmato, Senay Likke, and Haile Menkerios, as well as many other active members of the Ethiopian student movement, all came to the U.S. through what was known as the African Scholarship Program of American Universities.[28] The programme was set up by the precursor to the United States Agency for International Development (USAID), the International Cooperation Administration (ICA), in conjunction with the African-American Institute (AAI). The AAI itself was a multi-racial organisation, started in 1953 and led by black American scholars including Horace Mann

---

27   For an example of the work that InterAfrica Group has done see InterAfrica Group 1993.
28   For a list of the 93 Ethiopian scholarships students who were brought to the US on this
      programme between 1961–71, see African-American Institute 1976.

Bond and William Leo Hansberry (who had themselves experienced being
snubbed by the mainstream American academy). The aim of both the AAI and
the broader African scholarship programme was to provide training opportunities to the newly independent African countries until such time as these countries could set up their own institutes of higher learning.[29] The infrastructure
that supported the careers of those active in the Ethiopian student movement,
then, was enabled by the coming together of a civil rights agenda in combination with the US government's cold war commitment to modernisation projects
in the third world. Perhaps this also explains some of the atmosphere that
contributed to the themes that came to dominate this cohort of students' discussions. These included: 1) the need to both describe and address Ethiopia's
backwardness; 2) the need to develop a modern and scientific approach to dealing with Ethiopia's problems; and 3) the need to set forth a concrete programme
to transform the country. Although *Challenge* addressed a wide variety of other
topics including everything from current affairs to the role of the modernist
painter in society, the recurring concern was the need to find a prescriptive for-
mula to bring Ethiopia into the twentieth century. Here we see a profound sense
that Ethiopia is not coeval with the rest of world. The need to enter the twentieth century becomes the overall framework driving social scientific research
and discussion in *Challenge*, especially in the period between 1965 and 1969.

2   Our Collective Backwardness

> So we bluntly ask ourselves: Can't the Ethiopian youth help break the
> vicious cycle? If we are not to assume that Ethiopia will go on existing by
> the grace of the pathetic image she so admirably displays to the outside
> world, why can't we release ourselves and by the same token the entire
> population from the present passive and dormant state? How can we
> direct our potentialities along a more dynamic and constructive course
> without which no social progress is possible?[30]

These are the words of the first editorial that marks the beginning of the
transformation of *Challenge* from an organ of an apolitical social club to a
tool for political agitation. Written by Melesse Ayalew with editorial assistance from Dessalegn Rahmato, the editorial to the March 1965 issue of *Chal-*

---

29   African-American Institute 1976.
30   Ayalew and Rahmato 1965.

lenge is primarily concerned with describing Ethiopia as caught in a vicious cycle of unspecified evil, to which people have become accustomed. The essay expresses anxiety about the role of the educated youth in converting 'our three thousand year old civilization into a twentieth century civilization', with the constituent elements of twentieth century civilisation described as increased literacy rates, per capita income, and life expectancy.[31] Concomitant with their anxiety about the role of the youth in society, the editors also seem concerned with the lack of an internal force in Ethiopia that could usher in much-needed progress. The educated youth are imagined as both outside and inside the internal dynamics of Ethiopian civilisation, but what marks them as outside is their access to modern education. The editorial goes on to condemn the Ethiopian youth for not living up to the historic role that youth have played in other countries, and laments that even though Ethiopia is more backwards than elsewhere, until now the educated youth could be characterised as 'individualistic, egoistic, opportunistic and full of despair'.[32] Returning to the theme of the internal and external forces of change, the editorial team concludes that the vicious cycle of evil cannot go on indefinitely: 'it might not be too long before the silent millions begin to demand a share in the better life we are selfishly monopolizing'.[33] The role of the educated youth is to both articulate and manage the demands of the 'silent millions'. For this reason, the editorial argues that the educated youth can bring 'national coherence' to a population who until now had remained fixed in regional and ethnic affiliations. The students' special role as both an external and internal force in Ethiopian society is what will allow them to finally fulfil their historic role.

Later in the same issue of *Challenge*, we find another article entitled 'Unveiling the Paradox', written by Belay Kassa and similarly concerned with the context of modernity and the role of Ethiopian institutions in perpetuating what the author calls 'the complex of pseudo-modernity'.[34] It begins by commending the Ethiopian Orthodox church for preserving Ethiopian national identity, but says that this very success is what has hindered the church from creating an educated clergy capable of both 'theological compromise' and orienting the population towards a 'real philosophy'.[35] For the author, this educated clergy should be as important to the country as economists and engineers, yet the qualities of a 'real philosophy' are undefined apart from a linkage to modernity,

---

31   Ayalew and Rahmato 1965, p. 1.
32   Ayalew and Rahmato 1965, p. 2.
33   Ibid.
34   Kassa 1965.
35   Kassa 1965, p. 16.

rationality, truth, and law. When the author discusses the need to modernise the fasting and prayer rituals of the Ethiopian peasantry, he writes that these social practices 'interact with the ever-present nutritional deficiency and hamper the physical vitality of the individual, and consequently labor productivity operates at an exceedingly sub-optimal level even within the framework of the existing technology'.[36] The author therefore recommends church reform along the lines suggested by Habib Bourguiba, the first President of Tunisia, who is said to have warned against being too religious in the context of development and poverty alleviation.[37] It is interesting that the quote from Bourguiba used in the article is taken from Paul Sigmund's book *Ideologies of the Developing Nations*, which the author seems to have encountered in the course of his college studies.

Continuing the theme of Ethiopia's pseudo-modernity, in the August 1966 issue of *Challenge* we find an article by Girma Beshah entitled 'The Making of a New Ethiopia' that asks how an institution such as an absolute monarchy could persist in the twentieth century, 'especially in modern Africa'.[38] For the author the answer lies in the fact that such an institution is 'a necessary concomitant of a feudal society'.[39] That is to say, the explanation for the persistence of the monarchy can be found by connecting the political system that dominates Ethiopian social relations with the mode of production that dominates economic life. Given that the feudalist stage apparently dominates social relations, a monarchy is its necessary concomitant. The author then goes on to describe the history of modern Ethiopia from the consolidation of the nation-state under Minilik in the nineteenth century to the occupation of the country by Italy in 1935 as a period where Ethiopia rapidly emerged from isolation. One of the consequences of this is that Ethiopian society now has an enlightened segment he describes as the 'yeast of society'.[40] The problem with this educated elite is that until now they have learned to enjoy the habits of western Europe without reforming their country. This is why the author shifts his focus to the second generation of post-war educated students, arguing that sociologically speaking this new crop of students are 'of the people and for the people'.[41]

The article compares Ethiopia's educated students with the newly independent countries of Africa. The author explains that until now he had been taught

---

36   Ibid.
37   Kassa 1965, p. 17.
38   Beshah 1966, p. 41.
39   Ibid.
40   Beshah 1966, p. 47.
41   Ibid.

to think of Africans as inferior to independent Ethiopia, and yet it appears that the Africans 'are now ahead of us in the development of culture, economy and democracy'.[42] Beginning with a quote from the prophet Isaiah, the author then suggests that 'the [African] people that walked in darkness ... have seen the great light ... We Abyssinians are however, still groping in the thick of darkness'.[43] The author's criticism of Haile-Selassie calls for 'concerted action against our backwardness'.[44]

The topic of the backwardness of the Ethiopian people as compared to the newly independent African countries comes up repeatedly in the pages of *Challenge*. In his August 1966 review of Richard Greenfield's *Ethiopia: A New Political History*, Melesse Ayalew writes that the Ethiopian regime 'was not only inefficient and irrational in terms of reconciling its own contradictions and problems, but as events following the independence of Ghana and other African countries clearly demonstrated, it [the educated minority] was incapable of directing Ethiopia's glory, independence, and resources towards the requirement of the modern age'.[45] Melesse's interest in reviewing Greenfield's book is that the book demonstrates that the Ethiopian state, despite official talk of Pan-Africanism, continues to be steeped in a feudal political-economy that is fundamentally 'counterrevolutionary' and incapable of moving the country towards modernity.

By the August 1967 editorial of *Challenge* (still edited by Melesse Ayalew and Dessalegn Rahmato, but with editorial assistance from Hagos Gebre Yesus and Andreas Eshete) we begin to see less emphasis on a cultural explanation for Ethiopia's backwardness, and a deeper reflection on the economic and political structures that have inhibited Ethiopia's development. In particular, students begin to link the contradictions of the Ethiopian state with the attempt to reform the state in the post-World War II period. The editorial attempts to locate Ethiopia's backwardness in the 'internal disequilibrium' that has afflicted the feudal structure as a result of reforms to the state. Also targeted is the state's increasing dependence on western imperialism in order to survive.[46] This allows the student movement to begin to link Ethiopian social struggles with larger economic and political processes in Africa. In the August 1967 issue of *Challenge* three articles attempt to interpret the dynamics of the Ethiopian state within a global context. These include the editorial, entitled

---

42   Beshah 1966, p. 50.
43   Ibid.
44   Beshah 1966, p. 52.
45   Ayalew 1966, p. 60.
46   Ayalew and Rahmato 1967.

'Beyond an Ideology of Powerlessness'; an article written under the pen name of
G.B., which examines the futility of preparing economic plans within a feudal
economy; and a book review of Nkrumah's *Neocolonialism – the Last Stage of
Imperialism* written by Dessalegn Rahmato, which was originally published in
the *Iran Report*, an organ of the Iranian student movement based in the US.[47]
Clearly, Dessalegn's publication in an Iranian publication is an indication of the
ways in which the Ethiopian students were beginning to imagine their international linkages. Following the publication of Dessalegn's review in 1967 the
concept of neocolonialism becomes mobilised as a key analytic term by the
student movement when debating Ethiopia's place within the international
system. In particular, it is suggested that neocolonialism has made it impossible
for capitalist development to take place in Ethiopia.

This is why the 1967 editorial, 'Beyond an Ideology of Powerlessness', is
concerned with providing a framework to move beyond Haile-Selassie's self-
definition of his regime. First off, the editors tell us that while the Ethiopian
regime might be described as feudal, its existence is premised on serving 'the
interest of imperial domination by enshrouding itself with a new fawning
bureaucracy'.[48] Secondly, the editors warn us that despite the fact that ordinary partisans resisted the occupation of Ethiopia by Italy, the war ended up
strengthening and unifying the feudal class. Third, they argue that even though
the world order of colonial Africa was the world to which the Ethiopian state
had reconciled itself, after the war Ethiopian feudalism became aware that it
could not survive the second half of the twentieth century without altering
the basic structure of society. It was at this critical juncture that university-
educated men were recruited into the Ethiopian power structure. The editors argue that these new modern educated elite became 'the voice of the old
order speaking through its new recruits'.[49] Significant state transformation was
introduced in the post-war period, but for the editors of *Challenge* all of these
changes simply entrenched the authoritarian nature of Haile-Selassie's regime.
The reforms that were introduced simply amounted to the rationalisation of
feudalism and the strengthening of the hand of the landowners through a) the
formalisation of customary law in favour of landowners; b) the elaboration of
a state security system; and c) the increased repression by an increasingly centralised state. Finally, according to the authors of the editorial, all this involved
increasing international alliances with western imperial states.[50]

---

47   Rahmato 1967.
48   Ayalew and Rahmato 1967, p. 2.
49   Ayalew and Rahmato 1967, p. 4, quoting Peter Duval Smith in the *New Statesman*.
50   Ayalew and Rahmato 1967, p. 5.

Similarly, in Dessalegn Rahmato's review of Nkrumah's book on neocolonialism we begin to see the development of a theory of dependency, in so much as Dessalegn argues that imperialist monopolies not only draw huge profits from the underdeveloped countries but also retard their growth.[51] This sets the stage for an argument that persists throughout the life of *Challenge*, which amounts to claiming that in the context of capitalist imperialism it is impossible for third world countries to catch up to the west. This becomes the main justification for the turn to socialism and the popularisation of Maoist-style new democracy within the student movement. Dessalegn does criticise Nkrumah's book for not looking more closely at the relationship between the ruling classes of third world and imperialist countries, and he ends his review by recommending that the reader take up Nkrumah's book in conjunction with Fanon's *Wretched of the Earth*. Although he does not clearly state why these books should be read simultaneously, one can assume that Fanon's theory of the role of the comprador class in third world countries provides further justification for the turn to socialism within the Ethiopian student movement.

In the essay 'The Futility of Planning in a Feudal Society' we see the full articulation of a new trend in the students' argument about the backward nature of the Ethiopian economy. Central to this essay's argument is that the political framework that determines social and political life in the country is of decisive importance in determining whether any economic developmental goals can be met. As long as feudal social relations persist in Ethiopia, rational planning will be impossible.[52] What is different about this author's argument is that it takes for granted that Ethiopia has been reduced to a neocolonial state wherein both international and local political forces work together to perpetuate the existence of feudalism in the country.

'The Futility of Planning in a Feudal Society' begins by describing how Ethiopia introduced its first five-year plan in 1957, with the second five-year plan entering its final year of operation in 1967, and a third plan in the offering. Each plan was considered a phase of a longer 20-year development plan, whose main aim was to 1) increase productive capacity; 2) change existing technology used in production processes; 3) improve living conditions and provide social services; and 4) create a sound economic basis for national defence. This was to be achieved through modestly increasing GDP by just over 4 percent per year. According to the author, the implementation of the second five-year plan was doomed from the onset precisely because 62 percent of its planned expendit-

51   Rahmato 1967, p. 32.
52   B. 1967, p. 24.

ure in the industrial sector depended on US investments. This made the plan
dependent on doubtful sources, and so few investment plans were actually carried out.[53] The author then shows that there has been an overall decline in GDP
growth in the agriculture sector, and points to the land tenure system as the key
impediment keeping agricultural productivity low. A weak agricultural sector
prevents the provision of a labour force for industrial activity.[54] The author concludes that state-led development initiatives are a 'masquerade' in Ethiopia, as
their meaning is limited to the development of a bloated public sector. Until
the political framework that maintains feudal relations in the country can be
radically transformed, the ends of any development plan can never be met.
Imperialism then becomes the substitute force that stabilises the regime. What
is needed is the complete overhaul of the political system if any development
is to occur in the country.

If this article by "G.B." links the internal political conditions in Ethiopia to
neocolonialism, it also presents a particular theory of knowledge production.
This theory of knowledge production is best articulated in an earlier essay by
Hagos Gabre Yesus on land reform, where he argues that it is impossible to
actually recommend a development programme in Ethiopia since there is very
little systematic research on the landlord-tenant relationship in Ethiopia, nor
is there much information on the principles that govern agricultural production.[55] According to Hagos, suppression of knowledge is one of the outstanding
characteristics of the oppressive regime in Ethiopia. Rather than offer half-
baked recommendations on tenancy reform, the real question that development experts should be asking themselves is why there is a lack of information on the very topic they are meant to be researching. Hagos argues that
'correct analysis [is] always the indispensable prelude to action which results
in progress'.[56] The key to land reform in Ethiopia is political in so much as
any recommendation around land reform and tenancy that has currently been
produced by development experts takes feudalism for granted, and can be dismissed as unscientific. In order to produce correct knowledge about Ethiopia
a political revolution will be needed. In the meantime, all efforts towards land
reform must be dismissed. This is the same point G.B. makes when he says that
'the political framework is of decisive importance' in overcoming the futility of
planning the Ethiopian economy.[57]

53   B. 1967, p. 22.
54   B. 1967, p. 23.
55   Yesus 1965.
56   Yesus 1965, p. 6.
57   B. 1967, p. 25.

Another point in G.B.'s essay that resonates with the other articles in the August 1967 issue of *Challenge* is the author's contempt for the entire newly educated elite in the public sector who, he says, regard 'their job as more of a lucrative vocation than as a meaningful instrument for social and economic development'.[58] One could go so far as to say that what emerges from the pages of *Challenge* by the end of 1969 is a theory of the post-war educated class. For example, in a discussion of the 1967 anti-demonstration proclamation that was passed by the Ethiopian Parliament, the editorial team of *Challenge* describes their educated predecessors as deluded by the self-image of the student as 'a protected and pampered child under the paternal care of an imperial father presiding over a feudal establishment'.[59] This is juxtaposed to the self-image of the present student movement as shaped by a modern and scientific outlook. In the 1967 editorial 'Beyond an Ideology of Powerlessness', the editors advise that the aim of the present student movement is to not only expose the 'falsehood of all profits of despair' but to counter the ideologues of the state 'by creating forms of struggle in which the active participation of the betrayed masses of Ethiopia can be coordinated'.[60]

Here the primary purpose of turning to social scientific descriptions of Ethiopian society is to allow the student movement to develop a clear-headed programme of social transformation. The sense of obligation to transform the country is also partially motivated by the perceived failures of an older generation of students to address Ethiopia's passivity vis-à-vis a changing global context. This is also why, earlier, I identified the need to develop a modern or scientific approach to Ethiopian problems as an implicit but important theme within the pages of *Challenge*. In other words, as the editors of *Challenge* themselves tell it: 'The real issue is not between theory and practice. We [the editors] rather prefer to believe that the issue involves a choice between the welfare of the deprived majority of Ethiopians and the welfare of the small minority, between ourselves becoming additional problems and identifying and solving the already existing plethora of problems'.[61]

This insistence on a programmatic awakening is also linked to what the students call 'revolutionary renaissance', and is best understood as a reinterpretation of the universal significance of the European enlightenment for the Ethiopian context.[62] The editors of the August 1967 issue of *Challenge* argue

58   B. 1967, p. 20.
59   Ethiopian Students Association in North America 1967, p. 10.
60   Ayalew and Rahmato 1967, p. 6.
61   Ayalew and Rahmato 1965, p. 3.
62   Ayalew 1965.

that the importance of the French revolution is that it was part of a historic fight against 'medieval scholasticism, royal tyranny, and feudal landlordism'.[63] The problem with western European and North American societies is that they have strayed from their historical origins in the Enlightenment. This in turn has created a problem for the present-day Ethiopian intelligentsia in so much as it has learned its intellectual and cultural postures from 'this overstuffed and self-satisfied West'.[64] The editors of *Challenge* argue that the Ethiopian intelligent-sia have been mollified by a regime that closely resembles European regimes before the Enlightenment. Keeping with their programmatic agenda, the edit-ors also argue that since the Ethiopian intellectual 'derives his unquenchable sustenance from the glaring misery of his countrymen', he has no right to be indifferent towards the public problems of our time.[65] It is incumbent on the Ethiopian intelligentsia to produce a 'Voltaire, or Diderot, or Rousseau, or any of the great rebels against divine (devilish) absolutism'. In this sense the editors of *Challenge* understand themselves to be the vanguard of an approaching revolution that has long been forgotten as a lived experience in Europe.

   The link between an enlightened approach to thought and a programmatic agenda for social change is found scattered throughout the pages of *Challenge*. We see again in the 1968 editorial of *Challenge*, written by Dessalegn Rah-mato, a discussion of the manner in which the Ethiopian student movement had become solely interested in directing its attention to 'theoretical polit-ical issues', which are named as a concern for the principles of democratic government, popular rights, and national reconstruction.[66] This focus was not adopted out of 'loyalty to Western academic methodology', but to develop a forum where opposition to the Ethiopian regime could be 'expressed, stud-ied and propagated'. One of the original articles included in the 1968 issue of *Challenge* is by Abo Mabuza, a pen name for an Ethiopian student residing in western Europe. Abo Mabuza's article is one of the first essays in *Chal-lenge* to explicitly describe Ethiopian nationalism as a class ideology, while also describing the Ethiopian state as a heterogeneous multicultural Empire-state. The author's trepidation towards the forced homogeneity of the Ethiopian empire-state does not, however, temper his enthusiasm to create a 'political movement organized around a body of ideas representing concrete interests'.

---

63   Ayalew and Rahmato 1965, p. 4.
64   Ibid.
65   Ayalew and Rahmato 1965, p. 5.
66   Rahmato 1968.

Such a movement, for him, would be explicitly against 'tradition' as well as the 'backwardness, disease and ignorance' of the various segments of Ethiopian society.[67]

Similarly, in the 1969 editorial of *Challenge*, Alem Habtu claims that the literature of the student movement 'constitutes the most concrete, and scientific analysis of the social system which systematically continues to hold Ethiopia backward'.[68] It appears that one of the editorial choices made for the 1969 issue of *Challenge* was to increase the number of essays using the language and methods of the natural and the social sciences. This issue includes an article by Chikonaw Bezabih that describes in great detail the status of the public health system in Ethiopia; an article by Haile Menkerios on the problem of allocating economic surplus from agrarian production within a feudal economy; an article from Henock Kifle that uses the work of Maurice Dobb and Paul Baran to critique mainstream theories of economic development; and an essay from Senay Likke that attempts to link his PhD research in chemical engineering to attempts to efficiently improve small-scale production processes for coffee, grains, fruit juices, and minerals. Part of Senay's argument in this article is that it is important to improve the production capacity of small scale manufacturing without creating massive unemployment in the countryside. In his argument for the role of science and technology in Ethiopia we see a foreshadowing of what became the Agriculture Development Led Industrialisation (ADLI) policy adopted by the EPRDF-led government in the 1990s.

3   The Method of the Idea

This book argues that an enduring legacy of the Ethiopian student movement has been the method through which ideas have been linked to social change. Two articles from *Challenge* that clearly bring this out are Dessalegn Rahmato's discussion of the modern Ethiopian painter Afewerk Tekle in an essay called 'Art betrayed', and Hagos Gabre Yesus' book review of the anthropological work *Wax and Gold: Tradition and Innovation in Ethiopian Culture* by Donald Levine. Paying close attention to both Hagos' and Dessalegn's writing in these two articles gives us a clearer sense of the epistemological and ontological commitments fostered by the Ethiopian student movement when trying to bring about social transformation.

---

67   Ibid.
68   Habtu 1969.

'Art betrayed', by Dessalegn Rahmato, is a response to a meeting between the modern Ethiopian painter Afewerk Tekle and Ethiopian students studying in the Boston area, held at the Phillip Brooks House at Harvard University in 1965. The article is an attempt to tackle Afewerk Tekle's views on the responsibility of the artist to society, and what Dessalegn describes as Afewerk's 'naïve but socially harmful' perspective on the topic.[69] The article begins with a discussion about the cultural heritage of a nation, explaining that any given cultural object validates its historical existence in so much as it can be shown to have contributed to the nation's material or moral progress. In the article the author never defines what progress might be, although he refers to the ancient churches and obelisks of Ethiopia as examples of cultural objects that have contributed to the development of Ethiopian creativity, and states that the nation's pride is embodied in these works of art. Yet Dessalegn decries the present state of cultural production in Ethiopia as being 'untrue' to this heritage. Instead, for Dessalegn, artistic production in Ethiopia currently serves two primary purposes. The first is to help in the process of the self-aggrandisement of Haile-Selassie's regime, and the second is to help 'opportunistic pseudo intellectuals' pursue individual self-promotion within the halls of power. This, Dessalegn believes, is the result of an oppressive political atmosphere that stunts intellectual growth while promoting out-dated myths about Ethiopia's cultural heritage.[70]

What Dessalegn seems to oppose with regards to Afewerk Tekle is the artist's statement that the activity of painting is the only responsibility of the artist. Dessalegn counters Afewerk's claim by stating that even a monkey can be trained to splash paint on a canvas, which to him means that the idea of defining the artist through what Dessalegn calls the 'technical' capacity to paint is to reduce the artist to a mere monkey. An alternative definition of art as 'a medium of protest for progress' is therefore proposed. Art must be an attempt to grasp and visualise that which 'is denied by the established order' by apprehending what 'ought-to-be' rather than what is.[71] In this sense, art negates reality by first grasping reality and then visualising that which is denied by the established order. The artist must tear himself away from reality in order to consider misfortune, and is in turn also obligated to give form to that which ought-to-be. For Dessalegn, this shuttling back and forth between reality and the shaping of a transcendent order is the real task of the artist, and this is also what makes the occupation of being an artist dangerous.

---

69   Rahmato 1965.
70   Rahmato 1965, p. 19.
71   Rahmato 1965, p. 20.

CHALLENGE 113

Given that in Ethiopia the misfortune that the artist must face is the 'gaunt farmer', 'the emaciated children', and 'the wounds of the beggar', the task of the artist is acute and pressing. Dessalegn feels that Afewerk should be compared to an artist producing paintings of Louis XIV at the beginning of the French revolution. When Afewerk defines his occupation as simply being a painter he has become the monkey of a fanciful world, separated from the 'dialectics of creation' – that shuttling back and forth between reality and the transcending of reality – that ought to define the life of the artist.[72]

Dessalegn's polemical article did not go unnoticed, and in August 1965 Haile Fulass published a full response in *Challenge* that called out Dessalegn for his flagrant use of normative pronouncements as if there was common agreement on what an artist's role in society should be.[73] Haile Fulass also seemed deeply concerned with Dessalegn's lack of engagement with the content of Afewerk's paintings. He counters that if art is indeed a human activity imbricated in societal activity, then it must be that art can be defined in a myriad of different ways, including as a representation of ruling class interests. Although Haile Fulass shows that Dessalegn never provided concrete evidence as to whether Afewerk was an opportunist or not, he nevertheless asks – in a somewhat rhetorical fashion – if it is not possible for an opportunist to make good art. If it is possible, then perhaps Dessalegn's definition of art as a medium of protest cannot sufficiently cover what it means to be an artist.

Dessalegn did not take kindly to Haile Fulass' intervention, claiming in a response published with it that 'Art Betrayed' was never meant to be a discussion of a particular artwork, but was an attempt to discuss Afewerk's definition of the role of the artist. Dessalegn also seems to believe that Haile Fulass is being insincere when he claims incomprehension about what defines Afewerk as an opportunist. For Dessalegn, Haile Fulass' incapacity to condemn Afewerk is evidence of a 'vicious intellect', which like the Nazis is capable of rationalising wrongdoing through the language of hope. This then allows Dessalegn to return to his original assertion that 'Afewerk, as an artist and educated man, is among the few intellectually enlightened in our society, and it is his social duty not only to recognise but to express the needs and aspirations of his people in his work'.[74]

For Dessalegn, art is a social tool through which human societies can aspire to something that moves beyond present ideals. This desire to transcend the present is positioned as a human and universal proclivity that can best be

---

72   Rahmato 1965, p. 21.
73   Fulass 1965.
74   In Fulass 1965, p. 19.

expressed by the educated man, who Dessalegn seems to also conflate with the emancipated man. Dessalegn also assumes that the future goals of society can be accurately anticipated by the artist, while the movement towards achieving those goals can be managed as a process of moving towards that which self-evidently ought-to-be. Here art becomes part of the tools of social engineering.

In a strange way, Dessalegn's demand for a practical art of the future echoes the arguments that Hagos Gabre Yesus makes about the role of the social scientist in his review of Donald Levine's book *Wax and Gold: Tradition and Innovation in Ethiopian Culture*. The crux of Hagos' critique of Levine is that *Wax and Gold* mixes facts with values and is neither systematic nor scientific in its description of what Hagos calls 'the dominant feudal culture in Ethiopia'.[75] Ironically, what seems to bother Hagos the most about *Wax and Gold* is Levine's reluctance to unequivocally condemn Haile-Selassie's regime.

One example Hagos gives of Levine's making it difficult to differentiate between neutral social science description and political judgment is in Levine's account of the historical process that led to the domination by the Amharas over a variety of different indigenous groups in Ethiopia.[76] Hagos wonders why Levine incorrectly labels this historical process Amhara domination, when the term imperialism would have more accurately captured the dynamics of nineteenth-century Ethiopian history. Certainly, for Hagos, what is clear is that 'if one is against imperialism, against it as much as one should be against any other social evil, then no body of facts can demonstrate that one imperialism is better than the same injustice'.[77] Hagos believes that Levine has fallen victim to a fantasy of Ethiopian exoticness. But it is evident that Hagos also believes that a correct and scientific description of Ethiopian society can lead only to one true conclusion. For Hagos, since imperialism is taken for granted to be a social evil, the Ethiopian regime must be condemned on this basis.

Hagos rightly recognises that Levine's assessment of Ethiopia is based on framing social processes through the dichotomy of tradition vs. modernity. This allows Levine to catalogue Minilik's response to European colonialism and the subsequent process of the Amharisation of Ethiopia as part of Ethiopia's progress towards modernity. Hagos argues that modernity is not of one piece; some parts of it, including imperialism, must in fact be condemned, or else we will be unable to see that in essence Ethiopia remains a medieval society that 'has yet to free herself from monarchic absolutism'.[78] Although Hagos recognises

---

75   Yesus 1966.
76   Yesus 1966, p. 64.
77   Ibid.
78   Yesus 1966, p. 67.

the multiplicity of what modernity can be, for him the telos of social progress is not something that needs to be defined, interpreted or even argued over. In a strange way, Hagos seems to be arguing that the point of neutral value-free social science is to let us work more clearly towards eliminating social evil. Through this claim Hagos ends up evaluating Levine's rather complicated argument about Ethiopian culture in terms of whether it is a good tool to use to reach an end that is assumed, instead of explained or justified. In this sense, Hagos' condemnation of the Ethiopian regime seems nearly as arbitrary as Levine's celebration of it.

Hagos' review of Levine's book prompted a strongly worded letter to the editor of *Challenge* that questioned Hagos' assumption of a sharp divide between science and the processes of everyday life. The letter goes on to describe Hagos' review of Levine as either demonstrating a commitment to a blind positivism or a belief in a messiah who could perfect a world yet to come. Either way, it is clear to the letter-writer that Hagos assumes that human folly can be progressively separated from the processes of building a more perfect world.[79] This assumption is perhaps the most enduring legacy of the Ethiopian student movement. Within the literature of the Ethiopian student movement, the young intellectual is somehow in the world but also outside of it, able to effect a cause but without being changed by his or her relation to the cause. Any sense that the connection between subject and object is historical and fluid is replaced by the reduction of the present to something that must be managed, not for its own sake, but for a future end goal.

As agents of social change, the Ethiopian student movement seemed to perceive the work of linking theory to practice as the adoption of correct facts that would in turn lead to a new Ethiopian society. This seems linked to the assumption that theory is merely the logical connection between a series of already established facts. As a result, in Dessalegn's case the specificity of an artwork becomes negligible precisely because theory can decide whether a specific artwork is meaningful in terms of what it might achieve in the future. Similarly, Hagos rejects the specificities of Levine's arguments in their entirety, precisely because Levine's end goals do not match the goals of ensuring Ethiopian progress, however arbitrarily defined by Hagos. This is also not dissimilar to the argument presented in the article signed by G.B. on the futility of planning in a feudal economy. In that article it is assumed that because the correct political framework had not been adopted by the Ethiopian state, all attempts at planning were ineffective. The need for detailed engagement with lived reality is

---

79   Tekle-Tsadik 1967, p. 35.

dismissed precisely because the theoretical end goal of what is being examined is already known or assumed by the author. From my perspective, the end goals proposed in each of the articles I have just discussed appear quite arbitrary, but the authors do not permit them to be debated. Dessalegn dismisses his interlocutor as a vicious Nazi unworthy of dialogue, while Hagos must describe the letter addressed to him as both incomprehensible and self-contradictory, the result of an 'undeveloped superego'.[80] In both cases the present is read as a predictor of the future, but only in terms of its capacity to programmatically achieve a pre-determined end goal that is in fact outside the mess of lived and embodied human practice. If the student movement assumed that theory could be constructed by logically linking together already established facts, so too with the building of the future.

4 The Making of a Programme

The Ethiopian student movement took the programmatic task of building a new future for Ethiopia seriously. In the August 1965 issue of *Challenge* we find the agenda for the thirteenth congress of the Ethiopian Student Association North America that was to take place in September of that year. Reading the agenda items, we can see that five committees had been set up to lead discussion at the congress. These included committees on Ethiopian national affairs, education, the economy, student organisations and movements, and lastly a committee on international affairs. The sub-topics under the agenda items of each committee closely match the research articles presented in *Challenge* for that year. This shows how systematic the students had become in their attempt to build a theoretical discourse that would support their larger political goals. Under the committee responsible for national affairs there was to be a discussion on the nature of democracy, the need for an absolute monarchy vs. a constitutional republic, freedom of the press, the role of the church, and the question of tribal differences. In parallel, the committee on the economy would provide a review of the contemporary economic situation in Ethiopia with a particular focus on the subsistence economy, the condition of the peasantry, land reform, the role of foreign aid, foreign capital investment, industrialisation, and the development of trade unions. Also scheduled was a discussion on capitalism, capitalistic feudalism, and socialism. In terms of education, the agenda focused on the system of higher education, literacy rates, the role of

---

80   In Tekle-Tsadik 1967, p. 36.

government, the role of the volunteer organisations, the nature of math education, the problem of school dropouts, and finally the issue of public education
and mass media. The committee on student organisations was scheduled to
provide a history of the Ethiopian student movement, as well as lead discussion
on the reorientation of the student movement, including general questions of
policy goals and the quest for unity and cooperation among Ethiopian student
organisations. Finally, the committee on international affairs planned to give
a general review of world problems, including colonialism, neo-colonialism,
and imperialism, while discussing the specificity of events in Congo, Vietnam,
and other places, and to lead a discussion on Pan-Africanism and the recently
established Organisation of African Unity.

The thirteenth congress of ESANA was timed to coincide with the Fifth Congress of the Ethiopian Student Union in Europe, held in Vienna in September
1965. The resolutions from both events were published in the August 1966 issue
of *Challenge*, with a lead editorial entitled 'The Spirit of Solidarity'. Together
the resolutions from each congress marked an important stage in the history
of the Ethiopian student movement, in that the programmatic concerns of
the student movement shifted to be clearly about national development, with
equality and social justice as twin guiding principles. The shift is captured well
by Melesse Ayalew and Dessalegn Rahmato in their remarks in 'The Spirit of
Solidarity':

> Gone is the meaningless chatter about parties and social gatherings,
> drinking bouts and barroom girls that characterized the conventions of
> bygone days. Today, ... the youth of our country ... having gone through
> a mutation, has emerged as a potent force resolved to release the im-
> prisoned spirit of our people from the clutches of feudal tyranny.[81]

The 1965 congresses set an agenda for national reconstruction; yet it is remarkable that the ESANA resolutions contain very little language that would suggest
a socialist orientation.[82] This is not true of the ESUE resolutions, which start
with the world imperialist situation and then turn to what must be done in the
particular case of Ethiopia. Another striking difference between the ESANA and
ESUE resolutions is their take on land reform, with the ESUE position advocating for the public ownership of all land, while ESANA simply calls for land

---

81   Ayalew and Rahmato 1966, p. 1.
82   Ethiopian Students Association in North America and Union of Ethiopian Students in
      Europe, 1966.

reform whereby 'the owners can utilize the land for optimum production'.[83] The ESANA position seems to suggest that it is the ability to optimally use the land that should determine the size of land holdings in any redistribution programme. In addition, while both ESANA and ESUE call for the establishment of co-operatives, ESANA seems to understand this as the sharing of tools amongst rural peasants living with adjacent plots, whereas ESUE seems to have some sense that government-initiated collectivisation projects should be undertaken. What the two different sets of resolutions do share in common is the proposition that total transformation of the political system is needed before basic land reform can be undertaken.

In 'The Spirit of Solidarity' – the editorial that framed the printing of the 1965 resolutions in *Challenge* – the editors claim that the resolutions issued by the two student unions' congresses had already had a strong impact on the people of Ethiopia, as well as on Haile-Selassie's regime. The editors find evidence of this impact in the increased persecution of the student movement, including the banning of the National Union of Ethiopian Students (NUES) from university campuses in Ethiopia. The title of the editorial is derived from the fact that, despite increased state repression, since 1965 an increased sense of solidarity has been galvanising 'conscientious Ethiopians everywhere'.[84] Whether or not a new sense of student unity was fostered around the students' resolutions, in the 1965 resolutions, unlike the propositions on land reform that had recently been rejected by the Ethiopian parliament, the students were able to counter state discourse with a radical land policy of their own. One of the lasting consequences of both of the congresses held in 1965 was that economic development in Ethiopia was subsequently discussed through the twin rubrics of land reform and political transformation. If the actual details of the land reform resolutions remained vague in 1965, perhaps that too is part of the legacy of student movement. As we shall see later in this chapter, a certain nebulous quality remained a constituent part of what made up land reform policy in the post-1974 period as well.

Part of the story being told here is that both the resolutions of the student movement and the subsequent policy of revolutionary Ethiopia were developed through a history of unresolved contradictions and multiple openings, as well as multiple suppressed possibilities. These twists and turns in the formulation of policy recall Partha Chatterjee's disagreement with Benedict

---

83   Ethiopian Students Association in North America and Union of Ethiopian Students in
      Europe 1966, p. 9.
84   Ethiopian Students Association in North America and Union of Ethiopian Students in
      Europe 1966, p. 2.

Anderson and Ernest Gellner, who Chatterjee says read third world nationalist thought as a modular adaptation of European nationalism. Chatterjee counters the sociological determinism of both Gellner and Anderson by arguing that even if we can say that capitalism structures social relations, at the same time it is obvious that social struggle cannot be reduced to a sociological determinism. Precisely because the question of what to do with a 'backward peasantry' is the pressing economic and political problem of third world nationalist thought, the *sociological determinism* that is attributed to nationalism by the likes of Gellner and Anderson is actually internalised and assumed by third world nationalist thought. Even if third world nationalist thought is addressed to the 'people', it seeks to show that the 'people' can in fact modernise while retaining their cultural identity.[85] Chatterjee thus suggests that the question of managing cross-cultural relativism is built into the structure of third world nationalist thought and the post-colonial state.[86] Third world nationalism accepts the thematic of colonial thought even as it seeks to repudiate its problematic. How this contradiction is dealt with becomes the politics of third world nationalist thought and anti-colonial state formation. This dynamic is echoed in the writings of the Ethiopian student movement.

Between February 1970 and November 1971 five issues of *Challenge* were produced, and three of the five issues dealt with what was interchangeably called regionalism or the national question, while the other two issues focused on describing the social conditions of the peasantry and the question of neo-colonial and imperial policy in Ethiopia. While the editors who dominated *Challenge* in the period before 1970 continued to play an important role in the journal after 1970 and onwards, they were no longer able to act as if the student movement spoke with one voice. Instead, they published lengthy articles in response to ideological divisions within the student movement.

Perhaps the biggest issue facing the student movement in 1970 was how to respond to the Eritrean separatist movement, then led by the Eritrean Liberation Front. This was a particularly pressing issue since Eritrean students formed a substantial portion of the active members in the Ethiopian student movement. Yet despite their presence, the seventeenth congress of the ESANA (which by then called itself a Union) passed a series of resolutions against Eritrean separatism. However, by the nineteenth congress, the position of Ethiopian Student Union North America was reversed and a series of resolutions were passed in support of the right to secession for Eritreans. This prompted Senay Likke to

---

85   Chatterjee 1999, p. 30.
86   Chatterjee 1999, p. 28.

lead a walk-out of the congress that also included the long-time editor of *Chal-lenge*, Melesse Ayalew. One consequence of this was that for the first time in the history of *Challenge* the November 1970 issue of the journal – which reproduced the resolutions of the nineteenth congress – was edited by someone from out-side of the circle of men who had dominated the journal between 1965 and 1969.

In the next section of this chapter we will examine the arguments over the national question that led to the divisions in the student movement, and in so doing will discover how Ethiopian intellectuals imagined and also proposed to incorporate peasant populations into a developing nation-state. Many of the themes of backwardness vs. modernity discussed in the 1965–9 period contin-ued to shape the discussion of the nationalities question in 1970 and beyond. What shapes the debate on the nationalities question more than anything, per-haps, is the competing demands that the reader see a particular author or tract as more scientific and more correct in its analysis of Lenin and Stalin's positions on the national question. The period of 1970–1 in *Challenge* is also character-ised by both a more explicit turn to Marxist theory and a certain desire to reflect on the past mistakes of the student movement. For example, in the Feb-ruary 1970 edition of *Challenge*, the editor, Alem Habtu, informs his readers that the Ethiopian student movement is no longer an association of fratern-ities but a highly conscious political movement with articulated positions on the problems that confront Ethiopia today.[87] This is partially why the student association redefined itself as a Union. The editor also identifies the problem of regionalism as a central problem in Ethiopia, but suggests that the oppress-ive environment perpetuated by the feudal regime in Ethiopia has prevented public discussion of this problem. Throughout the editorial Alem never defines what regionalism means, even though he claims that it is a taboo topic, and that 'the Ethiopian student movement has been the first organised body of Ethiopi-ans to raise and discuss the question in full view of the public'. Alem goes on to mention that the student unions in both Ethiopia and Europe have had a number of discussions on the topic of regionalism over the last two years, and that the topic finally became an agenda item at the seventeenth congress. The February 1970 issue of *Challenge* not only reproduces the resolutions of the con-gress but also presents the four papers that were presented at the seventeenth Congress, on which the resolutions were based. Lastly, Alem warns that while the students' position on regionalism may change, 'what is constant is our com-mitment to revolutionary emancipation'.[88]

---

87   Habtu 1970a, p. 1.
88   Ibid.

In the same issue of *Challenge* there is a message from the Ethiopian Student Union Europe that also advises that the Ethiopian student movement has now reached a new level of revolutionary maturity. The ESUE sets out a series of goals that should be met by the members of the student movement. These include uniting with the masses, learning from the masses and teaching them in turn, adopting the way of life of the masses while also devising appropriate ways of imparting a scientific world outlook to them, and establishing a national revolutionary organisation to coordinate and lead the various forms of struggle waged on different fronts.[89] All of this is imagined as the natural evolution of the student movement. The ESUE writes:

> All natural and social change – from the weak to the strong, from the simple to the complex, from the inorganic to the organic – are governed by abiding laws of development. Similarly, the growth of our organization from infancy to maturity, from weakness to strength, from division to unity, from reformism to revolution displays the same dialectical development. Our future promises this same progress from lower to higher levels of struggle.[90]

Less optimistically, in the editorial for the July 1971 issue of *Challenge* Melesse Ayalew recalls that only three issues past the editorial team of *Challenge* had dedicated an entire issue of the journal to the question of regionalism, religion, and the self-determination of the Ethiopian people.[91] Melesse reminds his readers that the intention of producing that particular issue of *Challenge* was 'to generate an open and reasoned discussion' about the nationalities question; yet, according to Melesse, since that time there had been not a single substantive contribution that surpassed the preliminary studies appearing in that issue. Melesse feels free to reduce the subsequent writings on the national questions to a 'shrill insistence' for an 'instant solution' to the question of the right to political secession. Melesse also wonders if such an insistence has also 'led to irresponsible outbursts, stereotyped resolutions, and sectarian phrase mongering'. If the journal has to now return to the national question, this is only to unmask the petit bourgeois nationalism at the root of the current debate, which has served to divide the incipient left.

---

89   Ethiopian Students Association in North America and Ethiopian Students Union in Europe 1970.
90   Ethiopian Students Association in North America and Ethiopian Students Union in Europe 1970, p. 4b.
91   Ayalew 1971.

Later in the same July 1971 issue, we find an article entitled 'Mass struggle vs Focoism', which I mentioned earlier, written under the pen name Rejjim Gouzo, most likely by Melesse Ayalew.[92] Rejjim asserts that the student movement must discontinue the general policy of presenting a united front, given that there are tendencies within the movement that have now become liabilities.[93] Rejjim's main point in the article is that the turn to armed struggle within the Ethiopian student movement reflects a kind of revolutionary despair in so much as it denies the primacy of politics as the precondition and starting point of armed struggle. He then seeks to distinguish between revolutionary violence and (quoting Lenin) 'a theory of excitative terrorism', calling the visions and fantasies of the self-appointed Ethiopian ultra-Leftist 'a primitive version of the cult of focoism'.[94] Rejjim Gouzo is concerned that the student movement has begun to argue that repression in Ethiopia has made it impossible to do mass political work and, as such, it is only logical to focus on armed struggle as the sole path towards revolution. Rejjim's criticisms remind me of the maximalist demands discussed earlier – that no development planning is possible without total political transformation, or that no good art can be produced unless it serves very particular political purposes, or that all social science investigation in Ethiopia is corrupted unless it unequivocally serves the political goal of condemning the Haile-Selassie regime. Rejjim seems to be complaining that the student movement has come to dismiss the everyday reality of ordinary Ethiopians as the fertile site for the production of a popular political praxis. But the burden of this new insight must be placed alongside his own editorial style, which sacrifices the interpretive in favour of the programmatic.

The editorials and articles in the 1970 and 1971 issues of *Challenge* draw our attention to the shift in the stakes of the student movement after 1969. As we discussed earlier, commentators tend to interpret this moment as the period when politics within the student movement was instrumentalised for the sake of amassing power around certain individuals. While this may be the case, it can only be part of the story. My position is that even as power was amassed, these debates signalled the historical conundrums thrown up by the paradox at the heart of third world nationalist thought. The debates on the national question signify a creative and imperfect attempt to think through the problem of

92   During an email conversation with Alem Habtu he informed me that Rejjim Guozo was
       Melesse Ayelaw.
93   Gouzo 1971.
94   Gouzo 1971, p. 68.

post-colonial state-building in the Horn of Africa. Understanding these debates helps us to better recognise the ideas that have shaped present-day politics in Ethiopia and, to some degree, Eritrea.[95]

5   The Moment of Manoeuvre: Debates on the National Question

While the seventeenth congress of ESUNA was being held in the USA, activists and student unions in both Ethiopia and Europe were also discussing the problem of conflicts arising among people from different ethnic, cultural, linguistic, and religious backgrounds. Under the rubric of regionalism, writers and activists discussed the qualities that made up a nation, with some authors attempting to create a rough taxonomy of the social and political associations in the Horn of Africa that might qualify as fully-fledged nations. Importantly, activists also asked whether Ethiopia could be classified as a nation at all, and, if it was not a nation, what was it?

Probably the best-known essay from this period, which continues to have an impact on contemporary Ethiopian political debates, is Wallelign Mekonnen's 1969 essay 'On the Question of Nationalities in Ethiopia'. However, as Bahru Zewde has shown, an essay by Tilahun Takele (a pen name for Berhane Meskel) on the nationalities question probably had a greater impact on the student movement at the time that the debate was unfolding in the early 1970s. The bulk of Tilahun's essay is actually a response to an essay on regionalism by Andreas Eshete that appeared in the February 1970 issue of *Challenge*. Both Wallelign and Berhane Meskel spent the early part of 1969 in prison in Ethiopia, and Abdul Mohammed has suggested that it was probably the discussion groups held in prison that inspired Wallelign to pen his essay in the first place. When Wallelign's essay was published it prompted the banning of *Struggle* magazine from the university campus and an increase in state repression of the student movement. This included the assassination of the president of the USUAA, Tilahun Gizaw, in December 1969.

---

95   Perhaps the question of what to do about Eritrea was pursued because leading members of the Eritrean movement were part of the Ethiopian student movement until at least 1970. These include Haile Menkrios, Yordanos Gebre Medhin, and Bereket Habte Selassie (See Zewde 2010, pp. 66, 77). Both Bereket and Yordanos also became leading contributors to social science discourses on the Horn of Africa, with Bereket publishing a number of articles in ROAPE and eventually co-editing a book with Basil Davidson and Lionel Cliffe on the Eritrean question. See Habte-Selassie, Cliffe, and Davidson 1980.

Bahru Zewde has also suggested that the tumultuous events of 1969 in Ethiopia prompted two tendencies within the locally-based student union. On the one hand, some students decided that they would prepare to launch armed struggle by first going into exile, while on the other hand students and activists who remained in Ethiopia established clandestine discussion groups that were meant to form the building blocks of a revolutionary party.[96] An astonishing example of the exiled students can be found in Berhane Meskel, who collaborated with a number of other students to hijack an Ethiopian Airlines plane, which was then rerouted to Sudan. The group eventually took refuge in Algiers, from where they engaged in a number of activities that would eventually lead to the founding of the EPRP. Interestingly, in 1972, Wallelign would also attempt to highjack a plane, but this eventually led to his death, shot by Ethiopian security forces.

While Wallelign's essay has had a far-reaching impact, the essay itself is actually quite brief, and begins by saying that it should only serve as an introduction to the topic, especially since it was originally written as a speech.[97] Wallelign's main point is that, 'sociologically speaking', Ethiopia was not one nation but made up of multiple nations. Here a nation is simply defined as a people with a shared culture, language, way of life, and history. Given that participation in state institutions in Ethiopia, including going to school or holding a government job, requires that one must speak Amharic, Wallelign concludes that what counts as Ethiopian nationalism is in fact Amhara supremacy. Wallelign goes on to say that to be considered a real Ethiopian you must speak Amharic, listen to Amharic music, accept Orthodox Christianity, and sometimes even change your name to an Amharic appellation. He therefore calls for the equal right of all nationalities to participate in the state, and for the right of all cultures to preserve their language and way of life. This, he says, would make Ethiopia a genuine nation. Very programmatically, Wallelign's essay then moves into a discussion of how to achieve this goal, where he suggests two things. First, he warns against advocating for a coup d'état, since this will result only in a change in personalities; and secondly, he says that while he is not opposed to secession, he is opposed to the current secessionist movements operating in Eritrea, since they are led by the local bourgeoisie and, if victorious, will result in the masses replacing one master with another. Wallelign ends his essay by acknowledging that revolutionary armed struggle will be necessary if there is to be a

96   Zewde 2010, p. 179.
97   Mekonnen 1971.

genuine nation-state in Ethiopia, and that while the rebellion in Eritrea can be commended for weakening the centre, only socialism can guarantee the goal of genuine national unity.

Wallelign's brief exposé of the nationalities question moves so quickly over so much material that it raises as many questions as it answers. For instance, one wonders if Wallelign could not offer a more robust definition of what a nation is. His insistence on building what he calls a genuine Ethiopian nation seems to contradict the internationalist tendencies of socialism; and one wonders whether socialism really does have a role to play in building the kind of nation that he wants. That said, the main points raised in the essay – such as the right of Eritrea to secede, the role of armed struggle, and the role of socialism in fostering equality amongst different ethnic groups – became the main topics debated by the student movement in the coming years.

These are also the topics taken up by long-term ESUNA activists in the February 1970 issue of *Challenge*. Significantly, Andreas Eshete, Hagos Gabre Yesus, Alem Habtu, and Melesse Ayalew all contributed essays to this special issue on regionalism. Both Hagos and Melesse end up arguing somewhat simplistically that cultural and linguistic oppression are mere secondary expressions of the primary contradictions found in socio-economic conditions, with Hagos even reinforcing his position on the notion of Amhara imperialism – found in his review essay on *Wax and Gold* – to argue that Ethiopian feudalism is characterised by shifting strongmen whose power rests on military might rather than ethnic affiliation; Hagos argues that regionalism is a secondary antagonism of Ethiopian feudalism.[98] And yet it is odd that Hagos makes no distinction between the twentieth-century Ethiopian state and the nineteenth-century state, or for that matter the sixteenth-century Ethiopian state. Instead, all these are conceptualised under the broad category of feudalism.

Alem Habtu's essay also echoes these points; however, Alem locates regionalism specifically within the narrow-minded parochialism that he says is necessary for the reproduction of feudal social relations.[99] Here again, the problem of regional conflicts is reduced to a cultural symptom of the broader mode of production in Ethiopia, while the programmatic solution is said to lie in exactly the same place articulated by Wallelign's essay. More substantively, Andreas Eshete's essay, 'Problems of Regionalism and Religion: Some Theoretical Considerations', attempts to provide a robust theory for the analysis of regional and religious conflict in Ethiopia by first exploring the historical conditions under

---

98   Yesus 1970.
99   Habtu 1970b.

which the principle of self-determination has been invoked or applied elsewhere in the world, and then asking whether those conditions can be found
in Ethiopia.[100] After an exploration of the meaning of self-determination in
the French revolution, we are told that Ethiopian movements that appeal to
the principle of self-determination are 'perpetuating a fraud', since the historical conditions that would allow for the appeal to this principle do not exist
in Ethiopia.[101] In many ways Andreas Eshete's essay is an attempt to both synthesise and move beyond the discussion of regionalism in the other articles
submitted to the February 1970 issue of *Challenge*. The arguments offered also
provide the platform through which Tilahun Takele was able to refute the resolutions of the seventeenth congress.

The crux of the article lies in Andreas' appropriating Stalin's definition of a
nation as a 'historically evolved, stable community of language, territory, economic life, and a community of culture' in order to argue that all social and
political associations have the historical capacity to evolve into nations, and
that African people in particular are in the process of becoming nations.[102] This
also means for Andreas that Africans are capable of coming up with solutions to
the problem of regional conflict that have also been brought forth elsewhere in
the world. Andreas links the principle of self-determination to specific stages in
the development of human societies, and attempts to demonstrate that the historical origins of the principle of self-determination must be connected back to
both the bourgeois rebellion against feudalism and the expansion of bourgeois
property rights, which was most tangibly expressed in the French revolution –
for him the first moment in history where the idea of a people or nation was
linked to the principle of sovereignty. Following this, Andreas explains that the
principle of self-determination does not apply to the present-day context of
Ethiopia, firstly because there has been no bourgeois revolution, and secondly
because political unity flows from the monarchy. There is as such no sovereignty of the people, only the sovereignty of divine right.

Andreas also asks whether the principle of self-determination is relevant to
the Ethiopian bourgeoisie, but concludes that in the context of neocolonialism
a bourgeois revolution is impossible. What are taken to be the bourgeoisie in
a place like Ethiopia are actually just civil servants, bureaucrats, and military
men.[103] Andreas also examines the principle of self-determination in the con-

---

100   Eshete 1970.
101   Eshete 1970, p. 5.
102   Esthete 1970, p. 10. The citation Andreas provides for the Stalin quote is Joseph Stalin,
       Marxism and the National Question (New York, 1942).
103   Eshete 1970, p. 12.

text of the decolonisation of Africa, and here he argues that these movements can be understood as part of the historical movement of bourgeois revolutions, since these struggles were directed towards both political independence and the assertion of the sovereignty of the people.[104] From here he turns to the question of the right to self-determination of the Eritrean people, but in this case he rejects the description of the relationship between Ethiopia and Eritrea as colonial, since for him colonialism is defined by the supply of primary goods for industrial production, while feudalism simply entails conquest but not colonialism. Despite the British and Italian occupation of Eritrea, Andreas argues that property relations in Eritrea were never substantially transformed, and more closely resemble feudal Ethiopia than bourgeois private property. Moreover, the same structural hurdles that prevent a bourgeois revolution in Ethiopia prevent Eritrea from developing a bourgeoisie. While Andreas does argue that the principle of the right to self-determination must be defended, in the Horn of Africa this right rests with the 'toiling masses'.[105] He therefore argues that we must distinguish between the recognition of the right to self-determination and the exercise of that right, because in reality the demand for self-determination may be mobilised to defend the perpetuation of feudalism and imperialism. In the end, Andreas calls for a social revolution, and intimates that in any case the bourgeois revolution has historically proved itself incapable of solving the problems of regionalism. Thus, for Andreas, the claim to separatism by Eritreans is the equivalent of renouncing the struggle for self-determination for all of Ethiopia and Eritrea. He concludes that 'the freedom to renounce freedom is not a claim to freedom'.[106]

Andreas Eshete's essay on regionalism in Ethiopia also contains an interesting discussion of the role of the bourgeois social scientist in Africa, where he argues that the social sciences in general operate under the assumption that African societies are plagued with tribal and religious differences. Precisely because the social scientist describes the problem as such, he or she is keen to set up a bourgeois state through the language, culture, and religion of the ethnic group that is perceived to be dominant in any given country. This recalls Hagos Gabre Yesus' critique of Donald Levine's *Wax and Gold*, in that Levine's book identifies the Amharisation of the Ethiopian state with modernisation. Extending Hagos' critique of Levine, Andreas argues that the bourgeois social sciences take the problem of regional conflict for granted in Africa, and equates modernisation with a state unified through a dominant

---

104   Eshete 1970, p. 15.
105   Eshete 1970, p. 16.
106   Eshete 1970, p. 15.

ethnic group. In this sense, Andreas argues that bourgeois social science identifies the problem of regionalism without attempting to solve it. What modernisation means in Africa is the systematic violation of the principle of self-
determination.

In Andreas' discussion of the scramble for Africa, he argues that the principle behind the setting up of the colonial state mimics what he describes
as modernisation in bourgeois social science. Examining the process through
which the map of the Horn of Africa was redrawn in the nineteenth century, Andreas argues that European imperialism in the region was established
through collaboration with Ethiopian feudal regimes, so that the Amharisation of the Ethiopian state must be understood as the continuation of the
process of that collaboration. Looking at the post-war constitution of 1955 in
Ethiopia (the first-ever constitution was promulgated by Haile-Selassie in 1931),
Andreas shows that the centralisation of executive power in Haile-Selassie, the
establishment of the Orthodox church as the national religion, and the establishment of Amharic as the state language must be understood as addressing
the problem of regionalism through the biases of bourgeois social sciences.
Interestingly, however, Andreas actually never describes the contemporary
Ethiopian state as modern, although if we follow his argument, part of what
the state is modelled after are the principles of bourgeois social science. One
wonders – is the problem of regionalism in Ethiopia not more closely tied to
the problem of modernisation theory than to feudalism as such? And why does
Andreas insist on describing the nation-state as a stage in history that can only
be identified through the existence of certain historical conditions? Andreas
himself has outlined that one of the unique features of the twentieth-century
Ethiopian state is that it too is a response to the pressures of global imperialism
and capitalism. Rather than match the Ethiopian state to a set of teleological
stages it must conform to, it would be better to see the state-building process
in the context of complex international conjunctures. Modernity is not a set of
stages, but a set of historically constituted relations. The very fact that the centralisation of the twentieth-century Ethiopian state depended on the increased
use of roads, railways, and telephony, as well as a centrally controlled security
apparatus, makes the state something quite different from what it was in the
mid-nineteenth century. Because Andreas posits the nation-state as having a
fixed set of qualities, however, the principle of self-determination is dismissed
as irrelevant to the Ethiopian case. Instead, the nationalities question ends up
becoming a narrowly conceived debate that aims to empirically verify Stalin's
definition of the nation, while taking the concept for granted.

Tilahun Takele's and Andreas' articles on the question of nationalities differ
precisely in an ability to marshal historical evidence in order to better estab-

lish where nations do or do not exist in relation to Stalin's definition. Andreas and Tilahun share many of the same assumptions about the stages of capitalist development and the rise of the nation-state, with western Europe being said to have passed through the stage of nation-state formation in the eighteenth century, while Eastern and Central Europe led the way in the early twentieth century. For Tilahun, the Eritrean struggle and the various peasant uprisings then happening in Ethiopia must be understood within this telos as liberation wars based on nationalism.[107]

Tilahun names Andreas along with all the contributors of the February 1970 issue of *Challenge* as 'social chauvinists', who play into the hands of both the bourgeoisie and feudal landlords in Eritrea and Ethiopia. The point of Tilahun's article is to expose the North America-based theorists as lacking in proper Marxist analysis. Tilahun returns to Stalin's definition of a nation, but also includes the idea that a nation has a common psychological make-up, a characteristic that Andreas seems to have left out in his article.[108] While Tilahun argues that none of the characteristics that define Stalin's nation can alone constitute a nation, he also argues that there are numerous social groups in Ethiopia that do meet the criteria of being a nation. Tilahun also argues that Ethiopia taken as whole cannot be classified as a nation, as it has no common language, economy, or psychological make-up. Tilahun's essay makes a sharp distinction between tribes and nations, emphasising that a group that has the ability to trace its origins to a common ancestor must be identified as a tribe. Ethiopian ethnic groups are too large to be counted as tribes, and must be understood as having surpassed the communal or primitive stage of society; this also makes them fully-fledged nations. Tilahun's article concludes by declaring that the conditions which gave rise to nationalism in empire-states around the world are the very conditions that exist in Ethiopia today, most especially since it is obvious that an oppressor nation has imposed its language, religion, and culture on a variety of repressed and dominated nationalities.[109] It is therefore theoretically absurd for Andreas to suggest that the principle of self-determination could not be invoked because a proper bourgeois revolution did not exist in Ethiopia.

As argued earlier, both the older ESUNA group and Tilahun Takele (Berhane Meskel) understood the importance of connecting their theoretical conjectures to a program for resolving regional conflict. In the case of the ESUNA, the arguments advocated for in *Challenge* ended up informing the resolutions of

---

107   Takele 1971, p. 15.
108   Takele 1971, p. 8.
109   Takele 1971, p. 25.

the seventeenth congress of the ESUNA, which called for the recognition of the equality of all Ethiopian languages and cultures, while at the same time opposing all separatist movements. The seventeenth congress resolutions affirmed that the right to self-determination rests with the popular masses of Ethiopia, while calling out the leadership of the Eritrean Liberation Front as feudalist, comprador, and capitalist; it was claimed that the political platform of the Eritrean Liberation Front rested on the mystification of the socio-historical reality of Ethiopia.

Tilahun's programme, in contrast, denied Ethiopians the use of force in the case of a nation that wishes to secede. His essay called for the settlement of the question of secession on the basis of a universal, direct, and equal vote in the given territory wishing to secede, and called on all progressive Ethiopians to struggle against those who defend or sanction national oppression.[110] Tilahun Takele's essay was received with much disapproval and prompted a quick reply in the form of the July 1971 issue of *Challenge*, which contained only two essays: Tumtu Lencho's 'The Question of Nationalities and Class Struggle in Ethiopia' and Rejjim Guozo's 'Mass Struggle Vs Focosim'.[111] Tumto Lencho is an Oromo pen name for Andreas Eshete, although Dessalegn Rahmato apparently inserted much of the polemics of the essay after Andreas had submitted it to *Challenge*.[112] The essay reads as a collage of sorts, with Tumtu seemingly granting much ground to Tilahun's arguments even while calling Tilahun's essay a rag whose proper place was the wastebasket. In addition, Tumto Lencho condemns the entire student movement as 'infantile leftists' who have now foolishly reinterpreted feudal warlords engaged in armed struggle as part of the popular struggle.

Substantively, the major difference between Tumtu Lencho's argument and that of Andreas Eshete a year and half earlier is the focus on defining a national community as primarily established through a common market, with Tumtu arguing that until the establishment of the use of money as a standard of exchange, and not just as an object of exchange, there is in fact no home market that links economic producers.[113] Because exchange value has not been generalised, Ethiopian societies simply cannot be called capitalist. Tumtu also argues that this means that the disintegration of kinship relations amongst various ethnic groups in Ethiopia does not necessarily signify the existence of nations,

---

110   Takele 1971, p. 32.
111   Lencho 1971; Gouzo 1971.
112   The editorial process is discussed by Andreas in Zewde 2010.
113   Lencho 1971, p. 32.

as Tilahun Takele argues. What it does signify is the existence of nationalities, which for Tumtu is a stage in the evolution towards a nation, as defined by Stalin.

The other important intervention made by Tumtu Lencho is to explicitly argue that while imperialism exports capital to the 'oppressed countries', it does not alter the pre-capitalist relations in those countries. I will revisit this question when discussing the work of Jairus Banaji in Chapter 6, where I argue that the tendency to label as feudal that which appears backward in the wake of global capitalism fails to capture the manner in which smallholder farming turned the peasant into (an often failing) small proprietor. Tumtu Lencho argues that the class tasks of the toiling masses shift according to the world-historical epoch that shapes the relations between various economic systems, no matter the particular era in which an individual country might find itself. Here Tumtu seems to suggest that, because of the uneven development of capitalism, a sharp distinction can be drawn between the historical epoch of a particular country and 'the world-historical epoch in which the toiling masses everywhere stand against their class enemy', but the question of who is to fight and lead a particular battle and what importance is to be attributed to that battle must be centred on an analysis of the world-historical situation.[114] In a country like Ethiopia just entering the bourgeois-democratic revolution, the question of a direct transition to socialism comes up precisely because of the nature of the world-historical epoch. Even if Ethiopia might be in the bourgeois-democratic stage of rising capital, the nationalities question must be subordinated to the tasks of the era of world revolution. Tumto Lencho argues this by referencing the writings of Mao Tse-Tung. Both posit that after the victory of the 1917 revolution in the USSR, the era of bourgeois-democracy has passed. The task now is for the proletariat in alliance with the peasantry to carry the democratic revolution forward by seizing state power. This means that any national demand must be conditional on the need for a united party that can substitute bourgeois tasks with the socialist tasks of the proletarian era.[115]

Tumtu Lencho's essay is the first time we see the systematic introduction of Maoist thought into the debates in *Challenge*, along with an appeal to the theory of Chinese new democracy as the correct way in which the 'backward' and colonised countries should take up socialist tasks. The essay ends with Tumtu calling for the unconditional recognition of the right to self-determination of all the nationalities in Ethiopia (here understood as nations *in potentia*), and

---

114   Lencho 1971, p. 17.
115   Lencho 1971, p. 21.

for broad self-government for regions, which among other things should be demarcated in respect to nationality.[116] He also calls for the rejection of the territorial integrity of the Ethiopian empire-state and the political privileges that have been granted to certain languages. Ultimately, Tumtu Lencho reasserts that a commitment to class struggle must be the precondition for the exercise of the right of self-determination, and that the proletariat and the peasantry must be the leaders of the struggle. In this vein, he references *Al Hadaf*, the publication of the Popular Front for the Liberation of Palestine, which on 27 March 1971 carried an in-depth description of the emergence of a people's liberation front in Eritrea. This description proves to Tumtu Lencho that there are new fighting forces in Eritrea that respect the organisational unity of the toiling masses of all nationalities, and as such should be supported. He then goes on to claim that given the turn of events in Eritrea, ESUNA now stands vindicated in its initial refusal to support the comprador and conservative Eritrean Liberation Front.[117]

Tumtu Lencho's article helps us understand the shift at the nineteenth congress of ESUNA towards support for Eritrean secession, as well as the shift in the 'General Line' of ESUNA that was published along with the resolutions from the nineteenth congress in the November 1971 issue of *Challenge*.[118] The General Line includes a statement that endorses the two stages of the new democratic revolution, along with a new commitment to something called 'Marxist-Leninist-Mao Tsetung thought'. While quoting a number of Chinese revolutionaries, the 'General Line' also references Tumtu Lencho as a kind of foundational theorist for the new position of ESUNA. We also find echoes of the claim that in this new era of world imperialism the proletariat and its ally the peasantry must lead the struggle, and an assertion of the need for a revolutionary party that can seize state power and uphold the principles of new democracy. For the first time, we are told that the student movement should not be mistaken for a revolutionary party.

In turn, when we examine the nineteenth congress, we see that Tilahun Takele and Tumtu Lencho shaped the resolutions, which included a call for the unconditional recognition of the right to self-determination of all nationalities in Ethiopia, full equality of minorities, and self-government for regional nationalities. The nineteenth congress made a distinction between the recognition and the exercise of the right to self-determination by stating the conditions

---

116   Lencho 1971, p. 49.
117   Lencho 1971, p. 64.
118   Ethiopian Students Association in North America and Ethiopian Students Union in North America 1971a.

for its recognition, which included Tumto Lencho's proposal that a clear anti-feudal and anti-imperial programme led by the toiling masses must be the basic criteria for the exercise of said right. Support for the secession of a nationality was contingent on whether separation would clearly benefit the toiling masses in the seceding region, as well as the toiling masses in all the regions of the Ethiopian empire-state. As a result, the resolutions called for the support of the Eritrean struggle for self-determination including armed struggle, but acknowledged the difference between the people's forces in Eritrea and the forces of 'petty bourgeois reaction'.[119]

In examining the debates on the nationalities question in Ethiopia, we get a sense of the cross talk that allowed the Ethiopian student movement to appropriate the tools and concepts of a number of different political traditions, to both expand their membership within the Ethiopian state and to link their own actions to the world stage. But in all this, it is taken for granted that there is an objective reality, external to the very processes through which nations are politically established, that the concept of a nation can describe. What is never queried is how the concept of a nation, with all its inbuilt sociological determinism, allows insurgent intellectuals to connect with peasant populations who in turn come to form a national identity through the very process of insurgency. In the debates on the national question we can see both the ways in which theory transformed practice, and the ways that the practice of making a revolution changed the meaning of the theory that had been appropriated.

During the years when the nationalities question was being debated in *Challenge*, the journal also produced an issue that focused solely on the conditions of the peasantry in Ethiopia. Dessalegn Rahmato and Haile Menkerios were the two authors who contributed to this issue, and the main conclusion of both writers' articles was that the land tenure system in Ethiopia is 'socially exploitative and economically unviable'.[120] In the article written by Haile Menkerios, entitled 'The Present System of Land Tenure in Ethiopia: An Introduction', both the north and the south of the country come to stand in for land tenure classifications, with the north being described as communal, while the south is compared to the Hacienda system in Latin America.[121] In relation to the south, Haile focuses on the processes through which large tracts of land were granted to soldiers and aristocrats as a reward for nineteenth-century and early twentieth-century war-making and conquest. Haile Menkerios shows that this

---

119   Ethiopian Students Association in North America and Ethiopian Students Union in North America 1971b, p. 60.
120   Ethiopian Students Association in North America 1970.
121   Menkerios 1970.

reduced the local peasant populations to tenants on the land that they cul-
tivated. He therefore suggests that the problem of the land tenure system in
the north is the process of land fragmentation amongst numerous claimants
to communal property, whereas the problem in the south is the process of land
expropriation by the central state on behalf of newly made landlords.

The following article, by Dessalegn Rahmato, continues in this vein, showing that the communal nature of land tenure in the north is a myth, since
the peasant has little bargaining power within the legal system, and is often
relegated to an endless process of litigation in order to claim title to his or her
share of so-called communally held land.[122] Land fragmentation also means
that the peasant is reduced to strip farming with no ability to introduce extensive farming, and with little incentive to develop intensive methods on the plots
presently being tilled. For Dessalegn this means that the biggest problem with
the land tenure system in Ethiopia is that it blocks the emergence 'of a social
atmosphere conducive to innovation'.[123]

The research in Dessalegn's article is largely based on a critical re-reading
of reports from the Ethiopian Ministry of Land Reform. He mobilises statistics
provided by these reports to develop a discussion of rent and tax, and what
he calls 'the appropriation of surplus product'.[124] Dessalegn also provides a
description of the class structure of rural Ethiopia and the role played by the
church in constituting the social world of the peasantry. Ultimately, however,
Dessalegn eschews a psycho-religious explanation of the backwardness of the
Ethiopian peasant, and he also rejects the idea that the Ethiopian peasant is
simply loyal to tradition; rather, poverty and backwardness in Ethiopia can be
attributed to a social system that blocks experimentation and risk-taking.[125]
Not unlike Hagos Gabre Yesus' land tenure article of 1965, Dessalegn suggests
that better laws or clearer definitions of tenancy rights would not change the
conditions of the peasantry, and instead concludes that the relationship that
binds the producers to the appropriator of the produce must be destroyed:

> It is not the deficiencies of the system that create rural misery, but the
> system itself ... Only when the direct producers toil for no other but them-
> selves will they be able to attain emancipation ... In this connection the
> slogan land to the tiller is indeed subversive.[126]

---

122   Rahmato 1970.
123   Rahmato 1970, p. 38.
124   Rahmato 1970, p. 28.
125   Rahmato 1970, p. 37.
126   Rahmato 1970, p. 49.

In the editorial to the 1970 issue of *Challenge*, which examines the conditions of the peasantry, Alem Habtu tells us that the Ethiopian student movement has been articulating the needs and aspirations of the Ethiopian masses, and that from year to year the movement has moved from general statements to the analysis of specific forms of oppression and exploitation. However, Alem also reminds us that over the past five years no more than twenty people have contributed to *Challenge*, suggesting that members of the student movement and the readers of *Challenge* still know too little about the social conditions of Ethiopia. Alem then ends his editorial with a brief critique of the work and study methods of the movement, ultimately suggesting that the slogans of the movement have become a substitute for a lack of commitment towards serious investigations into the specific situation of peasants, women, workers, and even the lumpen-proletariat.[127]

It is striking that despite the fact that *Challenge* published at least five articles on the agrarian situation in Ethiopia, the day-to-day patterns of social reproduction of the rural areas remain opaque. In the end, we still don't know how farmers maintain soil fertility, or how and when farmers share tools and plough animals. Nor do we really know how farmers trade or barter with each other, how much they travel to acquire certain goods, or how they understand regional affiliations in these journeys. Even as the call for revolution within the student movement and in the urban areas becomes louder, the actual conditions of ordinary Ethiopians remain obscure, and what is provided is mostly concerned with fitting the peasantry into ideal-typical categories of social scientific thought. This in turn would shape the dramatic adoption of revolutionary rhetoric into the policy framework of the post-1974 period, while the specificity of what was needed in the country remained unstudied.

In 1973, the Ethiopian Student Union Europe (ESUE) used its annual congress to attempt to formally establish the World Wide Union of Ethiopian Students (WWUES). However, the conference ended up marking the final organisational break between the ESUE and what the North American Union had become after its nineteenth congress in 1971, when Senay Likke led a walkout from that organisation. In this regard, reading the August 1973 issue of *Challenge* is interesting, since the entire issue consists of a 40-page report-back on the failed attempt to establish the World Wide Union, and its subsequent replacement with an organisation called the World Wide Federation of Ethiopian Students (WWFES), which was dominated by the faction of the student

---

127   Habtu 1970, p. 2.

movement associated with Algiers, the ESUNA, and later the EPRP. The report also includes a history of the student movement that justifies the organisational break from the point of view of the federation, while at the same time offering a conciliatory note that suggests there was a minimum agreement amongst the various unions on anti-feudal and anti-imperialist principles. The report ends up framing the Europe-based union as petty contrarians with no good reason to leave the federation, and spends a considerable amount of time describing the procedural disagreements that eventually led to the ESUE's departure.

In recounting the history of the Ethiopian student movement from 1965 to 1973, the report also spends considerable time countering the accusations of ultra-leftism levelled against the homegrown student movement and those associated with the federation. These accusations include the charge that the student movement had attempted to usurp the role of the working-class party, and was quick to turn to armed struggle.[128] In response, the report details the recruitment of high school students into the student movement, and discusses the fact that both Ethiopian Airlines and sugar estate workers presented petitions to the congress of the National Union of Ethiopian Students. The report posits these latter cases as part of the intensification of the struggle in the face of increased repression from the Haile-Selassie regime, while also arguing that the recruitment of high school students into the movement should be seen as part of an overall shift in the class base of the student movement away from the elite university setting. Ultimately, the federation also argues that it was the homegrown activists in Ethiopia who first offered a critique of those who wished to subordinate politics to weapons, by arguing that guerrilla war is a war of the whole people and requires a minimum level of political preparation.[129] The report asks if it is ultra-left to emulate Ho Chi Minh in Vietnam or the Cuban revolution. Foreshadowing the upcoming civil wars, the report then concludes with two predictive pronouncements. First, the report tells us that 'the essence of a right policy is taking enemies for friends. The essence of an ultra-'left' policy is to take friends for enemies'.[130] Secondly, the report finishes with the declaration:

Long Live the Ethiopian Student Movement.
Victory to the Ethiopian Peoples
Victory to the Eritrean Revolution

128   Ethiopian Students Association in North America 1973a, p. 10.
129   Ethiopian Students Association in North America 1973a, p. 15.
130   Ethiopian Students Association in North America 1973b, p. 41.

Long Live the P.L.F. Revolutionary Vanguard
Victory to the African Revolution
Victory to the World Revolution

6   *Challenge* in the World

So far in this chapter I have attempted to use the journal *Challenge* as a prism
through which to examine the debates that dominated the Ethiopian student
movement in the 1960s and early 1970s. In the next section of this chapter I use
Challenge as a focal point to trace the passage of ideas from student debates
into public discourse, and to begin to suggest how this may have had a lasting
effect on Ethiopian policymaking. My approach has dictated that even as I try
to describe some of the historical events that surround the debates in the student movement, I have not wanted to write a history of the student movement
as such. Instead, this chapter is an attempt to work out what the social sciences
have been historically in Ethiopia, and to show what the social sciences can do
when they travel to the global south. In particular, I have tried to track how the
student movement reshaped Ethiopian politics through their particular take
on the role of ideas in society. One of the immediately obvious effects of the student movement on Ethiopian politics was the splintering of public discourse
into what would later become a civil war. Nearly every major political party in
Ethiopia traces its ideological roots to debates that unfolded in the 1960s and
1970s. In the next chapter I will return to the theme of the social sciences, focusing this time on the impact of the student movement of the 1960s and 1970s
on Ethiopian politics from 2005 and onwards. In the rest of this chapter I will
briefly discuss the immediate impact the student movement had on framing
the legislative outcomes of the 1974 revolution and setting the foundation for
the 1995 constitution ushered in by the present ruling EPRDF coalition. While
my discussion is highly descriptive, I am hoping to draw attention to the ways
in which the resolutions and programmes of the student movement filtered
into national policy formation in revolutionary Ethiopia. In particular, I want
to draw attention to how the resolutions of the 1965 ESUE and ESUNA congresses are reflected in the language officially adopted around land reform and
in the Program of the National Democratic Revolution. Later, as we discuss the
TPLF and its national coalition partners in the EPRDF, we will again see how
the nationalities debate framed the outcomes of the 1994/5 constitution.

The Derg-led revolution of 1974 is probably best known for its twin programme of converting both urban and rural land into the collective property
of the Ethiopian people. In fact, the March 1975 proclamation that provided

for the public ownership of rural lands was one of the first pieces of legislation introduced by the new revolutionary government, and reflects the student movement's demands for a radical decoupling of the link between social hierarchy and land tenure.[131] Specifically, the March 1975 law abolished all landlord and tenant relationships, while also granting former tenants possessory rights over the land that he or she tilled. The law declared that any person who was willing to cultivate land would be allocated rural land sufficient for the maintenance of their family, not exceeding ten hectares. Landlords were forbidden from quickly profiting by selling land before any redistribution programme had taken place while the tenant was freed from any previous payment of rent, debt, or other social obligations to the landowner. In order to ensure that the bonds of feudal obligation were not disguised through the wage-labour relationship, the proclamation also prohibited the hiring of labour to cultivate holdings. Peasants were, however, able to retain agricultural implements and a pair of farm oxen that previously belonged to the landlord for which reasonable compensation could be paid, although if the landlord had no implements of his own this was prohibited.

The new one-size fits all rural land reform was to be implemented through peasant associations (*Kebelle* in Amharic) that were also established by the March 1975 rural land proclamation. The main aim of the peasant association was to carry out the equitable redistribution of land by taking into consideration local conditions such as land infertility. Peasant associations each covered around 800 hectares and were small enough for members to know each other. All persons living within the area of a peasant association were mandated to join, with the exception of landlords, who were required to wait until the first round of land redistribution had taken place before participating in the association. The rural land proclamation also granted pastoralists possessory rights over land used for grazing and other agricultural purposes, and abolished obligations of payment for the use of land. However, pastoralists were only called on to form associations suitable for development purposes, not mandated to do so.

In December 1975, the Derg passed further legislation that was meant to consolidate the peasant associations as legal entities.[132] One of the justifications for such a move was that the newly established peasant associations were to be used as a forum to raise consciousness about the goals of the revolution. Peasant associations were described in the legislation as a meeting place where the activities of the broad masses could be expressed and where the government

---

131   Provisional Office for Mass Organisation Affairs 1975, pp. 18–29.
132   Provisional Office for Mass Organisation Affairs 1975, pp. 30–47.

could learn the needs and problems of the peasants. The December 1975 peasant association legislation was, thus, mainly concerned with establishing different committees and rules of operation, including the creation of youth and women's committees, and establishing the process of electing members from a peasant association's general assembly to the various committees. Peasant associations were meant to operate as an association-wide service cooperative through which agricultural extension services could be provided, in addition to collectively marketing the goods of individual peasant farmers. The new peasant association legislation also established elected defence squads as a first level of police within the peasant association, while also granting the peasant association judicial authority to hear petty offences that involved small amounts of money, conflicts over garden plots, family inheritance, and the division of common property between spouses.

The logic behind the various rural land proclamations was justified in the language of the student movement. The preamble to the March 1975 rural land legislation states that the aim of the new law is to 'liberate Ethiopian peasants from age-old feudal oppression, injustice, poverty and disease'. The preamble then explains that this is especially important given that in Ethiopia 'a person's right, honor, status and standard of living is determined by his relation to the land'. The preamble's conclusion also states that the development of the country depends on instituting basic changes in agrarian relations, so that 'the development of one becomes the development of all'.[133]

In a similar vein, the July 1975 proclamation to provide for the government ownership of urban lands begins by addressing 'the standard of living, right, honor and status of workers and the toiling masses', and also argues that the monopolisation of urban land by feudal landlords, aristocrats, and government officials had inflated the value of urban houses to the extent that an artificial housing shortage had been created.[134] The proclamation's preamble goes on to claim that this has reduced the lives of urban dwellers to misery, making it necessary to introduce legislation that will allow the government to plan the city in a systematic way so as to serve the majority of urban dwellers.

In the July 1975 urban land law, what this looked like was granting ownership of one house per person or family, with all extra houses becoming the property of the state. The urban land legislation also abolished private landlord-tenant relationships while granting possessory rights to tenants occupying extra houses. Tenants of the newly nationalised houses were, however, required

---

133 Provisional Office for Mass Organisation Affairs 1975, p. 18.
134 Provisional Office for Mass Organisation Affairs 1975, pp. 48–67.

to pay rent to the government at a standardised rate that was usually lower that what they had previously paid. At the same time, the legislation allowed a person or family the use of urban land of up to 500 m² for the purpose of building or residing in a dwelling. Spouses and children were allowed to inherit land use rights, while being prohibited from selling or mortgaging urban land.

The July 1975 urban land law also had a fairly elaborate section on the establishment of cooperatives for urban dwellers that had more or less the same powers as the rural peasant associations, and were also called *kebelles* in Amharic. However, it was not until a second Urban Dwellers Associations Proclamation was passed in October 1976 that the role and status of the urban cooperative societies were fully clarified.[135] Their new powers included the responsibility to provide municipal services such as collecting rent, organising people's shops, dealing with stray animals and domestic livestock, establishing public safety committees, and acting as the first level of the court system. The legislation also specifically designated democratic centralism as the main principle through which the executive, policy committee, and judiciary would operate within the urban cooperative. A greater emphasis can be observed in this latter legislation on the urban *kebelles* as a forum for organising people into government-initiated development projects, helping to raise socialist political consciousness, and mobilising support for the national democratic revolution programme.

In the Program of the National Democratic Revolution (PNDR) that was passed in 1976 we really see how national policy was shaped by the debates of the student movement.[136] Firstly, the program proposes a general theory of how a third world country ought to transition to socialism in the context of imperialism, and secondly, the program situates the Ethiopian revolution within the stages of that transition. The PNDR also evokes the language of the social sciences that we have become familiar with, echoing the notion that revolutionary advancement is necessarily linked to a correct understanding of current Ethiopian reality. Part of what that correct analysis entails in the PNDR is the capacity to distinguish friends from enemies. The current stage of the Ethiopian revolution is described as consisting of two broad coalitions: on the one side is the coalition supported by imperialism, made up of the feudal class, the comprador bourgeoisie, and the bureaucratic bourgeoisie, and on the other side is the coalition of revolutionary forces made up of the worker-peasant alliance and the petty bourgeoisie, which also includes individuals

135   Provisional Office for Mass Organisation Affairs 1975, pp. 68–96.
136   Provisional Office for Mass Organisation Affairs 1975, pp. 9–17.

who have transcended their class background. What is left out of this latter coalition is the lumpen-proletariat, who the PNDR describes as an untrustworthy social group easily mobilised into a reactionary force. Given the outbreak of urban civil war at the very moment that the PNDR was published, such a declaration should not surprise us. With friends and enemies delineated in such a clearly didactic fashion, it is clear that part of the purpose of the PNDR is to identify which parties and individuals would be included in its coalition of anti-feudal forces. At the same time, the PNDR's wider point continued to be confronting the contradictions between the peasantry and the feudal class and, to some degree, the contradiction between workers and the bourgeoisie within the context of global imperialism. This was to be achieved through the attainment of democracy for all oppressed classes, with the expectation that the national democratic revolution will 'attain its consummation through the subsequent socialist revolution'.[137] As such, the PNDR restricted the granting of democratic rights to what it called anti-feudal, anti-imperial and anti-bureaucratic capitalist forces. While the PNDR recognised the right to self-determination of all nationalities, it also insisted that unity between the different nationalities in Ethiopia existed through the common struggle against feudalism, imperialism, and bureaucratic capitalism. It is implied that reactionary forces representing the various nationalities would not be granted democratic rights. Another element emphasised in the PNDR that echoes the student movement's literature is the immediate task of organising, arming, and raising the political consciousness of the popular masses so as to defend the victories of the revolution. In this way, we can say that the Derg saw the institutions of the revolution as serving a top-down pedagogical role to awaken peasant consciousness and to ensure that ordinary citizens internalised the revolution.

The PNDR frames the passage of the rural and urban land proclamations as well as the nationalisation of major industries, banks, and insurance companies as major steps in the process 'of dealing deathblows to feudal lackeys'.[138] The early legislative outcomes of the revolution are also seen as releasing the productive forces of the country from feudal and imperial relations, which will allow the new democratic revolution to focus on basic developmental goals such as raising the standard of living, improving literacy, and providing public health facilities. The PNDR continues to assume that smallholder agriculture will be the foundation of any acceleration of economic development,

---

137 Provisional Office for Mass Organisation Affairs 1975, p. 9.
138 Provisional Office for Mass Organisation Affairs 1975, p. 10.

even while efforts are made towards establishing light industry. The PNDR only vaguely approaches the topic of the collectivisation of peasant farms or the need to establish large-scale government-run farms.

To someone unfamiliar with the debates of the student movement, the concepts used in the PNDR might appear eclectic and even colloquial. However, given our engagement with the ideas that shaped the journal *Challenge*, the language of the PNDR can be understood as the result of a longer and quite detailed debate. The PNDR has a striking emphasis on large-scale political analysis to the detriment of a specific programme related to actual relations of production in the country. As we can see, the student movement's proposal to create a radically new society was the ultimate goal of the national democratic revolution, and in a country where over 85 percent of the population was engaged in peasant farming, the abolition of all previous land tenure systems would at least guarantee the demolition of the old society. Undoubtedly, the legislation introduced by the Derg regime offered relief to peasants in terms of their social obligations to an aristocratic class, and in the south of the country the land legislation most certainly returned proprietorship to the indigenous residents and tenants of the region. But the question of increasing agricultural production was not really addressed by the PNDR, even though the 1973 famine was part of the reason the 1974 revolution had traction with ordinary people.

The total demolition of the so-called traditional land tenure system was easily accepted in Ethiopia, so much so that even in the liberated zones that were later operated by the EPLF and TPLF, land reform imitated the Derg-led initiatives. Perhaps this can be explained by the fact that land reform in Ethiopia hardly ever entailed the breaking up of large estates, since those were atypical in the Ethiopian political economy; rather, land reform simply released peasants from social obligations to a landlord class. At its most extreme, it implied the destruction of an aristocratic class without changing the production processes of ordinary farmers.

Whatever nascent commercial farming did exist, along with the opportunity to engage in wage labour, was lost as a result of the banning of wage labour in agriculture. Christopher Clapham and Dessalegn Rahmato have argued that seasonal migration to commercial farms was becoming an important source of income for peasants who relied on such earnings as a means to supplement subsistence-farming practices. They argued that one of the effects of land reform in Ethiopia was to crowd farmers into home regions and increase the fragmentation of land holdings in already over-farmed areas.[139]

---

139   Clapham 1990; see also Rahmato 1984.

In 1976 the Derg established the Agricultural Marketing Corporation (AMC) in order to collect surplus grain produce from peasant farmers. Its aim was to control the supply of grains from rural areas to urban areas and to the national army. Farmers were given AMC quotas that they needed to fill. However, since most of the grain produced in Ethiopia is consumed on site, with surplus agriculture production being limited to very few regional districts, the creation of the AMC created two new problems. On the one hand, a parallel black market in grains was produced that attempted to circumvent the centralised reach of the AMC so that better prices could be fetched in the open market, and at the same time farmers were sometimes forced to sell livestock to buy grain on the market in order to fulfil AMC quotas. Overall, this had the effect of raising food prices while stalling individual farmers' access to capitalist markets. This combination of events meant that by 1980 food production had fallen to below the level of the 1974 revolution, while annual population numbers increased by at least 2.5 percent.[140] John Cohen has cautioned that no one reason can be isolated to explain the decline in food production. What can be said, however, is that despite attempts at central planning, day-to-day life took revenge on the theoretical attempt to coerce it into empty formulations. The present defied revolutionary futurity. Where the country ended up was with another famine and increased civil war. A gargantuan effort was made to construct an intellectual problem-space that would allow participants to pose questions and receive answers that could address the country's historical predicament; and yet famine returned. Here we are back in the key of tragedy: the synchronic unfolding of events becomes less transparent, resulting in the loss of hope for 'an acceptable future'.

Running parallel to the capture of the central state by the Derg, the nationalities question loomed larger than ever after the 1974 revolution. I do not think that it is far-fetched to say that alongside the Ethiopian student movement ran a parallel revolutionary war with the Addis Ababa-based Derg regime during the 1970s and 1980s. Evidence that both the TPLF and the EPRDF understood themselves to be a legacy of the student movement and the Ethiopian revolution can be found in a number of brochures and policy documents issued by both organisations. In fact, the constitution adopted by the TPLF at its second organisational meeting starts with an introduction that includes subheadings such as 'Our Revolution and the World Situation' and 'Our People and Their Way of Life'.[141] Its introduction places the TPLF within the context of the 1974

---

140   Cohen 1980.
141   Tigray People's Liberation Front 1983.

revolution, but also identifies with the critique of Soviet imperialism. The TPLF constitution explains that the organisation stands against class exploitation, but is weary of battling both imperialism and local feudalism, a twin struggle the introduction identifies as a worldwide predicament of the third world. It goes on to define the struggle of the TPLF in terms of restoring national rights, but guided by a working-class ideology. Therefore, the TPLF claims that its main constituency are poor peasants and, to some extent, urban workers, students, and informal workers.

Later, in a 1989 brochure entitled *EPRDF: A Democratic Alternative for Ethiopia*, the current ruling coalition of which the TPLF was a founding member again describes itself as part of the 1974 revolution and its legacy, but also posits itself as finally able to resolve the national and class contradictions of the country raised by the 1974 revolution. In the brochure, the EPRDF also explains that the 1974 revolution lacked experienced leaders, which is why the democratic aspirations of the people could not be addressed. The brochure claims that 1974 turned out to be a mere military victory, whose major characteristic was a red terror. Accordingly, it argues that the question of self-determination for the nationalities contained within Ethiopia should be the starting and focal point for political organising, without undermining the class struggle.[142]

In the 1995 national constitution of the Federal Democratic Republic of Ethiopia, we really see the debate on the national question come alive. What is perhaps most surprising is that the language adopted by the constitution harkens back to the debates between Tilahun Takele and Tumtu Lencho, especially where they debated Stalin and Lenin's definition of a nation. The preamble to the 1995 constitution begins by locating itself in the nations, nationalities, and people of Ethiopia who have come together 'in full exercise of our right to self-determination, to build a political community'.[143] The constitution retains an evolutionary understanding of the development of nations. Accordingly, the constitution defines nations, nationalities, and people as 'a group of people who have or share a large measure of a common culture or similar customs, mutual intelligibility of language, belief in a common or related identities, a common psychological make-up and who inhabit an identifiable predominantly contiguous territory' (Article 39.5). This definition is a slight modification of Stalin's characterisation of a nation, which was so often discussed and contested within the student movement.

---

142   Ethiopian Peoples Revolutionary Democratic Front 1989.
143   Federal Democratic Republic of Ethiopia 1995.

The 1995 constitution also reflects the language and logic of the resolutions adopted at the nineteenth congress of the ESUNA, especially as they related to the question of Eritrean separation. The 1995 constitution sets out the process through which any nation, nationality and people can exercise the right to self-determination up to and including secession, and states that a simple majority vote in a referendum in the concerned region is all that is required for secession to be realised (Article 39.4.C). While the 1995 constitution sets up only nine self-governing regions, roughly organised around ethnic demarcations, it also grants that any nation, nationality, or people not already organised into a self-governing body has the right to establish its own state as set out in the constitution (Article 47.3).

'Rectifying the historically unjust relationships' and the collective rights of ethnic groups is also understood as the best way to ensure a common destiny of all the nations, nationalities, and people of Ethiopia (Preamble). The constitution also includes women as part of the historically discriminated groups (Article 35.3). In terms of social and economic rights, the constitution connects the practice of self-government to the question of land to the tiller, by claiming that land is 'a common property of the Nations, Nationalities and People of Ethiopia and shall not be subject to sale or to other means of exchange' (Article 40.3). However, some provision for the use of land by private investors is also guaranteed alongside the right to development, together with a state obligation to allocate increased sums to provide for public health, education, and other social services.

One of the more interesting aspects of the Ethiopian state today is that the present regime has retained the peasant associations and the urban co-operatives (*kebelles*) established by Derg regime as the main instrument in the so-called decentralisation of the Derg state. The *kebelle* is therefore the primary institutional space where citizens collectively organise the politics of daily life. Of course, it is also the first place where ordinary men and women encounter a top-down and sometimes coercive state. In this sense, one of the lasting legacies of the 1974 revolution is to have provided the apparatus for the state to penetrate the lives of citizens, but it did this by including ordinary citizens as participants in politics, even if coercion and corruption shaped state-society relationships. The 1974 revolution was where, for the first time in Ethiopian history, a highly disciplined nation-state was fashioned.

7   **Conclusion**

The Ethiopian student movement appropriated concepts from the social sciences in order to reconfigure the past as a useful tool to both think about the future and to act programmatically in the present.[144] This allowed insurgent intellectuals to create new narratives of social change that connected their own grievances to the grievances of peasant and poor urban populations. Yet a gap often remained between the needs of ordinary social actors and the social scientific formulas used to describe ordinary people. This can be attributed in part to the fact that the type of social science imported into Ethiopia homogenised different historical experiences into empty formulas.[145] The construction by the student movement of a new intellectual system served to provide answers about how to manage Ethiopia's place within a changing world system, and as a result that intellectual system deserves to be taken seriously. This has led me to attempt to connect the invention of an intellectual programme by the student movement to the larger processes of social change in the Horn of Africa. In this chapter I have attempted to position the intellectual project of the student movement as both constituting and responding to the social transformation that was demanded of it. To put this in simpler terms, I have argued that the student movement continued to grapple with the question, first raised in the late nineteenth century in Ethiopia, of what territorial sovereignty could mean in the Horn of Africa, while also addressing the contradictions of capitalism as they were playing out within the burgeoning Ethiopian nation-state. Haile-Selassie's regime proved incapable of speaking to these conundrums, and so the students provided their own answers. Even if many of the themes that came out of the revolutionary discourses of the student movement had resonance with debates from earlier periods in Ethiopian history, what was unique to the student movement in Ethiopia in the 1960s is that the students who made up the movement were the first group to have a collective self-consciousness of being modern, secular students. Importantly, this new social identity was often based on having access to scientific thought. One cannot make this claim about any other group of Ethiopian intellectuals prior to the 1960s, even if individual scholars might have gestured towards the scientific or the modern prior to the formalisation of the student movement in the 1960s.[146]

---

144   Here I think it is helpful to think about the legacy of radical scholarship in Africa through Jewsiewicki 1989.
145   Jewsiewicki 1989, p. 4.
146   See, for instance, Zewde 2002.

I end this chapter with a cautionary warning about the way a usable past has been reconstructed for the purposes of building a new future in Ethiopia. In Chapter 6 of this book, I argue that Marxism has often produced a developmental vision of the future rooted in a stageist understanding of the past, and therefore been unable to transcend the status quo. Similarly, in my investigation of the literature of the Ethiopian student movement I have tried to show that because the future was reduced to a set of predicable events tied to the present, social progress became limited to finding a way in which the Ethiopian population could be organised to produce that future. As a result, critical thought was reduced to a technique of social engineering rather than the abrogation of the regular and the habitual. What was missed in all this is that Marxism has always contained within it a dynamic critique of the legacy of positivism as dogmatically attached to the future (see Chapter 6).

CHAPTER 4

When Social Science Concepts Become Neutral Arbiters of Social Conflict: Rethinking the 2005 Elections in Ethiopia

The original impetus behind this research project was my attempt to make sense of the blogs, newspaper articles and academic accounts of the 2005 federal elections in Ethiopia. Given that both academic and popular descriptions of the 2005 Ethiopian elections continued to rely on a certain set of bifurcated metaphors, such as 'greed and grievance', 'patron and client', 'rapacious rule vs. innocent population', and so forth, I wanted to revisit the questions that Tobias Hagmann first posed in his criticism of Jon Abbink's assessment of the 2005 elections. To paraphrase Hagmann, can modern political parties such as the incumbent Ethiopian People's Revolutionary Democratic Front (EPRDF) and its founding party, the Tigray People's Liberation Front (TPLF), which fought a long civil war in order to institutionalise revolutionary democracy, be characterised as parties that simply 'represent a "personalized" and "traditionalist" form of domination'? Can contemporary Ethiopian history be reduced to notions in which politics is seen as part of a long tradition of authoritarian culture vs. democracy?[1]

In my examination of the literature of the Ethiopian student movement, I discovered connections between the policy choices of contemporary political parties and the animating ideas of the Ethiopian student movement. For example, the questions of 'land to the tiller' and of the 'self-determination of nationalities' continued to be two of the key debates that dominated the 2005 elections. However, I was truly surprised to see that there was a continuity of persons from the student movement up to and including the 2005 elections, in terms of the major players who were shaping policy debates. It seemed clear that many of the splits, openings, and fractures that divided the Ethiopian student movement not only shaped national policy during the period of the Derg regime and the civil wars of the 1970s and 80s, but continued to shape the content of the debates during the 2005 elections. At the same time, through the research I conducted for the previous chapters of this book, I also discovered that the historiography of the revolution played a constitutive role in legitim-

---

1 Here I am paraphrasing the discussion on page 607 of Hagmann 2006. See also Abbink 2006.

ising more than one side in the revolution. One of the consequences of this is that there has been a kind of silence imposed on any analysis of the student movement in terms of its policy impacts in the post-cold war period. Yet even the literature of the EPRDF/TPLF contends that the student movement constitutes the fore-history of both the Derg regime and the incumbent EPRDF. It is striking, then, that in the debates that circulated on opposition websites and blogs around the 2005 elections there is an absence of concern with the historical context that the EPRDF regime was aiming to address, particularly the legacy of the 1974 Ethiopian revolution, the student movement (which produced many of the ideas of the revolution), and the concomitant civil wars. Also missing from the discussion were the achievements and contradictions of the incumbent EPRDF in relation to this broader historical context.

Given this, I agree with what Sarah Vaughan has observed in her own work on nationalism in Ethiopia: that within the Ethiopian student movement a tradition was started whereby 'the historian's desire to explain that "it was so" melds with the politician's keenness to demonstrate that "it could not have been otherwise" and was thus "rightly so"'.[2] A kind of synergy exists within Ethiopian social science and political arenas, which to this day allows public figures to flip-flop between a primordial assertion of identity and an utter rejection of this primordialism by claiming that all previous knowledge has been produced through an instrumental framework (although of course all facts as such are manipulated narratives). This allows both the social sciences and social movements to be re-launched on the basis of a positivist commitment that things must become so.[3] This echoes one of the major findings of Chapters 2 and 3, which showed that historiography and political practice have been instrumentally connected since the 1970s in Ethiopia. What characterises the connection between intellectual life and political life in Ethiopia is the insistence that politics must transform itself to align with positivist truths discovered by social scientists (or that ideal-typical social science models are taken as laws of social development that the Ethiopian population must be adjusted to fit). Both the social sciences and historiography have become major battlefields where politics is played out. Following on this claim, in this chapter I argue that the 2005 election replicated a pattern of politicising social science knowledge that continues to be deeply connected to a form of knowledge production adopted by the Ethiopian student movement beginning in the 1960s. To this day, the student movement continues to generate a complex history of debate

---

2 Vaughan 2003, p. 19.
3 See also Sarah Vaughan's discussion of the relationship between positivism and ethnic self-determination within the EPRDF in Vaughan 2003, p. 203.

and conflict in the country, as well as to produce new social actors, who may be defiant of the terms set by the student movement but for whom the student movement is a condition of their own possibility. Even if many of the current practitioners of both social sciences and politics in Ethiopia reject the content of those early debates, they nevertheless continue to be deeply implicated in their positivist form. This is why I insist that it is only by seriously interrogating the claims of the 1960s and 1970s and linking them back to current debates in Ethiopia that politics in the country can overcome its overly fractious nature. This interrogation and linkage is some of what I hope to do in the rest of this chapter.

1   The 2005 Federal Elections

According to Christopher Clapham, the May 2005 national elections in Ethiopia took on 'the characteristics of "founding elections" akin to the 1994 contest in post-apartheid South Africa'.[4] Clapham makes this claim based on the fact that almost all observers of the 2005 elections agreed that they were conducted with an unprecedented level of fairness and openness.[5] For the first time in Ethiopian history, opposition parties and government spokespersons engaged in a series of debates on state television, which proved highly popular. In addition, opposition parties were allowed to engage in open mobilisation of their constituencies and fielded candidates in both rural and urban areas. As a result, the opposition parties did not engage in the boycott of elections that had become a common occurrence since the fall of the Soviet-backed Derg regime in 1991. Thus, even though the 2005 elections were the third set of national elections since the promulgation of the 1995 post-Derg constitution, they were the first elections in which multiple parties other than those affiliated with the incumbent party participated.[6] Nonetheless, the election ended in disaster, with many opposition leaders and their followers being jailed. The election has set the tone for how politics has played out in the past decade in Ethiopia. In fact, in the 2015 elections the EPRDF and its affiliate parties won 100 percent of the seats in the federal parliament.

The Coalition for Unity and Democracy (CUD) and the United Ethiopian Democratic Front (UEDF) were the two main opposition parties that participated in the May 2005 elections. Both coalitions were founded by prominent

4   Clapham 2005.
5   EU Election Observation Mission Ethiopia 2005.
6   See Lyons 2006.

members of the Ethiopian academic and intellectual scene, many of whom had also participated in the student movement of the 1960s and 1970s.[7] The popular Coalition for Unity and Democracy (CUD) was founded just before the elections as a coalition of four existing non-ethnic opposition parties, while the United Ethiopian Democratic Front (UEDF) was created in 2003 at a convention held in the United States and included remnants of some of the more active parties that came out of the ESM, such as the Ethiopian People's Revolutionary Party.[8] Two of its most prominent leaders and spokespersons (Merara Gudina and Beyene Petros) were professors at the University of Addis Ababa with clear roots in the ESM of the 1960s and 1970s.[9]

Most of the prominent founders of the CUD were Ethiopian intellectuals, many of whom received their higher education in the United States. This group included such prominent figures as Mesfin Wolde-Mariam, Berhanu Nega, and Yacob Haile-Mariam: the latter two had held positions as university professors in economics and business departments in the United States, while Mesfin was employed as a social scientist in the University of Addis Ababa system from the late 1960s to the early 1990s.[10] All of these opposition members had participated in the Ethiopian student movement in the 1960s and 1970s, with Yacob Haile Mariam working as an editor of and contributor to the student movement journals, while Berhanu Nega was a member of the EPRP. By the 1970s, Mesfin Wolde-Mariam was already well known as a professor in the Geography Department at Addis Ababa University (then called the Haile-Selassie I University) and was considered by many to be a progressive ally of the students, though more radical ones saw him as a 'bourgeois democrat'.[11]

The UEDF was composed of social-democratic-type parties, and as a coalition it tended to accept the 1995 national constitution as the correct political arrangement for the country. Thus, the UEDF's criticisms of the incumbent party mostly focused on the fact that the EPRDF paid only lip service to its own political and constitutional commitments. Given this basic political difference from the CUD, the UEDF played a much less controversial role in the

---

7   Lyons 2007.
8   The coalition included the following: the All Ethiopia Unity Party (AEUP), the United Ethiopians Democratic Party–Medhin (UEDP–Medhin), the Ethiopian Democratic League (EDL), and the Rainbow Ethiopia-Movement for Social Justice and Democracy (Rainbow). See Lyons 2006.
9   Abbink 2006, p. 181. See also Merera 2003.
10   Abbink 2006, p. 181.
11   Mesfin Wolde-Mariam's activities during the student movement are discussed in Balsvik 1994.

2005 post-election turmoil.[12] On the other hand, the CUD party platform seriously challenged the constitutional framework that has determined political
arrangements in the country since 1994. For example, the CUD challenged the
constitution's nationalities policy by calling for the full repeal of Article 39,
which guarantees the right to secession of all of the nations, nationalities, and
peoples that make up the federal republic of Ethiopia. The CUD also called for
the amendment of Article 40, which states that all land is vested in the state and
peoples of Ethiopia and cannot be subject to sale. Lastly, the CUD called for the
repeal of Articles 46 and 47, which determine that the federal system organise itself along ethnic jurisdictions. In effect, this meant that the CUD challenged the status of Eritrean independence, and also questioned the boundaries through which Eritrea was established. In addition, the CUD demanded
the establishment of a private land market and the loosening of state control
over banking and other financial matters.[13]

I have suggested that what characterises the connection between intellectual life and political life in Ethiopia is the insistence that politics must transform itself to align with positivist truths discovered by social scientists. What
I want to show now is that the attempt to use the social sciences to transform
political commitments on the ground helps account for the policy framework
set out in opposition to the EPRDF in the lead-up to the 2005 elections. If we
trace the intellectual work of Berhanu Nega and Mesfin Wolde-Mariam from
1990 to 2005, it becomes evident that they were involved in an intellectual project that aimed to shift the terms of the policy debate around land and the
nationalities question, in an effort to ensure that the newly popular post-cold
war notions of civil society and human rights would become hegemonic. Below,
I discuss how these scholars set out to do this, first through intellectual work
within civil society groups, and later by claiming the Ethiopian state as their
own when they declared victory in the 2005 elections.

To begin with, we need to connect discursive opposition to the policy framework set out by the EPRDF with the general rise in Addis Ababa of a number
of independent civil society organisations (CSOs) and research centres (NGOs)
that burst onto the scene in the mid-1990s. The ideas of these new social actors
are well documented in the publications issued by organisations such as the
Ethiopian Economics Association (EEA), the Forum for Social Studies (FSS),
the Christian Development Relief Association (CDRA), and the Organisation
for Social Justice in Ethiopia (SJE). These publications include *Economic Focus*

---

12   Lyons 2007, p. 538.
13   Kinijit 2011.

(a regular bulletin from EEA) and *Medrek* (the FSS bulletin), as well as one-off publications issued by these organisations. Most of the publications are compiled from the proceedings of regularly organised conferences and workshops.[14] They bear witness to the fact that NGOs in the 1990s and up until the 2005 elections regularly brought together major players on the Ethiopian intellectual scene. Under the rubric of civil society, therefore, a new intellectual culture was created, one that was moving away from the state-sponsored university setting and working largely under the umbrella of NGOs.

For example, in a variety of conferences and workshops we find Mesfin Wolde-Mariam working in tandem with other intellectuals, such as Dessalegn Rahmato from the Forum for Social Studies (FSS), to produce a persistent critique of the Ethiopian land tenure system as simply bringing about a 'Malthusian disaster' (their term).[15] These critics were also keen to point to the contradiction between the decentralised regional system governed by peasant associations (*kebelles*) on the one hand, and the operation of democratic centralism at the party level, on the other. An exemplary instance of the coming together of Malthusian-type critique of the land tenure system is found in the December 1997 bulletin of the Ethiopian Economics Association (EEA), where a roundtable discussion between Dessalegn and Mesfin Wolde-Mariam on 'Food Security and Rural Land Policy' is reproduced. Their argument rests on the claim that poverty has been manufactured by the land tenure system, precisely because that system does not lead to the consolidation of property. According to Dessalegn and Mesfin, this fact alone has led to a system of 'micro-agriculture' in Ethiopia, with plot sizes too small to bring about economies of scale.[16] Moreover, for Dessalegn, the fact that peasants are guaranteed access to land implies that the system does not encourage out-migration from the rural areas. Lastly, Dessalegn argues that periodic land redistribution through the peasant associations leads to tenure insecurity, which in turn implies that peasants are often unwilling to invest in long-term projects on their land. What is striking about the conclusions drawn here is that they stem from a series of ideologically-based logical premises about the rationality of human behaviour and private property.[17] So while Dessalegn Rahmato himself was an extremely active member of the ESM, including serving as editor of *Challenge*, and while

---

14 See, for example, Zewde and Assefa 2008; Areda 2007; Rahmato, Bantirgu, and Endeshaw 2008.
15 Rahmeto [sic] et al. 1997, p. 10.
16 Rahmeto [sic] et al. 1997, p. 8.
17 For a critique of the ideological nature of the land tenure debate in Ethiopia, see Wibke and Benedikt 2008.

he does not disavow the 1974 'land to the tiller' movement, his present critique ultimately rests on the idea that the Ethiopian peasant is a modern, rational economic actor, and as such the Ethiopian state should not be afraid to privatise land. At the very least, freehold will lead to the redistribution of economic incentives on behalf of those who can use them best.

The same issue of the bulletin also includes a vigorous rebuttal of the positions offered by Dessalegn and Mesfin by a number of audience participants who opposed this pessimistic condemnation of the Ethiopian land tenure system with a series of questions, such as: 'Who is food insecure?' 'Are all regions food insecure?' 'Is it possible to distinguish between chronic and transitory food insecurity?' 'Is the link between property rights and food security straight forward?' and 'Are there short term trade-offs that need to be considered in terms of the overall land tenure system?' In this debate that took place in the mid-1990s one can already begin to discern the fissures over land policy that would play out in the 2005 elections.

In terms of building an alternative intellectual community, the work conducted by Mesfin Wolde-Mariam and Berhanu Nega seems to have culminated in the February 2004 conference entitled 'Vision 2020', hosted by the EEA. This gathering included participation from all major Ethiopian intellectuals, particularly those involved in civil society research centres such as the aforementioned FSS (also founded in the 1990s). The proceedings were then made available in a bilingual (Amharic/English) newsletter also published by the EEA. The conference included much reflection on the recent history of Ethiopia, with the premier scholar of Ethiopian modern history and executive director of the FSS, Bahru Zewde, delivering a paper entitled 'What Did We Dream? What Did We Achieve? And Where Are We Heading?' This paper is significant in that it reflects on the past and present of the Ethiopian student movement.[18] In addition, Mesfin Wolde-Mariam delivered a fiery talk entitled 'Whither Ethiopia', which also reflected on the stagnant nature of recent Ethiopian politics. Berhanu Nega's speech at this conference in a similar vein, entitled 'Ethiopia's fate after one generation', continues to circulate on the Internet as a defining intellectual and political statement for opponents of the EPRDF.[19] At this conference a consensus seems to have emerged that transformative change was needed for the country; nonetheless, the overall tone was one of pessimism about the country's recent political history.

Coupled with the type of intellectual activity hosted by the EEA in the early part of the first decade of the twenty-first century, Mesfin Wolde-Mariam also

18   Zewde 2004.
19   Nega 2003.

became well known in Addis Ababa for his speeches at workshops, again hosted by various NGO groups. For example, in July 2003 he gave a speech at a CDRA workshop held at the Economic Commission for Africa headquarters entitled 'One Cannot Make the Donkey Move by Beating the Load: Breaking the Cycle of Recurrent Famine in Ethiopia', in which he repeats the theme of a Malthusian disaster awaiting Ethiopia, and then goes on to lambast the audience as morally weak for accepting the current land tenure system. Similarly, in 2002, Mesfin gave a speech at his alma mater, Clark University in the United States, during the inauguration of the International Development, Community and Environment Program, in which he argued that Ethiopia was still caught in the grip of a Leninist land tenure policy and simultaneously called on humanity to embrace American-style freedom and democracy.[20]

It is clear when reading through the documents produced by each of the aforementioned CSO/NGO research groups that they understand their own role as civil society groups as being the leading lights of the democratisation process in Ethiopia. They lay claim to this in a programmatic and prescriptive fashion, without ever explaining what they mean by civil society or democracy beyond formal definitions.[21] Civil society is not defined through looking at actual social processes specific to Ethiopia. Instead, it is defined by being programmatically able to achieve something, usually derived from what civil society has supposedly achieved globally. The definition of civil society is often taken unproblematically from organisations like CIVICUS, and then that definition is applied to Ethiopia.[22] Civil society *qua* civil society is seen as a catalyst for change, able to bring about the development of larger democratic processes and to quicken the drive for equity, and as having the capacity to engender innovative approaches to the rallying of public opinion. Within the literature generated by these groups, whenever there is some attempt to historicise civil society in Ethiopia, that history tends to refer to those local and international organisations that donors preferred to deal with given the civil war/junta of the 1980s. CSOs are collapsed with NGOs, and 1991 becomes a benchmark year for the formation of a modern civil society in Ethiopia. Political liberalisation is posited as an important moment when NGOs were able to operate with some

20   Wolde-Mariam 2003a, 2003b.
21   For examples of this, see Zewde and Assefa 2008; Areda 2007; Rahmato, Bantirgu, and Endeshaw 2008.
22   CIVICUS is an international alliance of civil society organisations that has been highly influential in a number of third world and former soviet bloc countries. Its aim is to promote citizen participation in local level, non-state-based organisations. CIVICUS sees this as an important way forward in order to amplify the voice of citizens on a global stage. See www.civicus.org.

degree of freedom. Moreover, the associational life that belongs to so-called traditional community organising patterns (for example, burial societies) is simply theorised as pre-civil society, whereas mass-based organisations such as peasant associations and trade unions are side-lined in the discussions at both the theoretical and practical levels, because they are regarded as simply party-affiliated organisations.[23] Thus, even in the descriptions generated by the CSO groups themselves, what we are really talking about as CSOs are donor-dependent NGOs engaged in development and service delivery. Even in their own reports, the CSO groups claim that their constituency base is small, with little or no capacity for policy engagement at the state level. Yet the CSOs continue to see themselves as a third space between the state and private life – a neutral space of knowledge production and human rights advocacy that can mediate social conflict. Not only do they assume civil society to be a neutral space that can mediate social conflict; these organisations present themselves as a space for the production of concepts that will mediate social conflict.

It is therefore striking, when reading through the research issued by these CSO groups, to find a seamless connection between their policy recommendations as advocates and academics and the policy formulated within the CUD party manifesto. Moreover, there is often congruence between World Bank policy as it relates to the land tenure question in Ethiopia, the writings of locally based Ethiopian intellectuals, and the CUD party manifesto. The CUD party manifesto includes ideas and language that seem to be directly lifted from a number of research papers issued by the previously mentioned researchers, especially the work of Mesfin Wolde-Mariam and Berhanu Nega, as well as the work published with the EEA.

By 2002 we see the EEA begin to work in tandem with World Bank activity in Ethiopia. We also find Berhanu Nega leading a major research programme on land tenure with the EEA and at the same time participating as a major researcher with the World Bank land tenure group, eventually producing a research report for the EEA that bears an uncanny resemblance to the policy recommendations coming out of the bank itself. Moreover, the opinions and conclusions in the EEA report are then echoed through Berhanu Nega's co-authored World Bank reports. In 2002 Berhanu Nega published the report 'Land Tenure and Agriculture: Development in Ethiopia' through the EEA; at the same time and in conjunction with this report, other EEA researchers led a review of policies related to landholding under the various political regimes in Ethiopia. Later, in 2003, the World Bank land tenure group published a series of articles

---

23   See, for example, Rahmato 2008.

on tenure security and land markets in Ethiopia with a research team under the direction of the well-known World Bank land researcher Klaus Denninger, along with Berhanu Nega and others.[24]

The EEA research report, 'Land Tenure and Agriculture: Development in Ethiopia', published in 2002, attempts to assess Ethiopian farmers' opinions and judgments of how the land tenure system has impacted their livelihoods. The primary method the report uses to do this is a gargantuan survey of 8,500 households in every region of the country except Gambela. The report also includes an assessment of 'stakeholders'' opinions of the land tenure system. By stakeholders the researchers primarily mean business persons operating within the private sphere, as well as policymakers within both government and the CSO sector, who mostly reside in the urban areas. Together, the overall aim of the two surveys is to try to connect the current land tenure system to its impact on the rural economy and agricultural development.

The household survey used a stratified random sampling framework, with questions written in English and then translated into Amharic and other local languages (depending on where the survey was being conducted). The researchers used local post-secondary students to conduct the survey. While the report discusses the limits to the survey in terms of outreach and representativeness, it never discusses the problems with the questions posed to the research subjects themselves. Indeed, the researchers take the questions asked to be self-evident in terms of what they might mean for the participants. For instance, the researchers asked the same questions in all of the regions surveyed and limited the answers to multiple choices so as to obtain comparable answers across the regions. However, the questions assume that an ethnically Somali pastoralist will have the same notion of what private property or freehold means as an Amhara farmer growing grain in the highlands of Gondar. As an example, the survey asks farmers to suggest alternatives to the current land tenure system, and the choices offered are limited to the following: 'a) free hold, b) a system that allows for better security, c) public ownership (secured rights), d) other'.[25] Another example asks if farmers who hold their land as private property would sell it if they had a bad harvest.[26] The farmers were given the opportunity to answer the question in a yes or no format; most answered 'no' to this question. The report uses this as evidence that farmers are rational actors who do not need to be protected by the state in order to maintain access to land. The report goes on to advocate privatisation of the land tenure system

---

24   See, for example, Deininger et al. 2003, 2004.
25   See question 23 in Nega 2002, p. 113.
26   Question 33 in Nega 2002, p. 134.

as more or less a good thing. However, because the survey also showed that farmers were not keen on unrestricted freehold – with a large percentage of them preferring state ownership of land with secure rights – the policy recommendation of the report offers a compromise between these two positions and advocates that the government ought to allow for the creation of a land rental market.

Starkly absent from the report is any attempt to think meaningfully about the notion that the individual farmers' 'rational' answers might easily be contradicted by day-to-day reality. The report never deals directly with the fact that the two answers cited above might indicate the existence of other kinds of social contradictions. It does not consider how, despite whatever logical choice the farmer might have made in the context of a survey, an individual farmer's choices are in fact conditioned by the political economy of the entire productive system in Ethiopia, in which agriculture plays a substantial role. Because the report's methodology takes the questions being asked as eliciting self-evident truths, the report must deny that a contradiction can exist between an ideally logical answer and an answer as it might play out in reality.

The EEA report therefore concludes that the government's emphasis on state ownership of land, framed by the policy of agricultural development-led industrialisation (ADLI), is wrong-headed – instead, it proposes that the whole 'social structure of accumulation' needs to be considered.[27] Here the report means to suggest that it is possible to produce an institutional context in order to change individual behaviour. However, it ought also to be noted that the peasant farmer is always referred to as an economic agent. Thus, if neo-classical economics is only concerned with the satisfaction of private ends as the definition of the public good, the EEA has a more classical, Adam Smith-type commitment to development, in as much as they assume that through promoting market-driven social relations one can create rational economic actors who engage in higher productive efficiencies, thereby establishing a collective social good. The development question and the political question for the EEA turn on how best to produce good entrepreneurs and risk takers.

Once again, the EEA report does not connect the individual to the context of the productive system in the country and the region as it actually exists. Rather, it assumes the need to equitably distribute economic incentives so that everyone can behave like economic maximisers, and suggests that the problem with the current land tenure system is that the right incentives do not exist because the system hoards the economic rewards that need to be freed

---

27   Nega 2002, p. 3.

up in the country. The economic and development conundrum for Ethiopia, from the perspective of the EEA, then becomes a question of how to reproduce the right kind of individuated person by rooting this individuation within the actual productive system of the country (what the EEA calls 'structures of accumulation'). The research report can be summed up as one in which the EEA's researchers presume the capitalist subject as existing a priori, through the establishment of some kind of pure capitalist social relations. When such a subject is not found, the EEA report makes the tautological claim that the landholding systems and their attendant peasant associations must be the reason behind the lack of rational economic actors. As I have already suggested, the problem with the theoretical and methodological commitment of the report is that it assumes what it wants to produce: the real nature of what it means to be a rational human actor.

The development quest for the EEA can therefore be equated with the problem of how to set up a situation in which people can behave like their natural selves – that is, a situation in which they can behave like atomised, self-maximising humans, but also a situation in which that type of human being is seen as transhistorical. Indeed, for the EEA, all Ethiopian peasants are in essence modern rational economic actors (this is also its definition of what it means to be human); it is only the current political system that keeps people from acting as their true selves. Politics must therefore be brought back into economics in order to set up a social system through which economically rational behaviour is produced (and in which politics can later on be separated from economic life). The overall argument is to create a moral framework from which the capitalist subject can fully emerge under conditions in which its behaviour will be rewarded.

In *Land, Poverty and Livelihoods in an Era of Globalization*, Haroon Akram-Lodhi and colleagues suggest that the current World Bank definition of what a good land policy ought to be includes such factors as promoting owner-operated farms, allowing for freely operating land markets, promoting the equitable distribution of assets, and recognising that there is a need to maintain some communal land holdings. Most importantly, for the World Bank, there is a need to secure transparent and enforceable property rights as the critical precondition for investment and economic growth. As such, the World Bank supports land reform in the effort to eliminate conflicts between parallel sets of rights.[28] Moreover, Akram-Lohdi and colleagues argue that, for the Bank, this somewhat heterodox land policy framework indicates that land considerations have become non-ideological and are now self-evident truths.

---

28   Akram-Lodhi, Kay, and Borras 2007, pp. 14–15.

Similarly (and based on a survey method that takes methodological indi-
vidualism as a given), the EEA report goes on to argue that state ownership of
land yields negative effects on land productivity and produces lower efficiency
levels than would be achieved if there was a working private land market. The
report argues that there is a need for entrepreneurial agents to access credit
and land (using land as a mortgage), and hence the need for a land market. The
report goes on to argue that marginal farmers should be encouraged to out-
migrate, the benefit of which will be to 'encourage accumulation of land in the
hands of entrepreneurial and economically successful farmers'.[29] In addition,
the report claims that land redistribution through the peasant associations
is too political, and as such creates tenure insecurity and prevents landowners from investing in sustainable use of the land. The report therefore argues
that the government places too much emphasis on agricultural extension programmes; that is, it is too technology focused.[30] Instead, the EEA argues that it
is necessary to change 'incentive structures', 'institutional configurations', and
'governance' and 'risk behaviour'.[31]

By the late 1990s, locally based CSO groups in Ethiopia took up this latter
claim as the common-sense position on the Ethiopian land tenure system, and
by 2005 this position became part of the official policy of the CUD party platform. The bulk of the policy issues in the CUD party manifesto circulate around
land privatisation and its connection to the nationalities question. A large part
of the manifesto is dedicated to a critique of the agricultural system in Ethiopia
and especially the land tenure system. The critique seems directly lifted from
the EEA research report. Using very similar language, the manifesto analogously
calls for 'the restructuring of patterns of accumulation', as well as arguing the
need to expand the banking and insurance sector so as to induce savings and
capital formation. Importantly, it calls for amending the constitution to allow
for mixed private, public, and communal ownership of land. Given that the
Ethiopian constitution embeds the land question within the nationalities question, the CUD party manifesto does not just call for the amendment of Article 39
but for its full repeal.

The CUD critique of the land and nationalities question centres on the fact
that the constitution protects people as members of a group (nation, nationality, or people) but not as individuals. The CUD manifesto claims that the
national constitution reflects the party platform of the incumbent EPRDF and
as such simply works in favour of revolutionary democracy. It therefore calls on

---

29   Nega 2002, p. 3.
30   Nega 2002, p. xv.
31   Nega 2002, p. 3.

the government 'to ... give capitalism more than lip service' and 'adjust to the world's new power alignment'.[32] In addition, the CUD accuses the TPLF/EPRDF of selling out national sovereignty to external forces. In the specific case of Eritrea, the CUD claims that the Ethiopian state has legitimate complaints about national maritime demarcation, border demarcation, and the status of Ethiopians in Eritrea. Ultimately, then, the CUD sees that the problem of ethnic conflict cannot be resolved with the policy of ethnic self-determination. To the CUD, such a policy is treason.[33]

Echoing the EEA report, the CUD party manifesto claims that the problem of the country is not one of natural endowment but one of good governance and democracy. It suggests that the current socioeconomic order thrives on poverty, with development itself being a threat to the ruling elite. The CUD claims that the EPRDF would rather endure the increased impoverishment of its people in order to maintain its own luxurious lifestyle.[34] In contrast, the CUD platform adopts a highly moral tone, claiming that there is a need for behavioural change in the Ethiopian political scene, and calling for the deployment of 'honesty and righteous human character' in politics.[35]

Fundamentally, the CUD is committed to liberal democracy, while it also 'combines useful values from social democracy and consensus democracy'.[36] It emphasises a commitment to individual freedom, and to free markets based on competition and on cultural and political change.[37] From a social-democratic perspective, the CUD adopts the idea of an equitable sharing of taxes and some kind of commitment to social welfare, but ultimately preaches the need to adopt liberal market economic principles into specific Ethiopian conditions. For the CUD, this is what will ensure a more equitable income distribution.

2   Discussion

During the 2005 Ethiopian elections, political groups were divided over the meaning and the legacy of the revolutionary process that begun in 1974. On the one hand, the current regime insisted on the need to transform the remnants of the pre-revolutionary state and society by following the historical traject-

---

32   Kinijit 2011, p. 43.
33   Ibid.
34   Ibid.
35   Kinijit 2011, p. 8.
36   Kinijit 2011, p. 9.
37   Ibid.

ory and policies initiated by the Ethiopian student movement. For the ruling
EPRDF, state institutions themselves were proposed as the arbiter of social conflict. On the other hand, the opposition insisted on the necessity of further sep-
arating state and society as the panacea for resolving social problems. For them,
civil society was proposed as a universally accessible space through which not
only could social critique be channelled but civil society itself could become
the arbiter of social conflict. The opposition then mobilised itself around a
number of key social science concepts drawn from the neutral space of civil
society as a way to promote hegemonic power around itself, while the EPRDF
held on to ethnic federalism and the right to self-determination within the
framework of revolutionary democracy as its transformative tool kit. It should
be noted that here again social science contestations paralleled conflict in the
social arena. Comparisons can also be drawn to the student movement, in that
the CUD also saw themselves as bearers of a modern form of universal knowledge, and for them it became necessary and just to organise society on the basis
of their newly found truths. Thirty years after the Ethiopian student movement
won its initial victory, this initial conceit was explicitly advocated by researchers who saw themselves as working within the realm of civil society.

The Ethiopian federal elections of 2005 have for the most part been situated between two poles that are of course analogous to the more universal
debates that one finds within African studies, whereby the state in African
politics is described as corrupt and patrimonial, as if Africans were just so
many backward people.[38] Moreover, the state is said to be hostage to patron-
client relations, with markets unable to develop or even just to free themselves
from tradition.[39] This debate has filtered into common parlance, and from the
point of view of international NGOs and bilateral aid organisations, the pre-
scription to end all of this African 'backwardness' is that state failure ought
to be corrected by weakening the state's command over its resources, while
autonomous civil society organisations should be strengthened as a buttress
against rent-seeking clients of the state.[40] Not surprisingly, these were also
the propositions adopted by the main opposition CUD party in the 2005 elections. As I have tried to illustrate in this chapter, the universal language of the
social sciences became the basis through which the CUD organised its platform.

---

38   Bayart 1994.
39   Hydén 1983.
40   At the time of the 2005 elections, reports from organisations such as the International
      Crisis Group and Amnesty International reflected this rhetoric. See International Crisis
      Group 2009; Amnesty International 2005; Human Rights Watch 2008.

One of this book's driving questions has been to ask what we ideologically reproduce each time we practice social science as a space of neutral meaning-making. In the discourses of the 2005 federal elections in Ethiopia, we see that the universalising conceit of the social sciences provides the overall epistemological framework for the claims made by both Ethiopian civil society advocates and the EPRDF. When liberal democracy is proffered against the Ethiopian regime's avowed revolutionary democracy – when it is praised for possessing the institutional checks and balances needed to rectify the problems supposedly inherent to an authoritarian African regime – liberal democracy itself is lifted out of the story of its own historical formation and is seen in purely formal terms. The Ethiopian regime is then discussed in terms of good and bad, where good and bad are measured by how close the regime has come to setting up the apparently universally recognisable institutions of liberal democracy. At the same time, what cannot be analysed is that the institutional processes connected to liberal democracy often entrench myriad odd forms of non-state and state-led dictatorship and rule in countries of the global south. The consequence of this is that bourgeois-looking institutions draw out social differences, instead of functioning as neutral peacemakers.

The question for us now is how to assess the processes of knowledge production that have attempted to tell us something about the ways in which people are living in Ethiopia, and in tandem have contributed to the overall attempt to change the structure of the state. Clearly, the activity of practising the social sciences is class-specific and based on the productive activities of a specific social formation, and is alienated from certain producers and classes within that social formation. Rather than pretend to produce neutral social science knowledge and so look for some abstract model of democracy for Ethiopia, it is important to trace the meanings of the different social relations and institutions that are embedded in society. In particular, we need to find out what the legacies of the revolution and the civil wars are, rather than simply saying, mantra-like, that the new regimes post Haile-Selassie are authoritarian. By definition, the struggle that led to the 1974 revolution and the resulting civil wars cannot be so vacant of meaning. Thus, for me, it is important not only to connect the state to a class analysis, but at the same time to circle back and place democratic structures into economic structures. Without this, democracy and elections become part of a technocratic toolbox for development rather than a substantive expression of real social forces and relations. To reiterate, the outcome can only be the kind of moralistic prescriptions that a supposedly neutral, positivistic social science claims to offer.

Gebru Tareke has reminded us that happy is the nation that still knows how to rebel, but also that 'happier still is the nation which utilises the historical memory of collective resistance to mold a more egalitarian and coherent community'.[41] This raises the particular question that Sarah Vaughan asked of the present regime:

> Can a revolutionary party with an evangelical belief in the superiority of its own political programme seek to establish a competitive electoral process as a desired goal in its own right? Could (should?) elections really be anything other than a means to an end, a process useful only for demonstrating anew the virtues of revolutionary democracy and democratic centralism? If the goal is winning at all costs, how can the contest be anything other than zero-sum, how can 'their gain' be anything other than 'our loss'?[42]

At the moment, it would seem that the question of elections is reduced to a zero-sum game. On the other hand, if the process of social transformation involves more than the mobilisation of social forces around the binaries of 'tradition vs. modernity', 'civil society vs. the customary', or 'intellectual vanguard vs. ignoramus', then perhaps an accounting of collective resistance to both oppression and exploitation would mean that elections could become something other than contests over whether abstract liberal freedoms can be established. Instead, they could become contests over the ways in which social policy could continue to be located in the possibilities opened up by the Ethiopian revolution, even as the revolutionary institutions are transformed. In this way, the social sciences in Ethiopia could also transform themselves into social criticism with a task – something opposed to what they are now, which is a coercive and technocratic ideological player masquerading as a neutral arbiter of facts. This latter transformation seems most urgent in Ethiopia, more than forty years after the beginning of revolutionary struggle.

---

41   Tareke 2009, p. xxiii.
42   Tronvoll and Vaughan 2003, p. 157.

CHAPTER 5

Passive Revolution: Living in the Aftermath of the 2005 Elections

Earlier, in Chapter 2, we discussed the limits placed on anti-colonial nationalist thought in relation to the economic and political conjunctures that demand the existence of such nationalism in the first place. We borrowed from Partha Chatterjee the idea that three ongoing moments shape anti-colonial nationalism as a developmental path towards passive revolution: the first is the moment of departure, when educated elites discover their own backwardness and attempt to create a political programme that would align the local nation-state with modernity; the second is the moment of manoeuvre, where popular forces are simultaneously mobilised and demobilised in order to restructure state-society relations; and the third is the moment of arrival, where anti-colonial nationalism now justifies the building of a state that has fully consented to managing an economy based on capitalist social relations. In this book, I have tended to see the movement towards passive revolution as a non-linear process. Nonetheless, in examining the rhetoric of the developmental state in Ethiopia since 2005 one gets the sense that we have now entered the moment of arrival: 'the passive revolution writing its own life-history'.

Evidence of this new life history can be found most clearly in the far-reaching efforts at urban reconstruction that have transformed the landscape of Addis Ababa (the capital city of Ethiopia) since 2005. These reconstruction efforts culminated in 2012 with a new proposed masterplan for the city. During the process of preparing the masterplan for Addis Ababa, the City administration was given the additional mandate of planning for a wider area that was identified as 'metropolitan' Addis Ababa. Under this proposal numerous small towns that fell under the jurisdiction of the Oromia National Regional State, and which stand outside the legislative purview of the federal government, were to be included within the boundaries of Addis Ababa (a city with its own autonomous status separate from any regional government).[1] Addis Ababa would expand its coverage from 54,000 hectares to an area as large as 1.1 million

---

1 The office in charge of developing this masterplan therefore changed its name to the Addis Ababa and Surrounding Oromia Special Zone Integrated Master Plan Project. See Haddis 2014.

hectares.[2] While high-level officials of the Oromo Regional State participated in the making of the masterplan, an overall technocratic approach to development meant that there was little consultation between city planners and ordinary citizens.[3] As a result, attempts in both 2014 and 2015 to implement the masterplan were met with fierce public protest as well as opposition from lower-level bureaucrats in the Oromo region. This forced the Addis Ababa City administration to abandon the masterplan in 2014 and again in 2015. It is clear that the masterplan was a key policy implement for the federal government if it was to effectively meet its economic targets as set out in its 2010 Growth and Transformation Plan (discussed later in this chapter).[4] The context of these urban protests can then provide us with one way to draw out the connection between social change, knowledge production, and passive revolution as set out in this book.

What is most striking about the urban renewal programme in Addis Ababa is that it has been supported through the piecemeal introduction of legislation that has made urban land available to private investors as leasehold. This in turn has allowed leasehold rights in urban areas to be sold on the free market. In addition, the introduction of a free market in urban land leases has guaranteed a bundle of usufruct rights to lessors that closely resemble private property rights. This is despite the fact that the Ethiopian constitution guarantees that all land in Ethiopia is vested in the nations, nationalities, and peoples of the federal republic and cannot be subjected to sale.

The first time the EPRDF introduced an urban land lease law in Ethiopia was in 1993.[5] However, at that time the federal constitution had not been promulgated and so the subsequent constitutionality of the law was in doubt.[6] It was not until the 2002 passing of the 'Re-enactment of Urban Land Lease Proclamation' that Addis Ababa began to engage in a process of urban renewal with leasehold as its fundamental policy tool.[7] It should be noted it was also in 2001 that Addis Ababa became a city with federal status, with its own charter and masterplan.

Reading through the 2002 land lease proclamation it is difficult to imagine that it was meant to address any other city in Ethiopia except Addis Ababa,

2   The number of 54,00 hectares was found in Ambaye 2013, p. 15. The number of hectares in an expanded Addis Ababa is suggested in Haddis 2014.
3   Haddis 2014.
4   The 2010 Growth and Transformation Plan can be found on the World Bank website accompanied by a comment from World Bank Staff. See World Bank 2011.
5   Transitional Government of Ethiopia 1993.
6   See Ambaye 2013.
7   Federal Democratic Republic of Ethiopia 2002.

since it is primarily concerned with establishing land lease use rights in accordance with a masterplan. Addis Ababa accounts for 25 percent of Ethiopia's
urban population, with the next largest city in Ethiopia, Dire Dawa, being 10
times smaller than Addis.[8] Moreover, until yet another land lease law was promulgated in 2011, the ability to acquire and possess land leases seemed to co-
exist with other urban land permits awarded to residents during the Derg era.[9]

It is now apparent that in the years leading up to the passage of the 2011 law,
the Addis Ababa City Administration was using the land lease law to expropriate land from residents who had established long-term usufruct rights in the
city. The city administration was able to do this by first stating that residents
could only claim usufruct rights if they used the land in accordance with the
city-approved master plan. If they could not, the land would be converted into
land lease and auctioned off through a tender system to investors who were
contractually obligated to use the land according to the city-designated masterplan. Expropriated residents did receive compensation for lost land, usually
in the form of an apartment located some distance from their former residence.
During the period of 2004–12, the government built approximately 97,000 new
apartment dwellings.[10] While the residents whose lands were expropriated
received compensation, the compensation was not equivalent to the potential
market value of the land. Thus, the land lease law not only had the effect of dis-
placing residents from the land, it also downgraded the class status of residents
to condominium dwellers without access to the means of production (land),
and without the social network that comes from belonging to long-established
urban neighbourhoods.

The other result of the 2002 law was that it led to increased land speculation,
with people first bidding for land through the government tender system and
then immediately selling the lease on the open market.[11] In order to address this
problem the Federal Government introduced the 2011 land lease law. While this
law addresses the issue of land speculation, it also greatly expands the scope of
the land lease law to include all urban centres in Ethiopia, now defined as any
town with a population above 2,000 people, and where 50 percent of the residents are engaged in 'non-agricultural activities'. The 2011 law also states that
there will be no other way to obtain urban land in Ethiopia except as detailed
in the 2011 proclamation. The issue of 'old possessions' is specifically addressed
in the new law, and what is ultimately concluded is that urban centres have up

---

8   Gorham 2014.
9   Federal Democratic Republic of Ethiopia 2011.
10   Ambaye 2013, p. 91.
11   Ambaye 2013.

to five years to convert old possessions into land lease. The law also states that any property transferred into land lease must conform to the masterplan of the urban jurisdiction or to the regional state plan for that urban area. This means that the law is now wide enough to expropriate residents throughout the country who do not conform to the urban plans for the region that they live in. It also means that peri-urban and semi-rural areas are now included under what is basically a law of expropriation and redistribution to 'investors'. At the same time, given that each land lease contract comes with stipulations on what the land must be used for, the law specifically addresses the problem of land speculation by detailing the manner in which leased land can be reclaimed by the government if the lessor is unable to use the land according to what is stipulated in the land lease contract. It is only after a lessor has added value to the land that leases can then be sold on the open market.

What is the point of such a large-scale land expropriation programme? On the one hand, the urban renewal policy fits into the overall Growth and Transformation Plan (GTP) that has been the guiding policy platform for the government of Ethiopia since 2011, divided into two phases: GTP I covers the years 2011–15 and GTP II covers the years 2016–20. The expropriation programme also fits into the Country Assistance Plan proposed by the World Bank and its partners for the years extending between 2008–16 and 2018–22.[12] What all of these plans emphasise is the need to provide security of tenure to investors and residents as part of an urban renewal programme. In addition, the major aim of the government's GTP is to transform Ethiopia into a middle-income country by 2023. This policy goal hinges on developing light industries such as floriculture, textiles, leather goods, and food and beverages in export processing zones (industrial parks near urban centres).[13] There has also been a policy shift to developing large-scale commercial agriculture in commodities such as sugar.[14] The overall stated aim of GTP I was to develop industries that use inputs from the agricultural sector and will in turn incentivise farmers to rationalise their agricultural practices by adopting new technologies; the hope was to build dynamic backward and forward linkages which will reward richer farmers who adapt to the needs of industry and the free mar-

---

12   See, for instance, World Bank 2012.

13   For a description of where the new industrial parks will be set up see: http://www.ipdc.gov
      .et/index.php/en/industrial-parks.

14   In 2005, the government introduced a new land lease law for rural areas, but it has been
      much less extreme in its attempt to expropriate farmers from rural areas. Most of the new
      commercial farming has been introduced in areas with low population density. See Federal Democratic Republic of Ethiopia 2005.

ket. In fact, fostering upstream and downstream links with industry was a key policy tool for GTP I, and through the emphasis on light industry the government hoped to bring about structural change in the economy. GTP II, on the other hand, much more clearly emphasises private sector development, with FDI playing an important role in developing export-oriented manufacturing.

Eighty percent of the Ethiopian population continues to reside in rural areas, with 85 percent of that rural population involved in smallholder agriculture.[15] In this context the goals of the GTP seem to leapfrog beyond what was articulated as the national development agenda under previous programmes, including the *Plan for Accelerated and Sustained Development to End Poverty*, which ran nationally from 2005–10 (PASDEP).[16] From 1994 and up to and including the implementation of PASDEP in 2005, the lead policy framework used by the Ethiopian government was Agricultural Development Led Industrialisation (ADLI).[17] ADLI emphasised the need to create the conditions for developmental take-off, rather than putting the industrial cart before the horse. Thus, there was greater emphasis on training agricultural and health-care extension workers, expanding roadway systems, increasing energy capacity, building schools and universities, and meeting basic services, as well as meeting the Millennium Development Goals. Agricultural co-operatives were emphasised as a key mechanism through which farmers could buy inputs such as fertilisers as well as sell products to domestic and international markets. There was also more emphasis on limiting rural-urban migration by developing a domestic economy linked through micro and small-scale enterprises.

According to the World Bank, during the period when PASDEP and GTP I were in operation, the Ethiopian economy maintained a 10 percent growth rate.[18] Given that the development agenda of PASDEP and GTP I was investment in public goods, and given the previous low level of productivity in what is essentially a subsistence economy, one can see how this growth rate would not be difficult to achieve. However, given that the PASDEP and GTP I period was also accompanied by runaway inflation, the increase in the real purchasing power of ordinary people is probably less than what might be expected given the increase in GDP.[19] Indeed, while PASDEP was able to reduce overall

---

15   World Bank 2012, p. 9.
16   Ministry of Finance and Economic Development 2006.
17   Oqubay 2015, p. 79.
18   See the executive summary in World Bank 2012.
19   World Bank 2012.

extreme rates of poverty, the absolute number of poor people remained steady at 15 million.[20] In the end, the stalled poverty, in conjunction with the fact that savings in Ethiopia continue to be low, seems to have led to a policy shift whereby GTP II begins with a sense of the failure of small-holder agriculture to produce the kinds of surpluses that would lead to industrial take-off. There has been much more emphasis on attracting FDI to government-built industrial parks so as to begin the process of setting up a manufacturing base in the country. More recently, the failure of these rapidly built industrial parks to meet expected revenue generation through the export of manufactured goods has meant that in 2018 the IMF reclassified Ethiopia as being at high risk of debt distress.[21] How then can the Ethiopian government achieve middle-income status by 2023? What might be the social costs of attempting to do so through the displacement of farmers in peri-urban areas?[22] After all, farmers close to urban centres are already linked into markets and would be the ones most likely to already be engaged in small-scale capital accumulation. Despite the rhetoric of the developmental state echoed in both GTP I and II, one wonders if the state is correctly identifying the right players in the economy to whom incentives ought to be distributed. Unlike PASDEP, the GTP seems short on detail in terms of engaging patterns of household reproduction. More worrisome is how little is said about the development of a well-articulated, self-sufficient home economy, even while the real estate and land development market is seeing unbridled growth, and small-scale farmers and poor urban dwellers continue to be displaced.

At the time when the 2002 land lease law was first implemented, the mayor of Addis Ababa was Arkebe Oqubay. In 2013 Arkebe was granted a PhD from the School of Oriental and African Studies (SOAS), where he wrote a doctoral thesis on industrial policy in Ethiopia. Later, the dissertation was published as a book titled *Made in Africa: Industrial Policy in Ethiopia*. As this book was being written, Arkebe held the position of Minister and Special Advisor to the Prime Minister of Ethiopia, in addition to sitting as the chair of the board of the Ethiopian

---

20   World Bank 2012.

21   In 2012 Ethiopia's external debt fell to 18% of GDP due to the debt relief received through participation in the Heavily Indebted Poor Countries Initiative (HIPC) and the Multilateral Debt Relief Initiative (MDRI) in 2006. However, by the end of 2016/17 external debts again stood at 30.7 percent of GDP. This correlates to the same period in which the industrial parks became the focus of government policy. See "Staff Report for the 2017 Article IV Consultation", *IMF Country Report No. 18/18*.

22   For an interesting study on the affects of urbanisation on peri-urban residents see Adam 2014.

Railway Corporation and the deputy chair of the board of Ethiopian Airlines; all are key institutions identified in the GTP as fostering economic growth.

In *Made in Africa*, Arkebe describes three core industries – floriculture, leather, and concrete production – that the Ethiopian government has focused on in order to grow the economy. Arkebe describes the Ethiopian state as a 'learning-state', currently in the process of identifying promising potential market players to whom they can distribute rewards and incentives. He also emphasises the strong potential for backward and forward linkages of the three core industries described in his case studies. Arkebe is keen to show how government policy can strengthen and foster those linkages; this overall strategy of identifying and creating linkages between industries, for Arkebe, is key to creating double-digit growth in Ethiopia. At the same time, according to Arkebe's own numbers, in 2011 manufacturing only accounted for the employment of 175,000 people in a country of approximately 85 million people.[23]

Through his descriptions of what he calls the Ethiopian developmental state, Arkebe Oqubay in his book is able to launch a convincing critique of neoliberal development policy. He also links that critique back to the ideological orientation of revolutionary democracy adopted by the EPRDF in the various party platforms that we have examined in previous chapters. At the same time, in Arkebe's plan, as for the GTP, '[F]irst, the only way for a country to develop is to industrialise; second, the only way for a country to industrialise is to protect itself; and third, anyone who says otherwise is being dishonest! "The developed economies do preach double standards". They preach free trade for developing countries, yet protect their own markets'.[24]

Clearly, what is at stake for Arkebe when discussing the merits of the developmental state is the need for Ethiopia to have the policy space to emulate the experience of the 'Asian Tigers', which for him sometimes include China and India. Arkebe appears certain that the historical experience of the Asian countries can be grouped together and then modelled into a technocratic project. As such, he conflates a critique of neoliberalism with the need to offer up the Asian developmental state as the only other alternative to neoliberal policymaking. What is left aside is the specific cold war conditions that gave a country like Korea access to US markets; as well, little attention is given to how international markets will respond to Ethiopian products. In this sense, Arkebe ignores the question of the ways in which Ethiopia is already inserted into the global economy and the global division of labour.

---

23   Oqubay 2015, p. 69.
24   Oqubay 2015, p. 296, quoting Ajit Singh describing something Nicholas Kaldor told him.

In addition, Arkebe ignores the voluminous research on the Green Revolution in Asia, which shows that, despite increased agriculture yields, two-thirds of the world's undernourished continue to live in Asia.[25] This can primarily be attributed to the fact that, while production has increased, poor people including poor farmers cannot afford to buy food. Rather than doing away with poverty, the adoption of Green Revolution technologies in a country like India has sparked a new set of development problems. Green Revolution technology has favoured already wealthy farmers, which in turn has led to the concentration of land amongst richer peasants, while creating a class of landless peasants who now find it difficult to feed themselves despite increased overall national production. In India today, both food production and income distribution are so uneven that the average caloric intake continues to be low. The Green Revolution has also led to a new set of environmental problems including the narrowing of biodiversity, which in turn has increased crop risks for diseases, dependency on fertiliser, and water table pollution. More recently we have also seen diminishing production outcomes.[26]

The history of the Green Revolution in India should be incorporated into Arkebe's modelling of the developmental state. After all, similar to India, the call to rationalise agriculture and light industry in Ethiopia is leading to a higher concentration of land and income amongst fewer people.[27] This in turn raises the question of what it means to displace farmers from the resource base that supports food production (land), while simultaneously failing to address the political problems raised by such displacements, including the consequent power imbalances in the reproduction of social and economic life.

Is industrialisation as described by Arkebe and GTP I and II the only option for a country like Ethiopia?[28] Certainly, GTP II no longer seriously considers the possibility of increasing the productivity of smallholder agriculture as a main policy tool that could produce linkages to contribute to the growth of a home economy, food security and poverty reduction. Nonetheless, it is still well worth asking the questions that are no longer being seriously considered: can state incentives be used in order to promote well-functioning ecosystems, including

25   Russet, Collins, and Lappe 2000.
26   Patnaik 1990.
27   Income inequality has generally been quite low in Ethiopia. Now, with an increased emphasis on development, the income gap has grown even if GDP has also expanded.
28   In fact, in a 2013 report by IFAD, it is argued that there is strong evidence that increases in crop yields lead to much higher decreases in the number of poor when compared to the effects of manufacturing and service industries. See International Fund for Agriculture Development 2013.

soil fertility, irrigation, pollination and pest control? Can a more modest form of industrialisation take the place of massive expropriation and redistribution of land?

In *Made in Africa* Arkebe Oqubay states that:

> Without wishing to provoke charges of policymaking hubris, I believe there is evidence of 'anti-fragility' in Ethiopian industrial policy. Anti-fragility is the term coined by Nicolas Taleb to describe the ability of a system to be strengthened by stress rather than collapsing under its weight (fragility). This is distinct from robustness, defined by Taleb as the ability to fend off threats and remain unchanged. To understand the sources of anti-fragility in policymaking, one must appreciate policy processes based on learning-by-doing and adaptability, characteristics rarely explored in studies of policy and performance in developing countries.[29]

Now, if the Ethiopian developmental state was anti-fragile, then how do we interpret the recent protests that successfully halted the implementation of the Addis Ababa masterplan? Perhaps, if political conflict can undo the goals of the developmental state, we need to rethink the relationship between ideas, state and society within the learning-by-doing developmental state. Was the developmental state just another positivist truth that has paved over alternative possibilities, and will soon be paved over by even newer truths?

In this book, I have tried to trace how ideas drawn from the social sciences have shaped social movements and state-driven policy in Ethiopia. I have argued that the success of the TPLF – when it was a rag-tag rebel force organising land reform campaigns in Northern Ethiopia – can be attributed to its ability to use its own iteration of Marxist theory to connect the needs of insurgent intellectuals with the needs of the Tigrayan peasantry. Again, we see echoes of that legacy in the attempt to graft an idea of the developmental state onto processes of restructuring state and society relations in Ethiopia. The attempt to instrumentally mobilise social science ideas to reshape state-society relations in Ethiopia is also a legacy of the student movement more generally. The discourse of those protesting the Addis Ababa masterplan also resurrects the language of the student movement of the 1960s and 1970s in two important ways. First, the protests ask if the EPRDF has lived up to its constitutional obligations to protect the interests of the nations and nationalities that make Ethiopia a multi-national federation, and second, the protests

---

29   Oqubay 2015, p. 242.

link the question of the rights of the various nationalities in Ethiopia to the question of rights of the tiller. For instance, in the opposition Oromo Democratic Front (ODF) statement that addresses the December 2015 protests, the ODF points out that the masterplan is a land-grab that will evict the Oromo people from their 'ancestral land'.[30] The statement also points out that the masterplan fails to address the historical grievances of the Oromo people, which began with the founding of Addis Ababa as a garrison town for Minilik's army. In addition, the ODF asks us to consider the consequent dramatic demographic shifts that have transformed the area now known as Addis Ababa from a place primarily populated by Oromo people to one dominated by residents from elsewhere in the country. They claim: 'The master plan further institutionalises the injustice committed against the Oromo people in the last century'.[31] Implicitly, and differently from Arkebe's developmental state, the ODF is also protesting the failure of the EPRDF to link the nationalities question to the right to not be subjected to technocratic development from a centralised authority.[32] Here we see that if the 2005 elections can be read as a contest between those who further wished to entrench neoliberal development policy, in contrast with the EPRDF's version of revolutionary democracy, the 2014/2016 protests can be understood as an attempt to offer alternative conceptions of the legacy of the student movement and its varied revolutionary ideas. If the virtue of the student movement from the 1960s and 1970s was that it attempted to theorise Ethiopia's place within global structural processes, discourses about the current protests in Ethiopia continue to be stalled around the centre-periphery paradigm that has dominated the historiography of the Ethiopian revolution since the 1970s. We continue to hear talk of 'Ethiopia's original sin', which refers to the formation of the Ethiopian nation-state under Minilik, while very little attention is given to the project of developing a historical consciousness that can explain the contradictions of inserting the Ethiopian nation-state into global capitalist relations – a problem that all political operators in Ethiopia have had to face since the late nineteenth century.[33] How then can we give political expression to the needs of ordinary farmers throughout the country? At this point, hasn't the centre-periphery paradigm become an exhausted debate whose real effects are the hardening of positions around 'ethnic' conflict in the Horn of Africa? It seems the region desperately needs new questions.

---

30   Oromo Democratic Front 2015.
31   Oromo Democratic Front 2015.
32   Oromo Democratic Front 2015.
33   Hussein and Ademo 2016.

Part of the problem here is that, if the student movement of the 1960s and 1970s had the temerity to construct an intellectual problem-space that could provide answers for the social crisis they faced, they also used the 'eternal' laws of the social sciences as weapons to silence their opponents. A positivist social science refashioned the intellectual's relation to his or herself and to his or her community, in addition to delimiting the horizon of political action. If we want to ask new questions about the region, we will need to adopt a more flexible notion of social theory, one where abstractions are understood as interpretative guides that could help us to provisionally describe something that is always concrete, historically situated, and relational. Theory itself is always partial, and a site of social struggle; its assumptions must be continuously accounted for and explained through multiple and varied historical perspectives.

This book has tried to develop this latter insight by positing the Ethiopian student movement as part of a creative attempt to address global economic processes. In so doing, I have been able to examine the contradictions in political thought recorded in the writings of the Ethiopian student movement by connecting that writing to the social conditions the students aimed to address. My concern has been to discover the epistemological principles the students relied on to make their arguments, and to connect those principles back to social forms of being. This is why I have been careful to show how the thematic of anti-colonial thought shaped the writings of the student movement. For me, the point has been to demonstrate the contradictions that are a result of the insertion of the Ethiopian nation-state into global capitalist relations. Yet the transnational aspects that have been so constitutive of what the Ethiopian student movement became have been downplayed within the secondary literature on the Ethiopian revolution. One consequence of this is that the literature has not taken up the particular manner in which the students aimed to address the global stage. The national question now appears to be an entirely internal debate, despite the fact that its genealogy was always linked to the question of how to relate the Ethiopian nation-state to a capitalist world system. For this reason I have tried to locate the questions raised by the student movement as African questions rather than simply Ethiopian. My description of the present attempt at urban revitalisation in Addis Ababa has aimed to show how a long-term trend to concretise the thematic of anti-colonial thought has become generalised as social practice in Ethiopia. This is the passive revolution.

The protests of 2014–16 never disappeared but were instead temporarily quelled by a ten-month state of emergency declared in October 2016. By the end of 2017 strikes within the newly constructed industrial parks, as well as sporadic but violent ethnic conflict, continued to present a growing problem throughout the country. One result of this ongoing political crisis was that in February 2018 the Prime Minister, Haile-Mariam Dessalegn, was forced to resign, even as a number of high-level Oromo political prisoners were released from jail. Nearly simultaneously, a second state of emergency that lasted for four months was declared. During this time, the Oromo People's Democratic Organization (OPDO), one of the four coalition parties that make up the ruling EPRDF, moved into the centre of the unfolding process, appropriating the rhetoric of the protests to demand reform within the EPRDF.[34] After a set of lengthy self-criticism sessions, in both December of 2017 and April 2018, the EPRDF executive committee elected a member of the OPDO, Abiy Ahmed, as its new chairman, and therefore as the new Prime Minister of the country.[35]

Since being elected, Abiy has participated in a series of rallies and meetings across the country in which he has emphasised national reconciliation between Ethiopia's diverse ethnic groups. At a popular level, he is perceived as a leader who was able to move the country away from the brink of civil war. In addition, he has released nearly all prominent political prisoners while inviting exiled opposition groups to return home to work with the EPRDF to build a new national consensus. Since then, the conversation amongst both opposition groups and the EPRDF has seemed to pivot around widening the space for ethnic representation within the context of electoral reforms, with questions of political economy seemingly 'conceptually separated' from the demands for democratic reforms.[36] This has in turn spawned a whole new wave of ethnic conflict at the local level, with ethnicity now becoming the primary framework through which collective grievances are articulated on the national stage. Six months after Abiy Ahmed came to power various relief organisations claimed that there are now over two million internally displaced persons throughout the country. It is also clear that the state-supported industrial policy of Arkebe has failed to deliver the increased levels of exports needed to sustain the overall

---

34   Over the past two decades the Oromo party within EPRDF came to be seen as complicit in the repression of Oromo leaders from various Oromo opposition political parties. Policy differences have now erupted in the context of the appropriation of Oromo issues by the OPDO/EPRDF. Symbolically, this is most evident today when travelling throughout the Oromo region where one mostly sees the flag of the Oromo Liberation Front rather than the official flag of the Oromo region that is associated with OPDO and EPRDF.

35   For a more detailed report on the machinations within EPRDF see, Hussein, Hassen and Mohammed Ademo, "Ethiopia: Is OPDO the new opposition party? An Appraisal". https://www.opride.com/2017/11/11/ethiopia-is-opdo-the-new-opposition-party-an-appraisal/ Nov 11 2017.

36   Here I am deliberately borrowing phrasing from Asef Bayat's book *Revolutions without Revolutionaries*, where he argues that the Arab Spring lacked an intellectual program and a strategic vision that connected with attempts by the urban poor to counter processes of dispossession. Bayat 2017, p. 18.

developmental trajectory set out by GTP II. In addition, while massive public investments (including increased external debt) were mobilised in order to
build the infrastructure of the industrial parks (which more and more relied
on imported inputs), exports from manufacturing remained far below targeted
results and in 2017 contributed only 3.6% to overall GDP. Unable to pay its debt
to outside lenders or sustain its import bills, in June of 2018 the EPRDF government began claiming that it would have to raise capital through privatising
state-owned enterprises – such as Ethiopian Airlines and Ethiopian Telecoms –
that continue to accrue both healthy profits and earn hard currency on behalf
of the state.[37] It has also become evident that the foreign exchange reservoirs
netted from traditional exports like coffee, oil seeds, legumes and qat have been
servicing the external debt that has resulted from a failed national industrial
policy. This again raises the question of what development might look like if
the surplus from agriculture was used to deepen links between domestic producers rather than link a nascent manufacturing base to the global economy.
One has to wonder if the strategy of displacement, expropriation and redistribution of urban and peri-urban land renders Ethiopian small farmers yet more
vulnerable to downturns in the global economy, as well as to natural disasters
such as drought, especially since 95 percent of small-holder farmers continue
to rely on rain-fed agriculture. These were the questions posed by PASDEP, ADIL
and even GTP I. Moreover, given that PASDEP and GTP I produced 10 percent
growth to the benefit of far more people than the attempts at privatisation currently advocated by GTP II, it seems that the legacy of the EPRDF will continue
to be contested. Yet all the current planning documents from the World Bank
and the IMF continue to presume that the funnelling of private FDI into manufacturing will become the main driver of growth in the country in the near
future. This is despite the fact that the industrial parks have been shown to be
politically contested sites of production that operate under capacity while also
underperforming in terms of export generation. The current round of privatisation and market liberalisation also signals the collapse of a tradition of state-led
industrial policy-making that prioritised long-term planning – a tradition that
is now to be replaced by short-term policy fixes (a one-time raising of capital).

As much as the current Oromo opposition mobilised the Oromo population and particularly the Oromo youth to resist land expropriation and Oromo
disenfranchisement, the one lesson that seems to have been learned from

---

37   See, Matina Stevis-Gridneff, "Ethiopia Opens Door To The World With Unprecedented
      Privatization Plan". https://www.wsj.com/articles/ethiopia-opens-door-to-the-world-with
      -unprecedented-privatization-plan-1528275922, June 6th 2018.

the election crisis of 2005 is that the opposition groups were organisationally weak on the ground. Tactically, this implied that the various Oromo opposition groups thought it would be better to bring pressure to bear on the OPDO (the Oromo party within EPRDF) in order to both fragment and transform the EPRDF from within. In this regard the Ethiopian reforms of 2018 echo Hazem Kandil's argument with regard to the Egyptian revolution, which suggests that conflict between various institutions within the state apparatus is what allowed for the collapse of the Hosni Mubarak regime.[38] In the Ethiopian case the marginalization of the TPLF within both the EPRDF and the wider party-state apparatus became possible when the OPDO leveraged their capacity to manage the social protests then taking place on the streets of Addis Ababa as a tactic to move their party into the centre of power within the coalition that makes up the EPRDF. By appropriating the Oromo protests of 2016, the OPDO and EPRDF were able to deliver Oromo political representation within leadership positions within the government while abandoning the other questions raised by the protests. Hazem Kandil's theorization of the Egyptian revolution often downplays the role of ideology in affecting regime change, but what we have been at pains to show in the Ethiopian case is that the thread that connects the Ethiopian state to the OPDO, and that in turn connects the land and the nationalities question to the EPRDF, is rooted in an intellectual genealogy that can be traced to the debates of the student movement. After all the legitimacy of the EPRDF political program has been that it can deliver answers to the land question through organizing the state around the nationalities question.

What seems to have come out of the EPRDF self-criticism sessions in 2017 and 2018 was an across-party consensus that the reformed EPRDF that emerged from the 2016 crisis would abandon revolutionary democracy in favour of economic liberalisation, while turning to the United Arab Emirates and Saudi Arabia as their new economic and foreign policy allies. This policy shift can be most clearly seen in the rapprochement between Eritrea and Ethiopia, with both the UAE and the Saudis playing a pivotal role in the negotiation process even as peace was locally driven and desired. Perhaps, then, Abiy Ahmed's rise to power can also be attributed to the wider international context of the war in Yemen and the need for Saudi Arabia and the UAE to secure stable allies in the Red Sea region. Ever since Eritrean seaports and its Asmara airport became strategically useful to the Saudi-led war in Yemen, Eritrea has been given new advantages vis-a-vis its relationship to Ethiopia. No longer a pariah state, it can now negotiate as an equal power within a changing regional configuration. In

---

38   Kandil 2012.

turn, these wider regional changes demanded a different type of leadership from the Ethiopian state – less friendly to China and more open to private capital and the Gulf region.[39]

It is ironic then that the OPDO was moved to the centre of power by what were essentially anti-privatisation protests, only to become the primary vehicle for an unprecedented program of economic liberalization, with the question of urban and peri-urban land use somehow forgotten. Once again, the EPRDF, the OPDO and the opposition party platforms all seem to be missing an intellectual programme that can link the demands for access to land and better working conditions with transformations within the structures of governance. In a sense, we have returned to the contradictions of the 2005 elections, but with the arguments for neoliberal reform now outweighing any vision of state-led development.[40] To reiterate some of our findings from Chapter 4, part of the problem here is that even where there might have been legitimate criticisms about democratic process under the EPRDF, too often 'authoritarianism' was equated by both the popular press, the academic literature and development organisations with attempts to use state power in favour of social outcomes. Since the rise of Abiy Ahmed, both the popular literature and the rhetoric of various opposition activists have coalesced around the twin tropes of authoritarianism vs. liberal democracy, setting up a false telos whereby it appears that the specificity of all societies can be rendered as a trajectory towards establishing liberal-democracy, but where the distinctive qualities of the Ethiopian case are also simply recast as backwards in this regard. A good example of this method of analysing Ethiopian politics can be seen in Renee Lefort's widely circulated August 2018 assessment of the leadership of Abiy Ahmed, where he writes that 'the emergence of a new Big Man, but in this case in a "softer" and more inclusive mould, would nevertheless be a remarkable step forward'. As we saw in Chapter 2, Lefort's approach to the study of Ethiopia is based on a kind of consensus amongst some Ethiopianists that even if the state tradition in Ethiopia is 'ancient', it is rooted in an Orthodox Christian culture of authoritarianism. Christopher Clapham is the best-known advocate of this position. Lefort posits that every new process of state formation in Ethiopia is really just an adaptation or new iteration of the ancient Christian Abyssinian state-form (see Chapter 5). Such an approach never has to deal with political thought in the country; nor does it bother to explain how different aspirations and pro-

---

39   See John Aglionby and Emily Feng "China Scales Back Investment in Ethiopia", *Financial Times*, https://www.ft.com/content/06b69c2e-63e9-11e8-90c2-9563a0613e56, June 3, 2018.

40   Please note that at the party congress in September of 2018, the Oromo Peoples Democratic Organization (OPDO) changed its name to the Oromo Democratic Party (ODP).

jects of development express themselves in real social tensions and conflicts. Instead, political contests are simply rendered as processes of social evolution within a determined end point. What is never taken seriously is the question posed by each subsequent regime since the student movement of the 1960s: how do you fashion a political collectivity in the Horn of Africa that can deliver social goods to its population while mitigating against some of the more deleterious effects of global capitalism? By all accounts, the TPLF/EPRDF delivered answers to this question, even if in answering this question new social contradictions were produced. Indeed, the point of the PASDEP, the ADIL programme, and even GTP I was to discipline capital so as to consciously embed economic transformation within social processes. However, as we have already seen, the overall approach to development by the EPRDF assumed you could reduce the problem of economic growth to a mere technocratic problem, while at the same time managing the introduction of new forms of exploitation and corruption (rent-seeking) as a problem of state engineering. As such the question of where social power lies within capitalist economies was left aside; or rather, capitalism was deemed a stable and knowable system with given rules and limits. Mastering those rules was the key to development. Politics was as such reduced to the capacity to promote a self-evident economic growth.

The resolution of the Oromo protests that began in 2014 in Ethiopia has coincided with the slow-down of national economic growth in the spring of 2018. However, if across the political divide, the shared project of Ethiopian social movements over the past fifty years has been the need to reshape the Ethiopian nation-state so as to deliver social justice in the form of access to land, education, health care, language and cultural rights, within the reformed EPRDF of 2018 social justice has simply come to mean using the state to open the country to capital. It is within this paradoxical situation – where ethnicity has become the ground for neoliberalisation – that questions of the legacies of revolutionary Ethiopia must now be posed. Where we are now was not inevitable: strategies of accumulation were not foreclosed; how and why the state rewarded certain classes and sectors of society was not pre-determined. On the contrary, the questions we must ask today are: why has there been a rush towards economic liberalisation? Can the abstract freedoms of liberal democracy provide a stable political framework that unites the multi-cultural nations and nationalities that currently make up Ethiopia? How does the false telos from authoritarianism to liberalisation foreclose more complex political questions or even address the fact that ethnic conflict has become the primary vector through which various groups now make claims on the central state? Why have the 2018 reforms produced more than two million internally displaced people, primarily as a result of ethnic conflict? Why is it now so difficult to talk about the social contradictions of the past fifty years except in highly polarised terms? Lastly, if the discourse of both civil society and ethnicity are equally part of how the anti-democratic tendencies within the African state are reproduced, then perhaps we should reframe the current reforms of the EPRDF as part of the constant pull of the African state between a supposedly culturally-based decentralised despotism and a top-down, urban-based authoritarian modernisation.

FIGURE 1   Revolutionary Square, Addis Ababa, 2001
             PHOTO BY THE AUTHOR

FIGURE 2   Revolutionary Square, Addis Ababa, 2012
             PHOTO BY LOULOU CHERINET

FIGURE 3   Revolutionary Square, Addis Ababa, 2013
            PHOTO BY LOULOU CHERINET

FIGURE 4   Revolutionary Square, Addis Ababa, 2015
            PHOTO BY LOULOU CHERINET

FIGURE 5   Revolutionary Square, Addis Ababa, 2017
PHOTO BY LOULOU CHERINET

PART 2

Theory as Memoir

∴

CHAPTER 6

The Problem of the Social Sciences in Africa

In attempting to temporalise the questions and answers of the Ethiopian student movement I have wanted to pose the question of whether it was possible
to open up the present – not by reimagining the future through new longings
for ideal-typical social science models, but through alternative conceptions of
our inheritance from the past. In order to think through this question, over
the past decade I have collaborated with the Ethiopian-Swedish artist Loulou
Cherinet to document and theorise the changing landscape of Addis Ababa.[1]
As part of this ongoing collaboration, since 2012 Cherinet has repeatedly visited
various sites in Addis Ababa in order to periodically photograph the same location from the same vantage point. Under the name *Big Data*, Cherinet presents
the photos of each site as a linear sequence of development that has taken
place between 2012 and 2017. Given the rapid changes to the landscape of Addis
Ababa, what makes the sequences compelling is that the content of each photo
is familiar and yet starkly different as each year passes by. Each sequence examines the sediments of an older modernity (earlier formations of Addis Ababa
architecture) that are buried under a new, more up-to-date version of what the
'modern' ought to connote.

Viewed together, Cherinet's *Big Data* documents the landscape of neighbourhoods bulldozed to make way for the coming skyscrapers that already dot
the margins of the old neighbourhoods. We see remnants of old houses and
old plumbing, as well as people who continue to eke out a living among the
rubble left after their houses were expropriated to make way for the newly
modern. In some photographs we find a single wall, a remnant of a house torn
down, somehow still standing, somehow still providing shelter. The everyday
life of the uprooted continues: women still cook and prepare food; herders'
animals linger amidst new condominium-style housing developments, while
traditional or old-style building techniques are used to erect structures made
of concrete and steel. Most startling, however, are the photos of the abandoned towers. Ghostly testaments: the abandoned towers speak of investors
running out of funds, and the already ruined landscape of the new utopian
moment that Addis Ababa was supposed to embrace. Overall, in these photos old and new dialogue with each other; the past is no longer silent, and

---

1   Zeleke 2010.

any sense of a seamless transition between past and present is interrupted. Here, one cannot behold new positivist truths discovered by the social sciences; instead the photos seek to reinterpret the present by examining the inheritance of contradictions that have come from the past. Similarly, in this book I have tried to draw attention to the wider attempt to transform social being in Ethiopia as a way to listen to what has been silenced in the very process of social transformation: lives cut short, bodies mangled by social violence. For me, this technique of listening has helped to convey something of the claustrophobia embedded in the social meaning of my case study: the loss of hope for a transformed present. In discussing the story of the protests against the Addis Ababa master plan I have, therefore, wanted to draw parallels to the way in which lack and longing once again confront each other as a social and personal experience in Ethiopia (what I called in Chapter 1 the problematic of Tizita). Any sense of a seamless transition between past and present is interrupted; the body searches for a method towards the redemption of the human bond with nature and other humans. Its method is found in the air that it breathes.

I began this book with a discussion of Dinaw Mengestu's novel *How to Read the Air*. I was particularly interested in the protagonist Jonas, who conjures unnameable ghosts that haunt him as a force-field. Through his imagination, Jonas juxtaposes his personal sense of loss with the more formal history of the objects he has lost. In the end, the exercise is not so much about an ability to reach back to the past to find the truth of what has happened to him or his family as it is about rendering strange the present mode of existence. No longer a part of natural history, not only is the present inhabited by the ghosts of the past, but the future is now opened up to new relations with the present.

In discussing Dinaw Mengestu's book I proposed that, as the narrator of this book, I am also Jonas. Starting from my own experience growing up in an Ethiopian household where politics was routinely discussed at the dinner table, I suggested that to live one's life as historical is to always be accompanied by a feeling of time as being out of joint with itself. A sense that the present cannot be limited to the forces that determine it also has a history in the tradition of critical Marxism. Methodologically, this book has been shaped by a notion of anthropological nature derived from the writings of Adorno and Horkheimer in the *Dialectics of Enlightenment*, as well as by Marx's discussion of the constitution of human knowledge in the *Economic and Philosophical Manuscripts*. In the rest of this chapter I argue through these authors that what it means to be human is to be given a self through historical relations with other human and non-human species. To transform social structures is to change those constitutive relations, and vice-versa. At the same time, to freeze human knowledge through subject-object identity is to freeze the very relationality that gives us human possibility. This of course matters in our study of the Ethiopian student movement since it is the assumption that theory and facts could coincide that led the student movement to dogmatically assert that the future ought to be constructed as a task of the enlightened social scientist. While historicism assumes that subject-object identity is the goal of social progress, I propose that human knowledge is produced through the abrogation of necessity assumed in the identity between subject and object.

Following the work of Michael Neocosmos in his book *Thinking Freedom in Africa*, I develop this latter claim by suggesting that we need to think of politics as having two dimensions: the first is concerned with how power is captured and structured by interests in society such that the relation between particular subjects and particular objects appears absolute, while the second is concerned with collective moments of disidentification from interests, and as such thinks political subjectivity as the universal subject of history – it is that which renews human possibility. Following these two different dimensions of politics, I insist that the work of imagining a world that is not a simple continuum of the present into the future entails tracing the dynamics of interest-driven politics as it is absolutised (and comes to stand in for politics as a whole). This book has tried to do this in the Ethiopian case by showing how politics has been shaped by a form of knowledge production adopted by the student movement in the 1960s and 1970s, which has become scripted into all major political debates in Ethiopia. By following the ideas and writings of various members of the Ethiopian student movement from 1964 until 2016, I have also been able to demonstrate that contemporary Ethiopian politics continues to be haunted by the social conditions the students aimed to address, but failed to resolve. This is why this book has also been preoccupied with questions of how to write and interpret the past while twinning that concern with a focus on the structure of capitalism, and how capitalism shapes both the past and the ways we talk about the past. It has been important for me to rid myself of a stageist definition of capitalist development while holding onto a notion of social progress. Implied in this notion of social progress is the need to move beyond a unidirectional sense of history to one where different experiences of time could co-exist and be thought about simultaneously. I insist that any attempt to move beyond an experience of time as a thoughtless continuum of past into present is not just the work of individual imagination but is bound up in collective social struggle: thought and practice together.

What, then, is unique about the Ethiopian student movement, and why devote an entire book to the political thought this movement has produced? After all, it is probably true that the commitment to total knowledge pursued by the Ethiopian student movement was also shared by many Marxist groups across the globe. The reduction of social progress to a process whereby an entire population could be organised to produce a knowable future closely resembled other attempts at social engineering taken up by positivist social scientists at the time. Throughout this book I have argued that the questions raised within the debates of the student movement were not unique to Ethiopia but must be situated in relation to both the scramble for Africa and the history of capitalism in Africa. Yet the initial establishment of the Ethiopian nation-state did not fully determine its future development. The histories of the questions and answers raised by the Ethiopian student movement show both innovation and uniqueness. What is remarkable about the Ethiopian student movement is that in 1974, and again in 1991, its ideas and even some of its persons reshaped the Ethiopian state, setting up new social groups, new class dynamics, new land policies, and new and unique ways of dealing with ethnic and linguistic differences. When we read the Ethiopian situation as strictly derivative or as a simple continuity of past into present, we lose sight of the contestation over the Ethiopian state in which political thought played a constitutive role. We also lose sight of how political struggles reshaped state-society relations in Ethiopia while also producing social and economic transformation (even if that change was not always for the better). This book is therefore arguing that what we have witnessed in revolutionary Ethiopia is a unique, creative, and understudied response to the aftermath of the scramble for Africa. From a comparative Africanist perspective, there is much we have yet to learn from the successes and failures generated by the Ethiopian student movement. Instead, Ethiopian developmental policy under the EPRDF has often been seen as a model for the rest of Africa to follow; or, more recently, it has been condemned as an ethnically discriminatory project.[2] This book has tried to show that between such dichotomies is a much longer history of state contestation, protest, and reconstruction. What is missing from either side of the debate on Ethiopian industrial and agricultural policy today is a serious discussion of how a capitalist world system has reshaped both African self-determination and the legacy of emancipatory movements. Here, I am reminded once more of Michael Neocosmos, who describes a democratic state as one that must constantly confront its oxymoronic character by affirming an egalitarian politics beyond the very interests that are represented in the state. As we move to the conclusion of this book, perhaps it is better if we think of social criticism as also having an oxymoronic character. After all, in tracing out the situated knowledge of the

---

2   See for instance Carmody 2017.

Ethiopian student movement I have shown that the attempt to construct an interest-free social science literature in Ethiopia has been at the very heart of what has closed down the possibility of criticism in the region. I have also tried to show that any alternative conception of social progress that goes beyond the student movement must be rooted in an examination of its history, thought and practices.

In *The Invention of Africa*, Valentine Mudimbe argues that when the social scientist asks about the local in Africa she inevitably ends up situating Africa as a sign of something other than itself. For Mudimbe, the social sciences are a paradigmatic cultural model that leaves the African social scientist with limited choices. In the end she must simply be ready for a positivist social science, while denying the exoticism inherent in any attempt to know Africa. Alternatively, Mudimbe advises that if we document the invention of this cultural model we can demonstrate the limits of social studies in Africa as a mode of knowledge production. In this book, I am trying to show how the commitment to science limited the capacity of the students to describe what Mudimbe calls the *chose du texte* of living and breathing Africans, which I discuss later in this chapter. By highlighting a link between the writings of the Ethiopian student movement and the social conditions of knowledge production I have also tried to connect the history of the west in Africa to the limitations in the writings of the student movement. This has provided me with a path towards a '*recit pour soi*' – an account of myself as a path towards personal survival.[3] Three questions immanent to this project remain: How does the story of the Ethiopian student movement fit into a larger story of how the social sciences have travelled to and become institutionalised in Africa? How are the origins of the social sciences in Europe bound up with the development of market-dependent social relations in capitalist societies? And what is the relationship between critique and the varied historical transitions to capitalism that Africa has undergone? These are also the questions the student movement asked themselves and I return to them here as a way to show that the problem-space both constructed and addressed by the student movement continues to be ours. Here, I am suggesting that we must attend to the historically specific questions of our present – our contemporary problem-space – even as we go beyond it. How do we posit new questions? Here my concern is to not only show that our present is contingent; more importantly it is pregnant with alternative pasts/futures. But this is also what it means to do theory as memoir. In my path towards personal survival, these are all the questions I needed to re-ask myself

---

3   Mudimbe 1988, p. 43.

in order to begin to make sense of the accompanying social violence of revolutionary Ethiopia. The body searches for a method in the air that it breathes:
*borrowing from tomorrow, renewing yesteryears, comes tizita (memory) hauling
possessions.*

1   The Problem of the Social Sciences in Africa

Since the 1970s, African studies has been going through a crisis, whereby it is
claimed that the explanatory frameworks for doing social science are either
overly universalistic or overly particular.[4] The relevance of both the applied
and theoretical social sciences have been called into question.[5] Scholars have
revised the field's normative frameworks and debated the nature of the production of social science knowledge in Africa.[6] This debate is well-known. For
instance, from Asad and Mafeje we know that African studies was at first largely
established by anthropologists, and that these anthropologists were inextricably tied to the colonial offices of both the British and French empires.[7] We
also have learnt the lessons that Mudimbe has taught us about the ways in
which our African epistemologies are inextricably tied with European ways of
knowing ourselves.[8] Moreover, Africanists have become aware that we must
be attentive to local sensibilities, relativising our own customs in relation to
these. However, what has been skirted are the ways in which practices within
the social sciences produce a very specific political subjectivity, a relation to
community and self as a form of knowing and acting, and that this is in fact
what is most troubling about social studies in Africa. There is a need to review
the debate on the nature of African studies in order to understand how and
why we have avoided this most crucial of issues: the ways that forms of know-

---

4   See Zeleza 1997. Here it is useful to recall Allen Isaacman's remark that nearly every presid-
     ent of the American African Studies Association has addressed their annual conference as
     if African studies was in crisis. Isaacman also points out that nearly every kind of Africanist
     scholar has, despite differences of method, political commitment or subject matter, framed
     African studies as crisis-driven. See Isaacman 2003. On crises in African studies see also Kitch-
     ings 2000; Postel 2003. For a good summary of the historical trends and capacities in African
     studies, see Sall 2003.
5   Mbembe 2002; Bayart and Mbembe 1994.
6   Mudimbe 1988; Hountondji 1983.
7   Asad 1973; Mafeje 1997, 2000. I am aware that this continues to be a contested point, with
     scholars such as Sally Falk calling for a more nuanced history of anthropology, but claims to
     generalisations aside I think the overall point more or less stands.
8   Mudimbe 2002.

ledge production constitute horizons of political action, and in turn how this has affected the kinds of questions we ask in the social sciences.

Social science studies in Africa must be analysed as an ideological discourse formulated around the twin concepts of modernity and tradition. More problematically, the debate on knowledge production that examines African social science studies must also be seen as itself centred on the conceptual dichotomy of tradition and modernity that lies at the heart of social science study in Africa. In our earlier discussion on nationalist thought in the colonial world I argued that the debates on knowledge production replicate the very terms through which social science practitioners in the African field take up and implement the discourses coming out of African studies. If we want to create knowledge that does not simply replicate the solipsistic foundation that so many critiques of the social sciences seem to be based on, then we must find a platform for critique that does not replicate the terms the critique wishes to transcend.

Where does this lead us? For me, it is an encouragement to begin to pick up on the static interpretive frameworks by which people continue to engage social processes in Africa. Particularly, we ought to focus in on the way these static forms of interpretation are born out of, and actually become part of social processes. I begin the next section of this chapter by asking what the conditions of possibility are for practising social sciences in Africa. I take this question to be a theoretical and practical, historical and philosophical problem. I also review the major writings that have contributed to the debates around knowledge production in African social science. Then, in order to move the debate on knowledge production out of a strictly epistemological framework and into one more concerned with social ontology, I suggest that we research the manner in which social scientists practice their craft in an African social formation, something this book has done by tracing the processes of social science knowledge production and dissemination in Ethiopia during a time of dramatic political change. This case study allowed me to follow the overall thrust of my original questions, connecting the practical ways in which knowledge is produced with the historical and theoretical questions in which these are embedded, ultimately helping me to trace the nexus between theory and practice in the Ethiopian context. Perhaps inadvertently, I was able to show that knowledge that is accountable to the communities it wishes to address is not produced when we resort to arguments about scientific objectivity, but neither can we assert the indigenous or the traditional as the authentic source of knowledge. Instead, knowledge production itself is a site of social struggle.

At the heart of my research project is the question of how to address the specificity of the African experience. As we have seen, this concern comes out of an existential regard for a place, but it also stems from a series of academic debates that began in anthropology in the 1950s and then came to engulf the entirety of the social sciences and humanities by the late 1980s and early 1990s. This debate in its most basic form has circled around the attempt to describe the constituent elements of the 'primitive mind'; in more polite circles it is said to have circled around the question of alterity. Crucial to this debate in English is the discussion generated around Peter Winch's work, which was particularly concerned with 'rationality' in the study of primitive societies and the philosophy of the social sciences.[9] Also important in this debate, and in conversation with Winch, was Robin Horton's 1967 essay 'African Traditional Thought and Western Science', which both affirmed and ethnographically established the possibility of the rationality of the African mind within the social sciences.[10]

Over time, the bulk of the debate with regards to establishing the rationality of the African mind was taken up by African Philosophy, an academic field that came into its own through the work of non-professional philosophers such as Placide Tempels and Alexis Kagame, and whose main concern was to demonstrate the systematic nature of African systems of thought. By the 1970s African Philosophy also began to be shaped by professional African philosophers whose works were anthologised in a number of ground-breaking and field-defining collections on the topic.[11] Thinkers such as Paulin Hountondji, Kwame Gyeke, and Kwasi Wiredu began to publish work that rejected the anthropological descriptions of the African mind provided by the early ethnophilosophers such as Kagame and Tempels, and instead engaged the western philosophical tradition in order to find a theoretical framework that would allow them to emplot African thought within universal principles of thought. For Paulin Hountondji, Althusserian science became the foundation for building an African philosophical practice, while for Kwame Gyeke and Kwasi Wiredu analytic philosophy offered the tools to prove the universalism contained in African vernacular traditions.[12] But even as professional philosophy became indigenised as an African academic practice, the discussion of African systems of thought within universal terms depended on rejecting 'an overplay of contextual relativism', which the new African philosophers read into the early

---

9   See Winch 1970. Also important was Winch 1964. For a collection of essays collected as a retort to Winch's thinking about primitive societies, see Brown 1979; Horton and Finnegan 1973.

10 Horton 1967.

11 See for instance, Eze 1997; Serequeberhan 1991.

12 See Hountondji 1983; Gyekye 1987, 1997; Wiredu 1996, 1997.

ethnophilosophical work of Tempels and Kagame. For them, the attempt to be universal must instead be seen as the 'intellectual quest [that] precedes and forms the foundation of the diversified attempts to deconstruct the old colonial sciences':[13]

> To appreciate fully the historical importance of earlier trends in the African philosophical movement, it is still vital to see that movement in relation to its origin as part of the entire [African] liberation movement based on race. Thus even the extreme cases of Césaire and Senghor's celebration of madness, emotionalism and irrationality as essences of Africanism must be seen as a metaphorical defense strategy, a rejection of reason and rationality as absolutist forms of Westernism.[14]

Masolo's claim here is echoed by the work of Valentine Mudimbe who, when asked to do a survey of African Philosophy, found that he had to ask himself what it meant to know Africa.[15] Differing from other professional philosophers, Mudimbe found that African systems of thought are always explained through constraints, rules and systems of operation that suppose a non-African locus.[16] For Mudimbe, African systems of thought cannot be made explicit within the framework of their own rationality, which is to say that even as Africans attempt to decolonise knowledge systems they remain caught in the trap of legitimising themselves within the protocols of the colonial knowledge system. This situation, for Mudimbe, is premised on 'an epistemological hiatus' created by the violence of slavery and colonialism, which in turn tore asunder the connection between the colonial and pre-colonial worlds except through European epistemological and social categories. To ask about the local in Africa is thus always to end up situating Africa as a sign of something other than itself. For Mudimbe, African traditional thought is unthinkable even if it exists as a 'chose du texte' for living and breathing Africans. But to live this 'chose du texte' does not detract from the fact that the representation of African alterity is always already 'a negative category of the same [Europe]'.[17] Indeed, for Mudimbe, to speak about Africans is to describe the process of inventing and conquering a continent and naming its primitiveness.[18] All African studies can be is a com-

---

13   Masolo 1994, p. 45.
14   Masolo 1994, p. 43.
15   Mudimbe 2002. See also Mudimbe 1983.
16   Mudimbe 2002, p. x.
17   Mudimbe 2002, p. 15.
18   Mudimbe 2002, p. 20.

ment upon itself within a paradigmatic cultural model.[19] This paradigmatic model is based on three genres: 1) exotic texts on savages (traveller's reports); 2) the philosophical interpretation of a hierarchy of some civilisations; and 3) the anthropological search for primitives.[20] This then creates a dilemma for the African, who finds herself trapped, standing before these three choices when producing knowledge about Africa. Either she must deny the exoticism inherent in any attempt to know Africa, or she must simply be ready for the practice of a positive social science; or, thirdly, she can simply be in alliance with science within its epistemological field.[21] On the other hand, Mudimbe proposes that we can resolve the problem of epistemological hiatus by taking the history of the West as our own. For him, this would allow us simultaneously to document the invention of the idea and practice of Africa and to both demystify and impoverish a notion of Africa.[22] This in turn would bring African philosophy to its limits within the social sciences,[23] not so much as a path towards truth, but as '*recit pour soi*' – an account of oneself as a path towards personal survival.[24]

What is at stake here is the lack of self-awareness embedded in the practices and history of the social sciences. Mudimbe is not interested in the problem of recouping an idea of African philosophy as indigenous to Africa, nor does he want the idea of Africa to become a usable myth for constructing political collectivities in the vein of Pan-Africanism, nor is he interested in offering a notion of collective action that is derived from engaging critical thought. Instead, Mudimbe rescues the social sciences in order for them to be a mere account of the self. There is an irony here, given that it was political independence and an alternative idea of Africa, historically rooted in pan-Africanism and the movement towards decolonization, that rapidly promoted the social sciences in Africa to the high status of the sciences of liberation.[25] Even if Mudimbe is able to reveal the conditions of possibility for an idea of Africa, he seems to be on less sure ground when connecting his own quest for survival with the political, material and social conditions for doing social science as a project of self-critical thought.

Within the social sciences, the reaction to the debate on African alterity has since the 1980s been in conversation with post-colonial writers, especially

---

19   Mudimbe 2002, p. 21.
20   Mudimbe 2002, p. 69.
21   Mudimbe 2002, p. 79.
22   Mudimbe 2002, p. 37.
23   Mudimbe 2002, p. xi.
24   Mudimbe 2002, p. 43.
25   Mudimbe 2002, p. 4.

those identified with subaltern studies (see especially the work of Dipesh Chakrobarty and Gayatri Spivak).[26] Moreover, trends identified with post-modern theory also influenced much of the critique of Eurocentrism within African studies.[27] We find evidence of the nature of this conversation and the abundant cross-fertilisation that was taking place between African studies and post-colonial studies in the pages of a journal such as *Public Culture*, where from the mid-1990s onwards most of the above-mentioned authors were either published or discussed in an incredible spirit of collegiality. The impact of the critique of African Philosophy can be seen in the way the debate was taken up in a special issue of *Public Culture* where the essay 'African Modes of Self Writing' by Achille Mbembe was discussed.[28] Mbembe's essay repeats much of V.Y. Mudimbe's insights but in a more pessimistic vein; for Mbembe there hardly seems to be an African self to rescue at all.[29]

Reading through these debates today, one cannot but be struck by how much the conversation is circumscribed by the need for the authors to distance themselves from the Marxist-inflected radical politics of national liberation that characterised much of the work of third world thinkers in the immediate post-independence era, and at the same time to treat the texts of the early anti-colonial thinkers as foundational to the third world context.[30] This, I think, speaks to the post-cold war context of the debate. Thus, if we compare the writings of third world scholars in a journal such as *Présence Africaine* – a journal that is representative of an older generation of intellectuals such as those taken to be canonical by post-colonial thinkers – to the works contained in *Public Culture*, we see a remarkable difference in the kinds of political commitments expressed by these two generations of thinkers.[31] In particular, the discussion in *Public Culture* seems to circle around the view that there is a crisis in practical politics and social theory in terms of rethinking the role of the state vis-a-vis decolonisation and its failures, with concepts such as 'civil society', 'locality',

---

26   See Spivak 1988; Chakrabarty 2000.

27   Eze 1997.

28   Mbembe 2002.

29   Speaking of African alterity Mbembe writes: 'in fact here is the principle of language and classificatory systems in which to differ from something or somebody is not simply to not be like (in the sense of being non-identical or being-other) it is also not to be at all (non-being). More it is being nothing (nothingness)'. Mbembe 2001, p. 4.

30   Examples of texts that have become canonical to a newer generation of post-colonial authors include Fanon 2004, 2008; Cesaire 2001; James 1963.

31   *Présence Africaine* is a pan-African Journal associated with thinkers such as Alioune Diop, Aimé Cesaire, Leopold Senghor, Jean-Paul Sartre and other leading francophone and anglophone intellectuals who supported the cause of decolonisation in Africa and Asia.

and 'discourse' forming the central basis of the conversation. This seems to be part of a wider trend in the post-colonial literature to focus on questions of cultural difference (incommensurability) and ethnographic techniques as a method for breaking with the practices of Eurocentrism.[32]

Thus, while Achille Mbembe repeats many of Mudimbe's questions in his essay 'African Modes of Self-writing' as well as in his book *On the Postcolony*, in his work there is a much greater attempt to find a form in which to write the true historicity of African societies, as well as to write about the African's relationship to itself.[33] Mbembe sees his project as part of an overall thrust towards provincialising whiteness, which for him comes under the name of the Universal, and misunderstands its own historicity. Mbembe therefore claims that 'social theory has condemned itself always to make generalisations from idioms of a provincialism that no longer requires demonstration since it proves extremely difficult to understand non-western objects within its dominant paradigms'.[34] Dealing with African society's historicity requires more than simply giving an account of what occurred on the continent; it also presupposes a critical delving into western history and the theories that claim to interpret it. For Mbembe the question of doing African philosophy is twofold: on the one hand we must account for the lines of separation and continuity that are the result of slavery and colonialism, and on the other we must come 'face-to-face with the opaque and murky domain of power, a domain inhabited by obscure drives and that everywhere and always makes animality and bestiality essential components, plunging human beings into a never ending process of brutalization'.[35]

Turning to Peter Rigby's exchange with Mudimbe, we can say that if this is true, the question of the possibility of an African or Asian philosophy cannot be a question of how to Africanise philosophy; rather, the question of African Philosophy must be how to create a space where the epistemological problems that arise from the historical experience of Africans can be problematised or even constructed.[36] If we accept this premise, then the task is not only how to make philosophy an object that is relevant as a research practice in Africa; it must also be the case that philosophy should provide a theory for action within a historical context.[37] It is obvious that for Rigby an African epistemology can-

---

32   See for example Marcus 1998; Marcus and Fischer 1986; Clifford and Marcus 1999.
33   Mbembe 2001, p. 5.
34   Mbembe 2001, p. 11.
35   Mbembe 2001, p. 14.
36   Rigby 1992, p. 257.
37   Rigby 1992, pp. 257–8.

not be found simply in theory.[38] Rather, it is in the relation between theory and practice embedded in society – which, as Rigby says, is what the ethno-philosophers such as Tempels and Kagame show us despite themselves:[39] 'culture as social labour'.[40] I believe that Rigby, unlike Tempels and Kagame, is also suggesting that a Marxian ethnophilosophical project can talk about particular world-views without pathologising one against the other.

Such a Marxian project would be inevitably indebted to the theory of knowledge production associated with the Frankfurt School, best described by Max Horkheimer's notion of Critical Theory as a non-metaphysical philosophical system. For Horkheimer, the critical theorist accepts the view that human reason is constituted through history; and yet, rather than relating reason to the enigma of life, the notion of life itself is relativised. Thus, rather than focusing on the metaphysical bias of one thinker or another, Critical Theory eschews all metaphysical thinking, choosing instead to trace the historical constitution of categories of thought and linking them to their genesis in social practice. The question for the critical theorist becomes how life has been mediated across time and space. Concepts taken to be eternal are thus shown to be historical. What is at stake in worldviews turns out to be a genealogy that shows that what was once taken as metaphysical can in fact be traced to an origin in specific groups of people and specific social relations: 'reality is society's work'.[41] Culture as such must be relativised, not to pit one set of people against the other but precisely so as 'to wrest tradition away from a conformism that is about to overpower it'.[42]

---

38   Rigby 1992, p. 288.
39   Rigby 1992, p. 289.
40   Rigby 1992, p. 295.
41   Horkheimer 1972, p. 203. I am paraphrasing Horkheimer's critique of Kant. Horkheimer writes: 'In accordance with the theoretical vision available in his [Kant's] day, he [Kant] does not see reality as the product of a society's work'.
42   Benjamin 1968, p. 255. What Benjamin writes here may remind the reader of Fanon's claim that 'custom is ... the very deterioration of culture', since its purpose is to eschew the rationality behind popular praxis in favour of upholding an image of African dignity or African primordialness. But Fanon also reminds us that the desire to attach oneself to tradition is 'not only going against history, but against one's people'. Indeed, the recurring images of an 'Indigenous Africa' that one sees for sale all over the world feel depressing in exactly this vein. In fact, those supposedly pro-African cultural forums that are interested in picturing 'Indigenous Africa' have the look and sound of coalition-building but really represent a sort of market of prestige and position. Though we find elegance and dignity pictured, what remains on sale is African misery mystified in the language of African dignity: that is, dignity as the counter-veiling tool for addressing social issues. For these cultural forums, the tools for discussion must never involve critique in the broader sense

Yet despite the clear applicability of these ideas to our discussion, the charge of Eurocentrism has often been levelled against Critical Theory, and particularly against its Marxist inheritance, so that authors such as Tsenay Serequeberhan can speak directly to the critical tradition and still claim that 'the time has come to ask where the philosopher stands in regards to the suffering of man, of which Eurocentrism plays a major part'.[43] Serequeberhan defines Eurocentrism as a mere 'pervasive bias that takes European life to be superior to all other forms of life'.[44] He goes on to call this bias a metaphysical belief, and states that Kant, Hegel and Marx are all committed to this metaphysical stance, since all three thinkers apparently claim European modernity as the 'real' to which all other peoples and places must aspire. As an example of this bias, Serequeberhan quotes a section of the *Communist Manifesto*, where Marx, referring to European industrialisation, says that 'at last man is compelled to face with sober senses his real conditions of life'.[45] To Serequeberhan, this implies that for Marx the figure of the human only appears under the conditions of European modernity. What Serequeberhan misses here is that for Marx, capitalism reveals that 'Man' is always that which lies at the bottom of all processes of production. In getting rid of extra-economic forms of coercion, capitalism in fact unmasks a simple truth: that Man is both the subject and object of history. For Marx, the point is to reassert an anthropocentric perspective on history. Missing this point, Serequeberhan fails to locate the term 'real' within the Marxist tradition. Accordingly, the 'real' in Marx is said to have the same metaphysical disposition towards the non-European other as in Hegel. Serequeberhan therefore collapses Marx's notion of the 'real' with 'European modernity'. Moreover, Serequeberhan does not see that Marx's overall project is an attempt to answer a question about the relation of the conditions of life to consciousness, and so misses Marx's point that capitalism is in fact the height of alienation, rather than the culmination of the 'real'.

A similar difficulty around the term 'real' occurs in a 2003 article by Achille Mbembe on necropolitics, sovereignty, and modernity, where he posits that for Marx the goal of revolution is to have 'unmediated access to the real'. Mbembe

---

of the word; and as such the discussions are doomed from the start. Thus, in contrast to the circularity of an intellectual discourse that deals with racism by an assertion of African dignity, this book instead seeks to retrieve the parts that make up Africa by examining history as a social process that has crystallised around the object we all recognise as Africa, and made it into a fetish object. Fanon 2004, p. 160.

43   Serequeberhan 1997.
44   Serequeberhan 1997, p. 142.
45   Marx and Engels 2006, p. 41.

further accuses Marx of blurring 'the all-important divisions among the man-made realm of freedom, the nature-determined realm of necessity, and the contingent in history'.[46] Again, what is missed here is that the very conflations Mbembe accuses Marx of making are in fact the conditions that Marx describes as the consequence of capitalist social relations. Thus, for Marx, the formality of reason that governs capitalist social relations becomes the formality of reason that subjectivity adopts under enlightenment thought. In this sense Marx is actually a post-enlightenment thinker. It is ironic, then, that Mbembe believes himself to be carving out a new philosophical field when he proposes that we think about 'life' as opposed to 'reason' as a less abstract, foundational category that can teach us much about the truth of the subject. At the very least, Marx's point in thinking through the problem of alienation is to understand the ways in which capitalism reduces life to a set of abstract principles. Indeed, as Horkheimer and Adorno teach us in the *Dialectic of Enlightenment*, the point of critical theory since Marx has been to trace out the totalitarian identifications between subject and object, nature and the human, and human and human. The movement of history might be described as anthropological nature, but history cannot be reduced to either nature or the human as its cause. In this sense revolution is the redemption of nature, but here redemption implies the reflective non-identity that subjectivity shares with nature and historical progress, and which nature in its own way has always demanded from subjectivity.[47] Using these ideas, we could say that all of this book has been concerned with mobilising the concept of anthropological nature to develop a theory of historically situated, embodied knowledge. In the section on anthropological nature, at the end of this chapter, I return to Marx and critical theory to show why a theory of embodied knowledge matters when critiquing the history of the social sciences, and to demonstrate that such a theory can be used as a counter to doing conventional social science.

For now, I would like to show that the charges against Marx and the critical tradition are not atypical of the debate that took place in the 1990s and early 2000s in reaction to academic Eurocentrism, especially as it relates to Africa.

---

46   Mbembe 2002, p. 20.

47   Interestingly, Mbembe claims that for both Hegel and Marx human progress is dependent on the reduction of nature to human neediness or humanised nature. For Mbembe, the problem with modern thought is that the non-identity of the subject with the object becomes that which must be overcome so as to have human progress. On the other hand, Adorno and Horkheimer invite us to think about revolutionary imagination and critical theory as that which traces the historical shape of reason when it is absolutised. See Mbembe's discussion in Mbembe 2002, p. 14. Also see the discussion in the chapter 'The Concept of Enlightenment', in Adorno and Horkheimer 1972.

In this respect Dipesh Chakrabarty's book *Provincializing Europe* is interesting, since it offers itself as a ground-breaking synthesis and an exemplary analysis of post-cold war trends in third world scholarship.[48] Indeed, much of the language and the concepts Mbembe uses in his writings are also in conversation with *Provincializing Europe*, sections of which were originally published in *Public Culture*.

Provincializing Europe addresses Africans as much as it does Asians, even if its specificity deals mainly with a Bengali context. In this book we are told that Europe is an imaginary figure that inheres in the everyday habits of thought within third world countries.[49] Chakrabarty then claims that Europe remains the sovereign subject of all histories, including Indian, Chinese, or African history.[50] As such, Indian or African history has merely become a variation of the history of Europe. According to Chakrabarty, this trend in thought 'subtends attempts within the social sciences' to address questions around the formation of political modernity in the third world; this includes addressing questions around the establishment of modern state institutions, as well as the development of capitalist enterprise.[51] At the same time, Chakrabarty claims that the politicisation of the populations of the third world that occurred through the process of decolonisation and the subsequent post-independence struggles created an irony at the heart of political modernity, as well as a parallel irony in the ways in which the social sciences addressed political modernity. The irony lies in the fact that those who were deemed the opposite of the political – peasants, the illiterate, women, Africans and Asians – demanded that the horizon of contemporary political action address their present, thus proving that history was not a unity set by the evolutionary trends of the more civilised European nations. As such, the twentieth-century popular movements of the third world also proved that the ancient gods and spirits of many a third world people could enter into the domain of the modern. Chakrabarty claims that even if capitalism has come to dominate global social processes, it is still the case that bourgeois social relations do not exist within the vast majority of countries in the third world. In other words, capitalism may have come to dominate the third world without third world societies producing a class able to fabricate a hegemonic ideology whereby its interests have come to look like the interests

---

48   Another book that is exemplary of this communitarian turn is Escobar 1995. In this chapter I am more concerned with Chakrabarty's text since it seems to synthesise many of the trends that typified the debate in the 1990s.

49   Chakrabarty 2002, p. 4.

50   Chakrabarty 2002, p. 27.

51   Chakrabarty 2002, p. 4.

of all (as was the case with capitalist development in Europe). Yet this does not mean that new class relations were not produced once capitalism touched the third world. Rather, Chakrabarty's point is that even if capitalism did not produce what looked like bourgeois social relations in the third world, we must not theorise what is there today as the mere anachronistic survival of an antecedent pre-capitalist culture. What we must do is challenge two ontological assumptions that lie at the heart of social science practice. The first assumption is that humans exist in a single and secular historical timeframe that envelops all other timeframes, and the second is that the human cannot be coeval with its gods – while for Chakrabarty, to be human is to live with gods. Chakrabarty concludes that if these two ontological assumptions can be dislodged, it must be the case that, rather than looking for preformulated transitions to capitalism in the third world, we come to understand capitalism as less than inevitable in what it produces. Instead, capitalism produces translations between different life worlds. History is not about opaque or incommensurable differences, nor is it the march of equivalents produced by the universalising logic of capitalism.

The challenge to these two social science assumptions are what Chakrabarty calls the challenge to historicism. For Chakrabarty, like most critics of Eurocentrism, historicism is the epistemological framework that lies at the heart of all social science practice, no matter from which side of the political spectrum one comes from, and is precisely what makes the social sciences an inherently Eurocentric project. Recognising that one must offer a history of capitalism in comparative perspective when trying to produce a theory about the third world, and also recognising that Marxist historiography is perhaps the most influential body of scholarship within the third world to have affected historicism as a trend in thought, Chakrabarty spends a considerable amount of time in his book critiquing the historicist tendencies within Marx's writings.[52]

I am drawn to take up Chakrabarty's reinterpretation of both Marx and the social sciences because I agree that social studies in Asia and Africa are a legacy of colonialism. Moreover, the social sciences inevitably treat the historical trajectory of African societies as always needing to be compared to Europe, even when the local is posited as a space of difference par excellence. As we have

---

52   That Chakrabarty takes Marx and Marxist questions seriously is part of the overall trend within the post-colonial and post-development literature to investigate the legacy of Marxism for anti-colonial thought, showing that in the end Marxism has less in common with the questions that face Third World people and more in common with right-wing Eurocentrism.

seen, this is not just a problem of colonial epistemology; rather, social science is inevitably a practice that attempts to produce a new relationship to know-ledge and a new way of being a person, without necessarily considering the historical and material conditions that allow the social sciences to exist in the first place. The question for us has been: how have forms of knowledge pro-duction constituted the horizon of political action, and in turn how has this affected the kinds of questions we ask in the social sciences? Answering these questions has meant paying attention to the ways in which power penetrates society, and how that power becomes the backdrop for carrying on the business of knowledge production within the social sciences. By rereading and rework-ing Chakrabarty's understanding of comparative capitalism and Marx I hope to build a theoretical framework for answering some of these questions in an Ethiopian context, and also to rescue the critical tradition from the charge of historicism laid at its feet by Chakrabarty.

For Chakrabarty, Marx builds into his critique of capitalism two trends from Enlightenment thought that also form the basis of most historicist thought, and which make Marx and historicism inherently Eurocentric. The first trend is a commitment to the abstract human as the goal of history (here Chakrabarty seems to define the abstract human as Kant's pure will). As such, Chakrabarty conflates Marx's notion of 'abstract labour' with the abstract bearer of rights in liberal thought. Chakrabarty writes that for Marx, 'the idea of abstract labour was thus a particular instance of the idea of the abstract human – the bearer of rights, for example – popularised by enlightenment philosophers'.[53] This leads Chakrabarty to (mistakenly) claim that Marx's revolutionary philosophy is calling for the full realisation of the liberal subject.[54] The second trend from enlightenment thought that Chakrabarty claims on Marx's behalf is a commit-ment to an idea of history as a unified unfolding. For Chakarbarty, both of these commitments within Marxism produce the thesis of uneven development, and in turn this thesis relegates the third world to the waiting room of history. In other words, according to Chakrabarty, it is always the case that for Marxism, as for the social sciences more generally, the third world is seen as backward when compared to Europe.

Chakrabarty also takes interest in Marxist thought because the question of the universalising tendency of capitalism that is so well articulated within Marxism also lies at the heart of all developmentalist discourses. In addition,

---

53   Chakrabarty 2002, p. 52.
54   For Marx, what in fact links abstract labour to the abstract human is the separation of the economic from the political sphere under capitalism. Citizenship for Marx is capitalist alienation. See Marx 1973, pp. 211–42.

Marxism has offered the most succinct theorisation of the relation of the universal law of exchange produced under capitalism to historical differences. Chakrabarty approaches this by telling us that Marx posits two histories. History 1 is where the universalising tendencies of capital are posited. However, he also claims that there is another history which capital encounters as its antecedent, and which has its own future outside of capitalism precisely because it cannot be presupposed by capital. This is what Chakrabarty calls History 2. History 2 is never sublated into History 1, but is what the worker brings to the factory prior to being reduced to a worker, and it is also other ways of being in the world besides as a bearer of labour power. Chakrabarty uses Marx's example of the pianist making music and thus producing the ear of the listener as an example of History 2. He claims that even though Marx recognises that there is a History 2, he has no way to account for the process of producing the ear. Chakrabarty calls this process of producing the listener's ear the story of historical belonging. He says that, in *Capital*, Marx delineates a universal history, and yet this universal history is an empty place-holder. Instead, according to Chakrabarty, the transition to capitalism must be theorised as a process of translation (of the ear). This, he says, 'enables a project of approaching social-science categories from both sides of the process of translation, in order to make room for two histories'.[55] In sum, then, History 1 is an analytical history that shows how every place becomes exchangeable with another (that is, History 1 is the history of capitalism). History 2, on the other hand, consists of a more affective history where life forms are not exchangeable, but where translation does take place. Here translation is understood as a process of barter between equals.

Chakrabarty claims that what interrupts and defers capital's self-realisation are the various History 2s. Moreover, social progress as such becomes the process for claiming the historical difference embedded in History 2. The bearer of History 2, who is also the antecedent bearer of labour power, does nothing to move universal history along; rather, the question of revolution is simply displaced by an effort at cosmopolitan largesse. But in the process, the question of social justice is also reduced to the problem of letting the native speak in their most literal of tongues.

Chakrabarty, following Marx, tells us that there is such a thing as 'real capital' or 'capital as such', and this is capital *being for itself*. On the other hand, the *becoming* of capital refers to the historical processes in and through which the logical presuppositions of capital's *being* are realised. Chakrabarty claims that

---

55   Chakrabarty 2002, p. 71.

the *being* of capital must exist somewhere before we can know capital's *becoming*. *Becoming* is the past logically posited by the category capital; in this sense *becoming* is only retrospective.[56]

This *becoming* is what Chakrabarty calls History 1. As an example of History 1, Chakrabarty tells us that free labour is both a necessary condition and a result of capitalism. History 1 is then a perspectival way to read the archives. On the other hand, History 2 is a past encountered by capital, but not as an antecedent established by the *beingness* of capital; rather History 2 has its own life form, it is something that exists without necessarily giving rise to capital or capitalism (both money and the commodity are given here as an example of History 2). Capital then has to destroy the first set of relations and meanings that have characterised the varied histories of the commodity or money (History 2) before it can incorporate them into its own self-reproduction; in other words, History 1 must destroy the multiple possibilities that belong to History 2.

For Chakrabarty, importantly, there is nothing inevitable about the subordination of History 2. Difference as such is therefore both external and internal to capital's *becoming*; yet difference remains for Chakrabarty the 'everyday, preanalytic, unobjectifying relations we have with tools [and the world]'.[57] Indeed, despite Chakrabarty's critique of Marx, History 2 remains 'the delusions of a madman'.[58] Here Chakrabarty seems to be suggesting that History 2 is that which is seen as irrational by capitalism. But at the same time, he is at pains to show that the existence of the delusions of a madman (History 2) proves the indeterminacy of capital to be interrupted by difference. But precisely because History 2 is reduced to the delusions of a madman, it follows that for Chakrabarty the possibility for disrupting the globalisation of capital is reduced to a 'Derridean trace'; it is the non-systemic within the system.[59]

At the same time, if the point of a critique of historicism is 'to get a glimpse of the finitude of capital's history',[60] this begs the question of how cosmopolitan hospitality towards a trace enables us to deal with the subjugation brought about by processes of accumulation in third world countries (even if those processes do not produce bourgeois social relations as such). To simply posit local practices in the global south as a trace external to the *being* of capital reduces the critique of capitalism to a hermeneutic project. Moreover, it misses the

---

56   Chakrabarty 2002, p. 63.
57   Chakrabarty 2002, p. 93.
58   Marx in Chakrabarty 2002, pp. 68–9.
59   Chakrabarty 2002, p. 93.
60   Chakrabarty 2002, p. 93.

point that historical difference must be theorised as that which is constituted by the relation between social forms of existence and human life itself. The weakness in Chakrabarty's argument is then that even if he recognises that History 2 can bring about a breach in the commodity form, he reduces that breach to a methodological problem of imagining what remains in the wake of capitalism's dispersion across the global as well as celebrating the autonomy of the local.

What I want to argue now is that both for Marx and for us the question of historical belonging lies in the relation between form and content that is constituted within capitalism and is at the same time mystified by capitalist social relations. Marx's starting point is in fact a critique of German classical philosophy and its incapacity to adequately address the question of human freedom. Difference (History 2) cannot exist as something that is both intimate and plural and yet in an external relation to capital (History 1), as Chakrabarty suggests.[61] Marx finds it important to build categories of thought that describe the layers of social reality from the ground up. His commitment to conceptual refinement is not about setting up hierarchies of social development; rather, it is an attempt to show that the question of the possibility of human knowledge is intimately connected to the possibility of human freedom. For Marx, this connection was suggested by Kant and later developed by Hegel; yet he shows that ultimately the question of the relation between knowledge and freedom in the capitalist era can only be answered by critiquing social forms of existence, which in turn must start with an analysis of political economy. When Marx wrote *Capital*, therefore, he was involved in a kind of ethno-philosophical project: at once critiquing bourgeois categories of thought and revealing the social and political conditions that produced them.

In contrast, Chakrabarty's attempt to draw out a universal history of capital, what he calls History 1, which can be separated from History 2, reduces the history of capitalism to a non-dialectical formalism. After all, categories that describe social reality have no essential meaning except as a specific set of historical practices that, through the contradictions that arise from their being lived and breathed, give way to varying aspirations. Yet Chakrabarty renders capital's becoming as something that can be identified outside of specific local history. In taking this position, Chakrabarty hopes to rescue local memory and practice from the universalising tendencies in capital. But in the process, the lack of bourgeois social relations in countries subsumed by capitalist competition can become theorised as the simple result of the continued existence of a

---

61   Chakrabarty 2002, p. 66.

local History 2. For me, in contrast, the creation or recreation of new forms of unfree and partially free labour must be seen as part of the processes of capitalist accumulation. Indeed, as Pablo Idahosa and Bob Shenton suggest in their essay 'The Layers of Social Capital', difference is the condition of appropriation for the accumulation of capital. Idahosa and Shenton thus write that 'the general tendency, spurred by capitalist competition and cooperation, to make labour homogenous by divorcing it from its historical attributes of race, gender, ethnicity, nationality, etc., is countered by the drive to find new forms of labour that, on the basis of these same historical attributes, can be paid lower wages'.[62] There might be two or more histories of capital, but this is not because each history is mutually constituted and yet external to the other; instead, changes to individual personhood and attendant social structures at the local level are premised on the effects that capital (and its varying regimes of production) have on already existing historical difference.

Chakrabarty shares in common with the debates on African Philosophy a concern with *how* the shifts brought about by capitalist social relations – often discussed only in terms of the arrival of modernity – interact with pre-existing local histories. This is a research problematic that has been central to the debates on the 'transition to capitalism' within Marxian thought. While some of these Marxist discussions have been marked by the stageist historicism Chakrabarty attacks, I continue to believe that this literature has much to offer to our attempt to think social change together with changes in the way the social has been theorised. I treat these debates in the following sections of this chapter. My suggestion is that if we return afresh to Marx and Marxist debates about the transition to capitalism, we can develop a theory of knowledge production that can accept the universalising tendencies of capital even while it escapes a Eurocentric telling of history. To this end, in the following section of the chapter I examine the writings of Jairus Banaji in his 2011 book *Theory as History*.[63] I am especially interested in the ways Banaji challenges the orthodoxies that have come to dominate discussions on transitions to capitalism. While I don't entirely agree with Banaji's approach to the history of capitalism, I find his work useful for reconstructing a history of modernity in the third world as both concomitant and mutually transformative with the history of modernity in the west. This requires us to rethink some of Banaji's own latent essentialism as it pertains to rural politics in the contemporary global south. In the last section of this chapter I then extend my interest in building a non-Eurocentric

---

62   Idahosa and Shenton 2006, p. 72.
63   See Banaji 2011a.

framework for knowledge production by drawing out what Marx describes as critical-practical thought and contrasting it with dominant forms of Marxist thinking that continue to offer us a stageist rendering of history. In particular, I argue that when Chakrabarty conflates the problem of historical necessity with Marxian thought more generally he in fact takes a Lukàscian philosophy of history to be Marx's approach to historical change. The key, then, in thinking past Chakrabarty is not to reassert a stageist view of history but to rethink what the relationship between rationality and history might be for Marx. We are ultimately concerned with how a Marxian method might help us address the problem of the relationship of the social sciences to its research subjects. This is particularly relevant to the attempt in the first part of this book to rethink the consequences of social science practice on the politics of revolutionary Ethiopia.

2 Rethinking Transitions to Capitalism

Within the literature on the history of capitalism there is a lively debate that seeks to explain the world-historical transition from feudalism to the capitalist mode of production. Substantial issues raised in this debate include the question of whether capitalism can be characterised as a mode of production dominated by the exploitation of free labour (Dobb); the role of international trade in the origin and development of capitalism (Sweezy); and the role of agriculture in promoting a transition to capitalism (Brenner).[64] Through the publication of two key texts in the late 1970s, Robert Brenner's proposition that capitalism had its origins in English agriculture came to dominate the transition debate.[65] Later, Brenner's work was popularised and extended by Ellen Meiksins Wood in essays that are best exemplified by her book the *Origins of Capitalism*.[66] Implicit in this debate is a conversation on the transition to capitalism for countries of the global south. For the most part, the global south is posited as being on a different developmental timeline than western social formations. More recently, a number of publications have sought to challenge the Anglo-centric and Eurocentric tendencies of the entire transition debate. One of the more influential of these publications is Jairus Banaji's *Theory as History*, and although Banaji does not call out Brenner and Wood by name he does directly challenge many of the orthodoxies associated with their work.

---

64   See Dobb 1963; Sweezy 1976; Brenner 1986.
65   Brenner 1976, 1977.
66   Wood 2002b.

From our perspective, engaging the debates on the history of capitalism in the west is important because it sheds light on the origins and structure of capitalist social relations in that part of the world. The debate also helps us understand the manner in which social difference and hierarchy is both theorised and operationalised under capitalist social relations, and this in turn helps explain the kinds of institutions that were built in order to address concerns over social difference and equity within the capitalist mode of production. Examining this debate should help us think through the problematic raised by Chakrabarty, which concerns how the social sciences form part of an institutional and historical matrix that 'subtends efforts to address questions around the formation of political modernity in the Third World'. I have argued that Chakrabarty's work either parses critiques of capitalism into a hermeneutic project merely concerned with a reading of History 2, or else encourages passivity to History 1 by claiming that capitalism is that which does not belong to the primitive. In returning to the transition debates, I aim to reopen the question of connecting historical belonging to social practice, hoping that in so doing we can also transcend the dichotomy between the local and the universal that seems so insurmountable when critiquing the practices of Eurocentrism.

Typical of the Brenner-Wood position is an attempt, when examining the early modern history of Europe, to disentangle *capitalist* subjectivity from *bourgeois* subjectivity.[67] Wood therefore juxtaposes the English ideology of agrarian improvement – best expressed for her by John Locke – against the ideology of the Burghers, the Enlightenment, and ultimately the French revolution. For her the Enlightenment can be recouped not only as one of many paths out of feudalism, but also as a path out of the universalising ideology of improvement first taken up in England.[68] One of Wood's key observations about the composition of society under capitalist social relations is that capitalism involves a form of appropriation of surplus production that is not directly dependent on juridical or political standing.[69] Economic and political life as such is split into two precisely because society is freed from the burden of politics and social power is designated through the market. Thus, for Wood, capitalism made possible, for the first time in history, a purely formal political sphere. This formal political space is also the space through which liberal democracy functions: after all, liberal democracy is premised on guaranteeing private property rights and thus never challenges the designation of social power through the market or the social property relations – and dispossession of the majority – that

---

67　　Wood 2002b, p. 14.
68　　Wood 2002b, p. 157.
69　　See especially her discussion of civil society in Wood 1990.

make generalised market relations possible. For Wood, not only is it important to differentiate between the values of the French revolution and the values of John Locke, it is also necessary to disentangle democracy from capitalism by critiquing civil society as the space through which authoritarian social relationships are reproduced. Couched in the Brenner-Wood position on the transition to capitalism is a debate about the role of the nation-state and of liberal democracy in equalising as well as maintaining social differences within western social formations.

The Brenner-Wood thesis on the transition to capitalism begins by typifying the sixteenth to eighteenth centuries as a period during which western Europe experienced multiple successful peasant rebellions that led to varied attempts to break with feudalism. These peasant rebellions were characterised by the fact that peasants were able to lessen the burden of tithe and tribute payments demanded of them, while also holding on to customary title of land. At the same time, Brenner and Wood argue that the trajectory of the fragmenting feudal economy took on a slightly different dynamic in sixteenth-century England. This is because even though peasants might have been successful at lowering tithe and tribute payments, landlords in England were able to deny peasants access to land. In order to continue to extract a surplus from their ownership of the means of production, landlords also began to rely on renting land to the highest bidder.[70] This in turn led capitalist tenant farmers to seek the adoption of economies of scale and the specialisation of production methods, as well as collaboration with peasants-cum-tenants to improve agricultural productivity.[71] The irony here is that the rationalisation of land also meant dispossession from the land for those small peasants unable to withstand this new competitive environment. Small farmers who might have fought to be free of feudal social obligation were now available to become landless socially free labour. Another consequence was that the imperative to improve agricultural production through intensive means resulted in the availability of cheaper food supplies to those who no longer had access to land but who were instead free labourers. Brenner posits that this also allowed the owners of industry (at this time those producing wool and other handicrafts) to hire socially free workers at a cheap rate.

What marks off the beginnings of capitalism as a specific historical period and social system from other periods and social systems is that in England from the sixteenth century onwards there was the establishment of an increasingly

---

70   Brenner 1976, p. 52.
71   Brenner 1976, p. 63.

integrated *national market* – what both Wood and Brenner interchangeably call
a *home market* – and that a key element in constituting this home market was
the establishment of a system of price-making markets that promoted dynamic
backward and forward linkages within the countryside, and between industry
and farm. The Brenner-Wood thesis thus importantly posits a particular set
of historical accidents as the trajectory for the establishment of capitalism in
England, implying that there was nothing historically necessary about the rise
of capitalism; rather, the displacement of people from the land, the growth
of free labour, and the growth of intensive agricultural production in England
produced a mutually reinforcing social dynamic that was the key instigator in
establishing a competitive market. Here, competition implies that survival and
reproduction of one's self is necessarily dependent on selling a product competitively. Producers must produce what is demanded at the socially necessary
rate of production (the minimum price), including selling and reproducing
one's labour at a competitive price. Moreover, to be able to produce at the
socially necessary rate, producers must continually cut costs by further specialisation, accumulation of surplus, and the adoption of the best available
production techniques. Accordingly, both Brenner and Wood define capitalism as the systematic tendency towards economic development through the
expansion of intensive innovation within the capitalist firm.[72] It is this spontaneous compulsion to systematically adopt intensive methods of production
in order to survive and reproduce that distinguishes the capitalist mode of production from feudalism.

According to Wood and Brenner, the English case raises an important set
of questions about the conditions necessary for individuals and societies to
engage in the logic of market competition. In a 1986 article entitled 'The Social
Basis of Economic Development' Brenner asks what would compel an individual to choose to improve the competitive capacity of their means of production when there is nothing inherently good about this method of production;
further, why would an individual choose intensive means of capturing surplus,
rather than extensive means? In so posing the question, Brenner hopes to highlight that the historical specificity of capitalism in England is such that one
cannot just assume that it is rational to 'maximize exchange values and produce all or most of your output for the market rather than produce the full
range of subsistence needs so as to maintain subsistence and beyond'.[73] Echoing Brenner, Ellen Wood suggests that:

---

72   Wood 2002b, p. 70.
73   Brenner 1986, p. 25.

The self-sustaining development unique to capitalism requires not just
the removal of obstacles to development, but a positive compulsion to
transform the forces of production; and this comes only in competitive
conditions, where economic actors are both free to move in response to
those conditions, and obliged to do so.[74]

An important corollary for Brenner and Wood is that even if there is commercial activity under a tributary mode of production, there is no systematic compulsion to improve productivity; rather, only surplus resources will be devoted
to specialised commercial production. The question of the origin of capitalism
is thus less about how commercial opportunities were expanded and economies freed to take advantage of economic opportunities, than it is about how
social relations were transformed so that the satisfaction of the most basic
needs could be met under an entirely new set of social arrangements characterised by market dependency. Neither growth in trade, nor colonisation, nor
incorporation into global markets can explain how the intensive rationalisation of the labour process becomes spontaneous to capitalism. Additionally,
neither profit in markets nor market exchange are markers of capitalist production; rather, it is competition that introduces the need for socially necessary
labour, eliciting as well the systematic investment in innovation. This definition
of capitalism also allows Wood and Brenner to think about the ways in which
both peasant and patron within a feudal or tributary system can often choose
to disengage from the market and still reproduce *systematic* forms of injustice.
On the other hand, under a capitalist system injustice is socialised through the
market.[75]

   Indeed, for both Brenner and Wood capitalism is nothing else if not total
dependence on the market for your self-reproduction. Competition becomes
logical when the only path towards production becomes organised through
what they call 'economically constituted property relations' instead of politically constituted property relations.[76] For them, what is particular to the social
dynamics of sixteenth-century England is that it was only there that land
was organised competitively, and only there was a transition out of feudalism
successfully established through economically constituted property relations,
while other western European countries, including France, were unsuccessfully
struggling with different paths out of feudalism.

---

74   Wood 2002a, p. 57.
75   Brenner 1986, pp. 31–2.
76   Wood 2002b, p. 76; Brenner 1986, p. 33.

According to Jairus Banaji, the distinction that Brenner and Wood draw so sharply between capitalism and feudalism is less clear when we examine the history of capitalism as a global phenomenon rather than something specific to England. Banaji often describes the tributary mode of production, which feudalism falls under for him, as a form of capitalism.[77] Banaji argues this by claiming that capital presupposes money, and that since capital emerges out of the circulation of money the emergence of capitalism presumes a necessary connection between money and capital. He then argues that you cannot simply contrast these forms (money and capital) by claiming that a historical gap separates them.[78] Instead, accumulating capital and turning money into capital is capitalism.[79] Moreover, since it was typical of the medieval era for feudal lords to 'thirst for cash' so as to take part in an international trading system for the acquisition of luxury items, it can also be presumed that the feudal lord was compelled to accumulate money and engage in some form of capitalism.[80] Standing in sharp contrast to the Brenner-Wood proposition that capitalism has its origins in England, Banaji therefore suggests that there is no singular and unique configuration of capitalism from which all other forms of capitalism derive, but a series of distinct configurations.[81] What Marx describes in England is neither the original form of developed capitalism nor its highest form; rather capitalism's origin is sporadic and all over the place, and there is no one transition to capitalism but multiple transitions. Subsequently, for Banaji, this means that the beginnings of capitalism in agriculture are insignificant.

At the same time, Banaji does periodise capitalism into historical capitalism and the capitalist mode of production, with historical capitalism being dominated by merchants, bankers and their syndicates, and stretching all the way back to at least the end of the Roman Empire and lasting until the eighteenth century.[82] The second period of capitalism, which runs from the eighteenth century onwards, is what Banaji calls the developed form of capitalism, which is what is analysed by Marx in *Das Kapital* and extrapolated in the works of Brenner and Wood. For Banaji, England remains a mere isolated case in the context of capitalism as an overall mode of production. At the methodological level this claim also allows Banaji to get out of a stageist and teleological retelling of capitalism's history.

---

77   Banaji 2011a, p. 2.
78   Banaji 2011a, p. 3.
79   Banaji 2011a, p. 9.
80   Banaji 2011a, p. 89.
81   Banaji 2011a, p. 9.
82   Banaji 2011a, p. 13.

Banaji suggests that even under a tributary mode of production, Asia and Africa, as well as the New World and Europe, were already integrated into a world economic network through which the import and export of basic commodities were organised. In the seventeenth century in the Atlantic World of Poland, for example, this meant that the slave plantations of the New World and the wheat-producing estates in Poland were connected through a complicated network of mercantile and financial interests centred in Amsterdam and London and premised on the import and export of sugar and wheat.[83] Here, commodity exchange at the local level resembled a capitalist enterprise insofar as the major share of the output was produced for national and international markets, yet the internal logic of the enterprise remained feudal.[84] If we take the slave plantations in the West Indies or the Polish wheat-producing estates as examples, we can say that neither was capitalistic because both were involved in the production of absolute surplus value. Accumulation was slow, sporadic, and dominated by the socially determined consumption needs of the lords and plantation owners, with investment itself being quite discontinuous.[85] This being the case, there was no systematic competition between the enterprises; rather, wealth was generated through the maintenance of a certain proportionality between income and consumption. But Banaji argues that what is significant about the consumption requirements of the nobility and estate owners is that the perpetual need to adjust the level of income to the rates of consumption was a 'determining force' that drew both landlord and peasant into production for the market, consolidating the feudal estate and at the same time forcing the peasants to access money in order to get simple commodities.[86] Therefore, the distinction between production for use and production for the market can be disputed, as can any notion of a *natural economy* used to describe agriculture production under a tributary mode of production.[87] After all, the wage paid under 'commodity-feudalism' came not as a wage in the way we understand it, but through further exploiting simple reproduction so as to compete in the global marketplace, precisely because increasing the lords' amount of sellable surplus would often mean reducing the caloric intake of peasants and workers through further taxation and tribute extraction.

If Brenner and Wood read the historical record in the sixteenth to seventeenth century as a witness to the decline of feudalism, Banaji reads these

---

83   Banaji 2011a, p. 72.
84   Banaji 2011a, p. 62.
85   Banaji 2011a, p. 69.
86   Banaji 2011a, p. 77.
87   Banaji 2011a, pp. 4–7.

same years as a period where feudalism came into its highest form by inter-acting with the international market and becoming what he calls *commodity-feudalism*. Typical of this period is that small peasant production no longer retained its former autonomy but functioned as a sector of simple reproduc-tion. For Banaji, it follows that over the long-term capital both reinforced and demolished feudal estates.[88] Capitalism as a mode of production is as such dir-ectly related to the demise of commodity-feudalism. But this demise itself arose from the fact that the medieval estate could only respond to the thirst for cash in three very limited ways: first by heavy borrowing; second by the liquidation of assets; and third by increasing the volume of output. Accordingly, the thirst for cash promoted unsustainable extensive methods of increasing productivity, including more debt and self-exploitation.[89] This means that the systematic adoption of intensive means for extracting surplus logically follows from the fact that the feudal system could not sustain its own thirst for money. Here we see that for Banaji the ascent of capitalism as a mode of production arises as a logical category of money.[90]

The larger point here is that capitalism embraces a wider range of relation-ships than just a wage labour system. As the foremost contemporary Marxist thinker to propose a non-Eurocentric reading of capitalist political economy, Banaji also finds it important to argue that the deployment of labour in the capitalist mode of production correlates with historical relations of produc-tion in complex ways, such that various forms of forced labour including chattel slavery can operate under a capitalist system.[91] The subsumption of historical relations of production into newer forms does not mean that Africans or Asians have a separate mode of production that articulates with capitalism; instead, the historical forms subsumed into capitalism simply show how capitalism has always worked.[92] Banaji therefore goes as far as to reject the need for a debate on the articulation of different modes of production with capitalism (here one gets the sense that he is addressing Samir Amin and the dependency school). In this sense, for Banaji, within the history of capitalism there can never be a History 1 or History 2.

And yet, thinking back to Brenner and Wood, the ability to retreat back to simple reproduction is evidence that feudal systems of production are non-capitalist, since it indicates that socially necessary labour time is neither sys-

---

88   Banaji 2011a, p. 88.
89   Banaji 2011a, p. 91.
90   Banaji 2011a, p. 87.
91   Banaji 2011a, p. 41.
92   Banaji 2011a, p. 66.

tematic nor spontaneous. Anticipating this critique, Banaji argues that Brenner and Wood posit spontaneity as a necessary law of history when it should instead be seen as the contingent outcome of class struggle and more specifically the outcome of legal battles.[93] For Banaji the retreat to simple reproduction is evidence of market dependency; after all, as we have seen, this retreat is compelled by the market. For Banaji, value-producing relations of production conducted through archaic or pre-capitalist forms of subjection of labour may sometimes successfully compete with other forms of capitalist subjection and sometimes fail, which means that the stages between free or unfree labour are not chronological. Additionally, spontaneous moments of capitalist innovation are not periods of a kind of pure capitalism that occur after primitive accumulation, but moments that come and go, and are intrinsic to the reproduction of capital. Rather than making spontaneity a law of capitalism, Banaji claims that the laws of motion of capitalism always include 'so called primitive accumulation'.[94] Here we see that even though Banaji rejects Brenner and Wood's supposition that the spontaneous adoption of intensive production techniques is a fundamental law of capitalism, there are a number of laws that he does suggest are trans-historical and necessary to the development of capitalist social relations.

From my point of view, synthesising Banaji's position with the writings of Brenner and Wood, it is important to acknowledge that in the sixteenth century England was a part of a global trading system, and that the growth in world trade must have affected agricultural producers in England as it did elsewhere in the world. At the same time, contrary to Banaji, to me it seems that the fact that peasants in England were part of a social dynamic that, by the sixteenth century, afforded them much less access to land than their European counterparts does seem to have produced a specific set of social institutions that dramatically altered the world trading system. The question of systemic and global market dependency seems tied to the development of generalized economically constituted property relations in England in the early modern period. Yet these social relations were co-constituted through a world trading system. Indeed, it seems undeniable that the beginning of the growth of economically constituted property, the rise of New World colonialism, the rise of commodity-feudalism, and the growth of the trans-Atlantic slave trade were not merely coincident but in fact constitutive of each other's occurrence, and that their historical correlation led to their mutual transformation as well as to

---

93   Banaji 2011a, p. 13.
94   Banaji 2011a, pp. 43–4.

the transformation of the social formations that participated in these activities. Capitalism does seem to have produced a necessary link between the thirst
for money and the subsumption of production into socially necessary labour
time. Yet it seems that Brenner over-emphasises his point about trade. Even if
an internal set of consequences accidentally led to the development of market
dependency in England, there is still question of how trade impacted internal
class structures in England and elsewhere. Wood herself says:

> There is, of course, much that Brenner does not do. One especially import-
> ant point demanding exploration is that, although the commercialization
> model may be fatally flawed, capitalism did emerge within a network of
> international trade and could not have emerged without that network. So
> a great deal still needs to be said about how England's particular insertion
> into the European trading system determined the development of English
> capitalism. England arguably transformed the nature of trade by creating
> a distinctively integrated national market (centred on London), perhaps
> the first truly competitive market.[95]

Setting aside the debate on the articulation of different modes of production,
we can bring Samir Amin's insights on African incorporation into a global economy into this analysis. He claims that the primary way global trade impacted
internal class structures in Africa was through the export of chattel slaves to
the Americas. During the period between 1600 and 1800 a new class of African
elites engaging in international trade, became increasingly dependent on the
market for commodities and money.[96] This was accompanied by the fragmentation of those reciprocal economic ties that once connected kings to subjects –
after all, the source of wealth was now elsewhere. As such, there was a concomitant breakdown of older forms of social organisation common to tributary
societies. In Africa, then, the structural relationship between this new class
and ordinary people was pernicious, as the fragmentation of the old tributary
system led to a growing thirst for cash on the part of elites through their participation in the slave trade, while at the same time elites engaged in the slave
trade had no market incentive to improve economic productivity. Unlike its
European counterpart, the social fragmentation of the tributary mode of production in Africa did not produce a wage labour class in Africa, nor did it lead
to the adoption of a dynamic system of intensive production; instead there was

---

95   Wood 2002b, p. 67.
96   Amin 1972; see also Inikori 2002.

the growth of chattel slavery, which meant that Africans were traded as fixed capital, rather than having a part of their body/time commodified as variable capital, as was the case in England. At the same time, there was the enrichment of chartered companies based in Europe that were conducting trade between Europe, the New World and Africa; and lastly, and as a direct result of the enslavement of Africans, the rise of a plantocracy in the West Indies and the southern USA, etc. Thus, by the 1880s Africa's incorporation into the global economy was cemented through the establishment of formal colonialism. Moreover, if settler colonialism was unsuccessful in the 1600s in Africa, it was successful in the latter half of the 1800s precisely because African societies had become weakened by their engagement with the slave trade.[97]

The most important point here for our discussion is that in Africa global capitalism affected internal class relations, which in turn meant that wage labour and capitalism were tied together in very complicated ways, so that capitalist social relations in Africa are made up of a complex mix of customary social relations and processes of commodification. As Henry Bernstein has argued, this 'mutual effectivity is what accounts for many of the historical specificities of patterns of commodification, including limits to growth'.[98] This also means that there can indeed be people labouring under a number of different social arrangements in order to make goods for the capitalist market, but who have not been transformed into wage labourers. Social reproduction then happens partially in the informal sector, with farming often subsidising the poor wages received from engaging in the monetised economy.

Anyone familiar with the dynamics of production in the third world has known for some time now that peasants are no longer simple subsistence farmers working within a tributary economy, nor are peasants working in an economy in transition. Instead, peasants are tied into a capitalist system as both workers and petty commodity producers. Despite being owners of the means of production (owners of land), they are also petty commodity producers who are dependent on the market in that they rely on it to access seeds, fertiliser, credit, and other basic commodities. However, it is only the intensification of self-exploitation (lowering costs of feeding themselves, etc.) that allows them to produce a surplus. Banaji's observation that capitalism is indifferent to the mode of exploitation through which it subsumes workers seems to be accurate when thinking about how labour in Asia and Africa has been incorporated into the global economy.[99] He observes:

---

97   See the discussion of African Social Formations in Amin 1977, pp. 317–18.
98   Bernstein 2004, p. 123.
99   Banaji 2011a, p. 11.

When the process of production of a small-peasant household depends from one cycle to the next on the advances of the usurer – when, without such 'advances', the process of production would come to a halt – then, in this case the 'usurer', i.e., the monied capitalist, exerts a definite *command over* the process of production. This control or command is established and operates even when, as in this case, the labour-process remains technologically primitive, manually operated, and continuous with earlier, archaic modes of labour. The purely formal and stereotyped conceptions of 'capitalist production' that see in its basic relations only the glitter of technological advance (machinery, fertilizer and so on) have very little in common with Marx's understanding of capitalism ...

Let me pose the question more sharply. Is the domination of capital over the small producer – that is, the extortion of surplus-value from small peasants, artisans, etc. – compatible with the forms of the process of labour specific to these households? Both Marx and Lenin answered, quite clearly, 'yes'. For, 'the fact is that capital subsumes the labour process as it finds it, developed by different and more archaic modes of production' (*Capital* Vol. 1, 1021.) This is a theme that Lenin had to constantly emphasise against the Narodniks in Russia ... It follows that, in these forms, based on the 'formal subsumption of labour into capital', the small peasant is a 'simple commodity owner' only by way of his attributes.[100]

To be clear, the point here for me is *not* the claim that the past 1,000 years can be divided into historical capitalism and a capitalist mode of production, but rather that there can be multiple and different paths out of the tributary mode of production, and that those paths are neither linear nor are they ever complete. Following Brenner and Wood, I would suggest that we ought to be wary about drawing conclusions about the necessary laws of capitalism from the decline/destruction of feudal or tributary systems. But we ought to be cautious about following both Brenner and Wood too closely, for instance when Brenner claims the contemporary political ramification of his theoretical propositions in relation to the third world peasantry is that peasants are not capitalist since they do not bear the characteristics of the English mode of capitalistic production, most especially because they are neither doubly free, nor committed to spontaneous and intensive investment in production.[101]

---

100   Banaji 2011a, pp. 308–9.
101   See Brenner 1977.

Brenner's position here is strangely coincident with what Henry Bernstein has described as the more mainstream position on development that suggests that Africans lack the right motivational structure for economic growth, so that Africans are seen as risk averse and involved in an economy of affection based on kinship.[102] Indeed, within this paradigm of thought the African peasant is posited as supposedly moving in and out of markets at their own discretion, more concerned with the accumulation of prestige and power than acting in the interest of rational self-maximisation.[103] In other words, for mainstream development, the problem of African backwardness can be reduced to the fact that *homo economicus* does not exist in Africa. Moreover, the African state is posited as a key site in the economy of affection, so that what appears to be a form of irrational behaviour is theorised from their point of view as a specific form of African rationality, where ethnicity and regional associations form the bases for accumulation.[104] Of course, what differentiates Brenner from this more mainstream position is that he understands capitalist rationality as also having a historical specificity. He therefore advocates northern solidarity with the African peasant in order to overcome global capitalism (no need for them to go through what we have gone through). On the other hand, mainstream development theorists advocate that Africans could become rational self-maximisers if only they were given the right conditions – infrastructure, marketing, price information, appropriate technologies, models of good governance, and a rebuilt civil society – in order to be rational. Under this model the objective is to support rather than invent the African as *homo economicus*.

Banaji has the merit of pointing out that the peasant (subsistence farmer) in the global south is an integral part of how capitalism operates today. The problem is that, for Banaji, the dissolution of the tributary mode of production is never explained except as a logical category of fully developed capitalism. For him capitalism proposes an essential relationship between wages and capital, even if he acknowledges that capital incorporates gender, race, ethnicity, town and country into complex social forms. Banaji is able to argue this because he shows that capitalism has always paid a wage to what appear to be subsistence farmers, even if the wage paid is not always as direct as when it is paid to a wage labourer. This claim about wages becomes interesting when it connects to Banaji's interpretation of political action in contemporary politics. If we take a cursory look at Banaji's writing about Indian politics today, we see that he is able to argue that the peasant is a member of the proletariat. This

102   Bernstein 2004b, pp. 117–18.
103   Here the mainstream theorists referred to by Bernstein are exemplified by Hydén 180.
104   Bernstein 2004b, p. 118. Here Bernstein refers to Chabal and Daloz 1999.

seems to be a crucial point, because it is important for Banaji to include the peasant into the telos of universal socialist struggle and the dictatorship of the proletariat. Thus, rather than think through the unique social forms that are the result of the different ways capitalism has developed across Asia and Africa, Banaji advocates contingent struggles around law and liberal democracy precisely because it is here where capitalism takes its shape,[105] and it is here where the peasant/worker develops the self-capacity for organising against capitalism.[106] Banaji thus emphasises the need to build up the structures of civil society against capitalism, emphasising trade union activism over and against thinkers such as Arundhati Roy who support social movements such as the Naxalites and who claim that democracy in India can only serve the interests of capitalism.[107] For Banaji, Roy represents an overly romantic understanding of the peasant as a pre-capitalist subject. What the Naxalite movement fails to understand is that as citizens of India they are the inheritors of a democratic state, and that this state contains no necessary contradiction within it except as a site for social struggle. Banaji writes:

> As a historian I know at least this much – that capitalism and democracy are not functionally related, not even historically, but systems in conflict. Capitalism seeks to limit democracy through its use of the state apparatus. For the democratic left the crucial element of democracy lies in the ability of the masses to shape their lives through the political system, and that in turn requires mass organisations like unions, workers' councils, and popular committees of the kind we saw in the recent upsurge in Egypt especially.[108]

If, as Bernstein and even Banaji have pointed out, customary social relations and the commodification of the peasant economy are not intrinsically opposed, then, as Bernstein demonstrates in his article on the changing nature of the agrarian question in the twenty-first century, this forces a new set of labour questions upon us.[109] After all, capitalism now needs a much smaller labour force when it expands industrialisation, so that even if capitalism promotes a world proletariat it cannot accommodate a generalised living wage. Instead, social reproduction happens under insecure and oppressive conditions, and

---

105   Banaji 2011a, pp. 13, 15.
106   See Banaji 2011b; Brenner 1977.
107   See Banaji 2010.
108   Banaji 2011b. For a more thorough critique of Banaji's idealism see Javed 2012.
109   See Bernstein's discussion of the new labour question in Bernstein 2004a, pp. 203–6.

often in the informal sector, with labour frequently migrating between town and country in a continuous circular and seasonal fashion and with subsistence farming subsidising industrial workers, even as cash wages subsidise the subsistence economy. In other words, despite the fact that capitalism impoverishes people, poor people's survival is premised on their reliance on antecedent social forms, regardless of the movement of capital. Again, it turns out that Chakrabarty is not incorrect in pointing out that capitalism is mediated by the social forms that it finds whenever it establishes itself around the world. But for us the continued survival of History 2 is premised on the fact that the local generates new forms of personhood and subjectivity that must be theorised as the changing meaning of History 1. History 1 and History 2 co-constitute each other and are coeval, even if they operate in an uneven terrain and with varied temporalities.[110] On the other hand, for Banaji the past is simply reduced to a logical category of capital. History is as such reduced to exploitation and struggle. What Banaji's analysis of capitalism loses when he theorises *homo economicus* as burgeoning everywhere all the time is the specificity of the multiple social forms that are the result of capitalism's mediation across time and space. As a result, the problems of epistemology raised by Chakrabarty simply disappear.

These issues reappear for us in how in Africa and Asia the distinction between liberalism as a 'failed project' and a 'failure to transition to capitalism' has been elided. After all, even though from its inception capitalism has been co-constituted with the global south, it seems apparent that the liberal subject has yet to arrive in Africa. Thanks to Banaji's own analyses, we can conclude that this is not because the global south is non-capitalistic. There is no essential backwardness in the global south whereby the removal of blocks to transition would magically result in the right kinds of social relations (and individuation) that would allow *homo economicus* to stand tall. But this means that capitalism is not always accompanied by the forms of law, freedom and personhood that allow for capitalism and liberal democracy to 'work' in the west. Banaji fails to follow through on the methodological issues he raises when he points out that the subsistence farmer is both a petty commodity producer and a worker receiving a wage under a capitalist system. For Banaji it suffices to simply posit the peasant as a proletarian; and by so doing he is able to include the global south into the motor of history as well as the overall fate of trans-historical labour. Thus, for me, both Banaji and Chakrabarty – albeit from opposite directions – have only one-sidedly linked the way social facts come to bear on

---

110 For more on the relationship between time, coevality, and Marxism see Osborne 1992.

the hypotheses we build about society. What is needed is to bring together the partial insights of both Banaji and Chakrabarty by more accurately mapping African social forms of being onto the development of capitalism, and then returning to the claim that the social sciences are a Eurocentric discourse.

Chakrabarty's critique of the social sciences relies on the claim that they have a universalising tendency that sublates all of human history into the telos of capitalist development. My argument here is that even while capitalism has a universalising or totalising tendency that is mimicked by the social sciences, a gap exists between the intentions of capitalist logic and its failed realisations. That gap is not the result of a disruptive hermeneutics that juxtaposes use value against exchange value (History 2 and History 1) but, instead, is the consequence of other possible futures sedimented within the tyranny of History 1. The world is the world co-constituted by all of us together; coeval across differing temporalities. This is why Benjamin asks us to explode the homogenous empty time of capitalism: not so that we can assert History 2 (forms of use engaged in by workers) as ontologically separate from capital but instead so that the worker can transcend the mystification of their own labour (and social reproduction) under a capitalist system.[111]

While it has been the intention of this book to begin to interrogate the framework for knowledge production in African social sciences, I also argue that in the context of building critical thought for an African context it is both necessary and possible to develop a theory of knowledge production to which a notion of social progress is immanent. A working definition of capitalism and its history in Africa is essential to that project. At the same time, I argue that even as we maintain this claim, we must also insist that knowledge can and must be relativised. Combining these two dispositions, my hope is to demonstrate that it is possible to move beyond an Africanist social science practice that tends to define Africa and knowledge about Africa through the static and positivist parameters of tradition, modernisation and indigeneity.

3   Knowledge Production in Africa

In his book *Citizen and Subject: Contemporary Africa and the Legacy of Late Colonialism*, Mahmood Mamdani suggests that African social sciences tend to be

---

111   For more on how family life, gender and other aspects of everyday life are part of the processes of reproducing capitalism, see Bhattacharya and Vogel 2017.

polarised around two clear tendencies, the first communitarian and the second modernist.[112] In the modernist camp we find a body of scholarship obsessed with the idea of civil society, and tending to be anti-tribal and anti-traditional. In addition, the modernists are keen to discuss social justice through the rubric of universal human rights. On the other side are the communitarians; this group tends to be dominated by Afrocentric, back-to-the-source types. Here, scholarship tends to champion the cultural heritage and cultural capacity of Africans. What is original about Mamdani's book is that, rather than reject either position, through his research practice he aims to sublate both. Mamdani achieves this by showing that the forms through which Africa is described are rooted in colonial language; in so doing he links the forms through which we know Africa with the forms through which Africa has historically been governed.

Mamdani argues that the language of custom, tradition and modernity is derived from the practice of indirect rule that was instituted by all colonial governments. Thanks to this system, the origins of civil society in Africa were not the result of processes of commodification but the direct result of the urban settlements of the colonists. Here commercial and civil law were imported from the metropolitan nations in order to govern colonial settlers. Meanwhile, colonial rulers governed over the vast majority of natives who resided in the rural areas through a codification of customary law that was in turn institutionalised through the establishment of native authorities, native courts, and native chiefs (in the case of Ethiopia similar processes were initiated under Minilik, the Italians, the British and then Haile-Selassie's state building project). In the rest of Africa this meant that customary law more closely resembled the anthropologists' fantasy views of Africans than it did the modes of organisation of daily life. Indeed, Mamdani argues that, as a form of governance, indirect rule tends towards decentralised despotism for its subjects, those living in the rural areas, and centralised despotism for those who tend to be urban-based and members of a nascent civil society. This means that the language of custom vs. modernity has its historical genesis in the need to describe the social objects created by indirect rule. Even if these objects are real enough, we can say that the language of the social sciences in Africa tends to take these objects for granted instead of linking them to their historical constitution, if not invention. Thus, in Africa, the language of tribe and custom and the language of civil society are twin concepts. But while civil society has universal pretensions, the tribe is seen as parochial and fleeting; it is that which must become universal.

---

112 Mamdani 1996.

Through indirect rule, a universal civilisational mission in Africa was ironically set up through the tribalisation of Africa. Mamdani's study thus traces how indirect rule as a form of power, as well as a way of describing people, tends to fragment its victims' sense of experience and hence their capacity for political resistance. Mamdani concludes that in Africa (as elsewhere) abstract universalism and intimate particularism – as a form of rule as well as a philosophical, scientific and ideological practice – turn out to be two sides of the same coin: 'both see in the specificity of experience nothing but idiosyncrasy'.[113]

Mamdani's work stands out for the way he spends time linking the forms through which we know Africa to the social processes through which political actors penetrate society. Accordingly, when he locates the languages of rights vs. culture in their historical context, he is attempting to both deracialise and detribalise what is quite literally the language of a civilisational mission. For Mamdani this is, of course, an urgent task, precisely because the language of the customary (tradition) vs. civil society (modernity) has created an impasse in terms of practical politics in contemporary Africa. Thus, within the democratisation debate in Africa, the terms 'tribe' and 'civil society' are often operationalised and taken for granted in such a way as to reproduce a form of power and knowledge that originates with colonialism. And yet, if we follow Mamdani's argument carefully, we note that the language of patrimonialism vs. civil society has a historical and institutional precedent. The relatively recent discourse that approbates civil society is one part of the evolution of the dichotomy in colonial rule that Mamdani points to as reproducing the tradition-modernity discourse. This discourse in fact explains away the historical processes that allow the state to penetrate society in a myriad of ways, without saying very much about these processes.

To this day there is very little work that theorises the specificity of civil society in an African context, even if, as we have seen, there are a multitude of works that define civil society in programmatic and prescriptive terms. This lacuna is striking, given that the notion of civil society is a central focus in sociology's foundational texts; moreover, it is also a key concept in the history of modern European political thought, whether in the writings of Adam Smith, Hegel, or Marx. Indeed, as Ellen Wood has pointed out, civil society is a key concept for the above-mentioned thinkers precisely because the concept came to capture an important moment in Europe's transition to a capitalist mode of production.[114] Caporaso and Levine have argued that the ideas of the

---

113   Mamdani 1996, p. 11.
114   Wood 1990.

early practitioners of the social sciences are embedded in the late eighteenth-century European perception of a shift within European society in the way private wants were being satisfied. This shift in fact led to a realignment of the terms used to describe social order. It began to be emphasised (particularly by political economists) that society now organises itself through its own social laws, processes and imperatives; these new social laws and processes are what came to be called civil society. Social and political thought was less concerned with establishing an account of political processes, conflicts and deliberations, than with establishing an historical account and description of the unintended consequences of private interests and activities. Politics as such was no longer emphasised in terms of accounting for large historical processes, but was rather seen as slavishly following forces immanent to society. The early thinkers of the social sciences, therefore, saw the rise of civil society as being in contradiction and opposition to politics.[115]

If the early practitioners of the social sciences disagreed about the ways in which society can come to terms with the social effects of capitalist social relations, what was not disputed – and this is instructive for the history of civil society for developing economies today – is that as capitalist social relations developed in Europe, workers were less often obligated to work through extra-economic compulsion. Civil society as such was seen as the space opposed to extra-economic coercion (overt political coercion).[116] In Marxist parlance, the capitalist worker/wage-labourer is said to be free from the social bonds that tied them to a traditional community (feudal social relations), while at the same time the worker is free to sell his labour to whomever he likes.[117]

What is specific to capitalism in western Europe is then that the mystified separation of the formal political sphere from civil society produced in this double freedom of the worker a form of social freedom that was entirely new. Both the experience of this freedom and its theorisation have been central to the constitution of modern social thought. Civil society as a modern concept was thus invented to both describe and explain the immanent social forces linking otherwise independent producers.[118] But as such, civil society is a concept that is central to constituting the practice of the social sciences: it is the space

---

115 Discussed in Caporaso and Levine 1992.

116 See Wood 1990.

117 Here we might also note that in *Capital* the more Marx emphasises that this 'freedom' pivots on the separation from land and other means of production, the more he begins to qualify the term free worker with the phrase 'so-called' and other qualifications (including sarcastic jokes). See Marx 1976.

118 Caporaso and Levine 1992, p. 37.

of being doubly free that allows knowledge of society to be assumed and also produced when we practice social science. I would also argue that today we assume this very same freedom whenever we produce social science knowledge. Indeed, we can say that most of the thinkers we now take to be the founders of the social sciences were in fact struggling to come to terms with the new phenomenon that we have come to know as civil society.[119] The rise of the modern concept of civil society is therefore a central social phenomenon that also coincides with the founding of the social sciences as a set of academic disciplines.

This raises an interesting paradox: how it is possible that social life can be separated from formal political life, and yet reproduce collective experience across generations? Another way of putting this conundrum is to ask: how can political subjectivity simultaneously be a site of both objective and subjective meaning-making and yet claim to be apolitical? The invisible hand of capitalism is always tied to political and legal forms of being, even if those rules are not overtly coercive. For me, this *apolitical politics* is embedded in both the concept and practice of civil society in the west, and it allows the doubly free subject to be assumed as something universally attainable, rather than a social form specific to a historical moment. Being doubly free then becomes a space of neutral knowledge production – it is what allows social science to parade itself as neutral. This intellectual posturing is ideologically reproduced each time we practice the social sciences; it is in fact what makes social science knowledge possible in the first place.

At the same time, Mamdani's work raises crucial questions about the relationship of capital to labour, and of the history of capitalism to democracy. In a country with an established civil society, the social sciences become at best the science of the forces immanent to civil society; more importantly, though, they can appoint themselves as a neutral arbiter of the relations contained within civil society. But in a country like Ethiopia, where approximately 80 percent of the population is self-employed through smallholder agriculture, how can we talk about something like civil society?[120] As we have already seen, in Africa and Asia capitalism to this day relies on extra-economic forces (politically constituted property relations) in order to function, even if a wage is indirectly paid to the farmer/petty commodity producer. Following Mamdani, I would suggest that civil society in Africa is a form of power rooted in urban areas and obsessed with the idea of itself as anti-tribal and anti-traditional,

---

119   Caporaso and Levine 1992, p. 34.
120   Issa Shivji makes this argument more clearly in Shivji 2006.

but that in fact it has none of the historical attributes of a European civil society. If this is true, so many of the comparative political and economic questions that the social sciences ask about Africa will inevitably lead us to a dead end unless they can account for actually existing African and Asian developmental trajectories. First and foremost, then, I want to acknowledge that liberal democracy and civil society as they appear to us in the west are, in the global south, rarely the space of progress they are often claimed to be – and that this has everything to do with history of production in that part of the world.

The point here is that private property relations are not the primary legal relation that secures the reproduction of capitalism in Africa. Rather, Mamdani shows that the domination of capitalist social relations in Africa is more likely to be found in the complicated relationship between statutory law and so called 'customary law'. That struggle, in turn, is expressed in the constant flip-flop of the African state between decentralised despotism and centralised despotism. Both land and labour are treated as a set of interlocking obligations and relations, and the struggle over those relations often comes in the demand for reform of customary law (modernisation) or in the struggle for decentralisation (the promotion of ethnic autonomy), without resolving the fact that cultural identity in Africa is the form through which relationships between the capitalist market and the non-market are mediated.[121] Thus, the wound of the "tribal" in Africa is that it is actually the site where extra-economic coercion is fought over and negotiated, not in some narrowly reductionist manner but because, since the nineteenth century, the customary and the tribal was never meant to be anything more than the place from which coercion was advanced. All this demonstrates clearly that force and market relations are not separable. In Africa, force is not the pre-history of market relations but is tied into the very way capitalist market relations are reproduced.[122]

Connecting this history back to the debates about civil society, we can now claim that, in Africa, civil society is a supremely political space, but that the specificity of its politics lies not so much in its structural defects but in the crystallisation of a form of power that continually reproduces the binaries of rural vs. urban, customary vs. modern, tribal vs. civilised, etc. The problem with civil society in Africa is *not* that it separates the economic from the political so as to continually recreate the space of bourgeois neutrality, but that it must deny the social differences that are rooted in the way indigeneity, ethnicity and

---

121   Mamdani 1996, p. 137.
122   Mamdani 1996, p. 144.

the native have been historically constructed and reproduced for the sake of colonialism and capitalism. The consequence of this is that bourgeois-seeming institutions, instead of functioning as neutral peace-makers, reproduce a form of power that draws out the differences we have mentioned so that formal democratic institutions become anti-democratic machines. Inevitably, a social science practice that takes its own bourgeois neutrality for granted will map onto and even formalise the anti-democratic tendencies that structure forms of rule through forms of knowing. Knowledge production then crystallises around political contests over the rural and the urban, the modern and the customary (for example in the 2005 federal elections in Ethiopia).

Thus, unarmed with or indifferent to a theory of the history of capitalism, many contemporary social science researchers in Africa become part of a social process that justifies attempts to reconstitute man as a self-maximizing individual, something that in reality only very specific capitalist market relations have created. At the ideological level the social science researcher becomes the equivalent of the social theorist who assumes the freedom of the doubly free worker as a universal goal, and at the epistemological level the researcher assumes bourgeois freedom as both the condition and the goal of their intellectual activity (despite whatever personal claims are made to the contrary).

Mamdani situates the originality of his research project against Fanon and that part of African studies that overemphasises the racial legacy of colonialism.[123] Instead, Mamdani wants to show that decolonisation achieved the de-racialisation of civil society, whereas ethnic segregation has been politically maintained in post-colonial Africa. This implies that what is important in contemporary African politics is not race but the manner in which the native question has escaped reform by the post-colonial state. In arguing this, Mamdani also hopes to show why the perspective of political economy is less useful when trying to draw out a history of the African state. Key to Mamdani's argument is that, historically, civil society and the native question were co-constituted through the gratuitous violence of the scramble for Africa. This also helps us understand that civil society in Africa is not maintained through the type of hegemonic consent that we have come to expect from civil society, given the programmatic ways in which the term is applied today. Rather, if the conflicts stemming from the relationship between the cities and the rural areas of Africa are one of the institutional legacies of colonialism, part of that legacy is the incorporation of anti-tribal violence into civil society. This violence, for me, ultimately rests on racial fictions.

---

123   Mamdani 1996, p. 4.

As we have seen, Mamdani argues that post-colonial statecraft continued to govern the rural areas through some kind of 'indirect rule', resurrecting 'invented tradition' as a method for maintaining and lubricating state and society relations. Tribalisation and citizenship are in that case still co-dependent terms that rely on racial categories for their definition; but this time, race is veiled through a discourse of the city as modern or civilised. This implies that there was no de-racialisation of the urban areas, but merely an upliftment, reform or *evolution* of the black as citizen, while the tribal subject or the ethnic remains the black as tribal. The notion of a de-racialised and urbanised African citizen which deals with its rural subjects as tribal can then also be read as the moment where African nationalism incorporates anti-black violence into its project of governance.

Is it possible that Ethiopian studies and Ethiopianist social sciences are more deeply implicated in the silences in African historiography precisely because state sovereignty is premised on being both anti-colonial and anti-black at the same time? Is it not the case that knowledge production under a modernist African state must vigorously deny the blackness of being African, while at the same time the standard that constitutes the horizon of its legitimacy is based on not being like other Africans, but in fact being more civilised? Social studies in Ethiopia aim to prove that the state's horizon of legitimacy can be based in an Ethiopian reality, and yet it must efface that which appears to be too black.

4   Anthropological Nature and the Possibility of Critique

We have expanded the historiography of capitalism to include the global south. But, our thinking through of Eurocentrism still leaves unresolved the problem of what to do with a rendering of history as a set of necessary logical problems, a view of history that is as prevalent in Banaji's work as it is central for the transition debate more generally. In this section I try to work through the difference between Lukàcs and Marx in terms of the two notions of politics offered by Neocosmos (mentioned earlier in this chapter). I argue that Lukàcs represents a form of identitarian thinking common to the critical tradition that is primarily concerned with drawing a correspondence between stages of development in society and revolutionary subjectivity. He is therefore unable to offer a vision of emancipatory politics that goes beyond the regular and the habitual. On the other hand, I argue that if we return to a Marxian notion of anthropological nature we can unearth a non-identitarian notion of political revolution and human progress. The critical tradition contains a reservoir of ideas that can help resolve some of the paradoxes that are at the heart of the debates within African philosophy and post-colonial theory more generally so that we can 'think' once more about freedom in Africa.

In *Provincializing Europe* Dipesh Chakrabarty states that in his previous work he had misread Marx's notion of 'real' labour (vs. 'abstract' labour) as referring to a 'Rousseauian "natural"', whereby the individual could be posited as an ahistorical subject with naturally different endowments.[124] Chakrabarty now realises, he says, that the concept of the 'real' actually serves to question the nature/culture divide typical of bourgeois thought by referring to that which cannot be fully dominated by the commodity but which still has a social existence. What the 'real' now allows Chakrabarty to think about is the gap that exists within the scene of commodity production, whereby 'real' labour is never fully subsumed by the commodity form. The history of this gap allows Chakrabarty to say that something like History 2 exists, and it is also why he claims that History 2 is another history which capital encounters as its antecedent and which has a future outside of capitalism. What Chakrabarty is referring to as the 'real' is what Marx calls 'use value', but also the 'sensuous human activity' that Marx describes as constituting all of human life. Yet when Chakrabarty claims that we can separate the history of 'use value' from History 1 (the history of the law of exchange), what he ends up doing is positing 'use value' as an object that is separable from the transformations wrought by its relation to History 1. What we actually get from Chakrabarty is a one-sided praxis divided from itself. I have argued that Chakrabarty is especially interested in constructing a narrative of History 2 because he has understood the problem of historical transition in Marxism to be one where the linear progress of time is reduced to the movement of fulfilling and realising bourgeois social forms. I now want to follow up on this claim by showing that when Chakrabarty identifies Marx's writings with historicism he is in fact only describing a form of Marxist historiography that is best exemplified by Georg Lukàcs' essay 'Reification and the Consciousness of the Proletariat'.[125] Even though Lukàcs' essay represents one of the most skilful syntheses of the critical tradition, it still falls into the trap of reading the whole of human history as stages of a fantasised European history; therefore, to my mind Lukàcs' essay demonstrates the problems that need to be addressed if we wish to rescue the critical tradition for non-Eurocentric purposes. It also seems to me a worthwhile project to return to the ways in which Marx himself connected history to the nature/culture divide, and to juxtapose these with how

124   Chakrabarty 2000, p. 92.
125   Lukàcs 1988.

both Chakrabarty and Lukàcs develop their own philosophy of history. Again, the hope here is to overcome the practice, common to both the social sciences and the humanities, of using critical theory to discuss Africa in a stageist and Eurocentric fashion.

In taking up Marx, Lukàcs insists that his own work is an extension of classical German philosophy that for him starts with Kant and ends with Hegel. Characterised by a belief that rationality can master reality, this philosophy for Lukàcs is also the best of all bourgeois thought. What is redeemable about Kant is that he initiates a *critical* turn in human thought. Kant achieves this when he resolves the antinomies between Hume and the positivists by showing that objective knowledge comes from human rationality. As such, Kant demonstrates that it is no longer tenable to ask if there is a one-to-one correspondence between facts and nature, nor can we simply suggest that facts are established through custom (repetition of a norm); rather, human activity consists of the rational self creating a coincidence between its thoughts and the objective structures of pure reason. Kant's subject can therefore create a human reality, even if that subject cannot (re)create the world. Moreover, that there can be coincidence between objective conditions (pure reason) and the subject proves that there can be subject-object identity. This capacity allows Kant to say that the human can be both autonomous in his decisions and free from dogma. To master one's self is to be equated with the mastering of reality. History, here, becomes incidental to ethics, while the world appears as a set of natural and inexorable objective laws.[126]

What is problematic about Kant, according to Lukàcs, is that the question of what constitutes a thoughtful act (in addition to its possibility) is resolved by proving that thought can act on itself without any need for the world. Lukàcs points out that even if the mind in this scenario can proceed formally, its result is thought without content; quoting Hegel, Lukàcs advises that 'pure duty is ... absolutely indifferent towards every content and is compatible with every content'.[127] Following Hegel, Lukàcs concludes that Kant's theory of action, rather than a theory of praxis where freedom and autonomy can tell one how to act in the world, is a theory of how to contemplate the world. Either the philosophical problem that arose for Kant when dealing with the antinomies of pre-critical thought must be resolved by returning to the claim that reality is irrational, or else one must follow through with the critical tradition inaugurated by Kant and bring content into formal praxis. If Kant asks what human activity can do

---

126   Lukàcs 1988, p. 124.
127   Lukàcs 1988, p. 125.

in reality, philosophers must now extend that question, first by refusing to see the world as nature and thus as a thing-in-itself, and secondly by asking what the conditions are in which objects come to exist. Classical German philosophy asked whether knowledge built reality; moving away from an elaboration of the internal conditions for knowledge, human culture must now be investigated as a kind of second nature:

> Man in capitalist society confronts a reality made by himself (as a class) which appears to him to be a natural phenomenon alien to himself; he is wholly at the mercy of its laws, his activity is confined to the exploitation of the inexorable fulfillment of certain individual laws for his own (egoistic) interests.[128]

For Lukàcs, this implies that concepts in capitalist societies must be recognised as behaving in the manner of commodities; they act as natural forms, rather than a particular moment within a larger movement of totality. As such, the human remains an object rather than a subject – what the human creates (including forms of thought) act on him like a law indifferent to his specificity. Put in Lukàcs' terms, this means that the human's mind is reified. At this point one begins to realise that Lukàcs' genealogy of classic German philosophy is also a genealogy of the self. This in turn must be understood as an attempt to extend Marx's notion of commodity fetishism, for if Marx understands that the commodity is a particular physical manifestation of a complex of social relations, Lukàcs now argues that as a consequence individuals and the forms through which they act also become static things like objects.

One of the more striking claims that the reader is confronted with in Lukàcs' essay 'Reification and the Consciousness of the Proletariat', is that Chapter One, Section Four of Marx's *Capital* 'contains the whole of historical-materialism and the whole self-knowledge of the proletariat'.[129] In extending Marx's work Lukàcs also claims that he is sketching the whole process of mankind's movement towards self-consciousness. Most notably, his primary concern is to elaborate the qualitative consequences of universal quantification; and to a quite remarkable degree he does just that. However, in the section of the essay entitled 'The phenomena of reification' we begin to see that Lukàcs begat a theory of bourgeois individuation as both a theory of history and a theory of revolution. This section gives an account of the history of a number of objects,

---

128 Lukàcs 1988, p. 135.
129 Lukàcs 1988, p. 170.

all of which are now, in the bourgeois era, ready to achieve self-consciousness. The most important of these objects are the commodity, consciousness, and society. Each narrative sketch that delineates the history of one of these objects is similar to the next: history is the story of the development from organic unity to distortion, crowned by 'undisturbed' objecthood, and finally to self-consciousness.

Similar to Marx, Lukàcs sees that commodity exchange existed prior to capitalism. However, while Marx sees this as inconsequential to an elaboration of capitalism except insofar as commodity relations dominate social relations in capitalist societies in a manner unique to such societies, Lukàcs argues that 'subject-object commodity relations' have always existed.[130] This suggests, for Lukàcs, that a context of organic totality prior to capitalism not only resembles capitalist social relations, it is structurally an early version of it. As such, for Lukàcs, even in early organic societies there has already been a falling out between the identity of subject and object. He insists, however, that in primitive societies commodities only exist at the borders of communities. Here, the surplus left after subsistence is traded for the surplus of another community.[131] Lukàcs then goes on to say that what grows out of this are more elaborate modes of commodity production such as the feudal system of the Middle Ages. This implies that under feudalism conditions of labour are concealed in relations of servitude, but this is still not a true subject-object dichotomy; rather, it is only when the doubly free worker of commodity relations comes onto the scene of history that the law of equivalency becomes universal, and it is only under these circumstances that the subject becomes totally severed from the objective structures of society, including the objects it produces. As such, the identity between subject and object finally becomes utterly fragmented. The commodity, then, comes into its own as an object that embodies all of the shattered fragments. If under previous modes of production the commodity was little understood, now it can be grasped 'in its undisturbed essence'. This is also a claim about history and consciousness:

> Only in the context of [commodity relations] does the reification produced by commodity relations assume decisive importance both for the objective evolution of society and for the stance adopted by men towards it. Only then does the commodity become crucial for the subjugation of men's consciousness.[132]

---

130   Lukàcs 1988, p. 84.
131   Lukàcs 1988, p. 85.
132   Lukàcs 1988, p. 86.

Thus, as the commodity enters into the objective evolution of society, consciousness also becomes an undistorted universal object. This is because 'the fate of the worker becomes the fate of society'.[133] Lukàcs therefore suggests that it is precisely the case that under capitalist social relations self-consciousness of totality becomes possible in a way that was never possible before.

One of the keys to unravelling Lukàcs' philosophy of history lies in an examination of the manner through which he draws a distinction between bonded labour (slaves and serfs) and the proletariat. While this may seem like an obvious Marxian differentiation, on this point Lukàcs misinterprets Marx – a misreading that allows us to understand what Lukàcs means when he says that Chapter One, Section Four of *Capital* contains the whole of historical materialism and the whole self-knowledge of the proletariat.

One of the first things to be noted about the slave as described by Lukàcs is that he or she can never be an object in the way the proletariat are always objects. The slave is never alienated from his or her own creation. Under capitalist social relations the proletariat and the reified mind in general contemplates reality, while the slave, on the other hand, lives in an organic totality. The consequence of this, for Lukàcs, is that only the proletariat emerges with the consciousness of an individual. After all, the slave's fate is personal, and thus neither atomised nor individualised. As such, the slave's fate is in fact outside the evolution of human society, whereas the thoroughly fragmented self of capitalist social relations belongs to a 'unified structure of consciousness that embraces all of society'.[134] Referencing Marx, Lukàcs therefore says that the proletariat has the consciousness of a Robinson Crusoe.[135] The problem for the worker, then, is that he lives in a contemplative relation to the world, while the slave is less than contemplative.

What we are concerned with here is not what this reveals about Lukàcs' theory of the slave (he does not have one), but what it says about his views on the doubly free worker of capitalist social relations. For Lukàcs, the worker who is free from social bonds and free to sell their labour as a commodity is also 'the rigid epistemological doubling of subject and object' as represented by bourgeois consciousness.[136] This comes to mean that the proletarian subject has a specific ontological makeup that is delimited by the cultural and historical moment in which they live, a fact that distinguishes them ontologically from the slave. What is remarkable and specific about the proletariat is that their personality is divided:

---

133   Lukàcs 1988, p. 91.
134   Lukàcs 1988, p. 100.
135   Lukàcs 1988, p. 135.
136   Lukàcs 1988, p. 169.

[I]n slavery and in solitude the ruling powers appear as the 'immediate mainsprings of the production process' and this prevents labourers
enmeshed in such a situation with their personalities undivided from
achieving clarity about their social position. By contrast, 'work which is
represented as exchange value has for its premise the work of the isolated individual. It becomes social by assuming the form of its immediate
antithesis, the form of abstract universality'.[137]

Later, Lukàcs adds:

> Even when in antiquity a slave, an *instrumentum vocale*, becomes con-
> scious of himself as a slave this is not self knowledge ... for he can only
> attain to knowledge of an object which happens accidentally to be him-
> self. Between a 'thinking' slave and an 'unconscious' slave there is no real
> distinction to be drawn in the objective social sense.[138]

For Lukàcs, abstract labour today can tell us something qualitative about labour
yesterday. We also gather from this passage that it is only under capitalist social
relations that work becomes universal and, more importantly, social. In fact,
following from this, Lukàcs claims that it is only through exchange value that
the 'living core' of society (labouring men) begins 'entering into the evolution
of society'.[139] This is possible only because Lukàcs takes labour to be a trans-
historical object of society; yet as an object it does not enter into the dialectics
of history until exchange value fully appears in history.[140] Accordingly, trans-
historical labour only becomes an object that can be part of history when it
becomes an object dominated by commodity relations. Further, it is because
commodity relations have produced labour as historical labour that labour
can now move from being an object in itself to an object for itself (a free subject).

---

137   Lukàcs 1988, p. 168.
138   Lukàcs 1988, p. 169.
139   Ibid.
140   Lukàcs' own words speak clearly in this regard: 'On the one hand, this transformation
      of labour into a commodity removes every "human" element from the immediate exist-
      ence of the proletariat, on the other hand the same development progressively eliminates
      everything "organic", every direct link with nature from the forms of society so that social-
      ised man can stand revealed in an objectivity remote from or even opposed to humanity.
      It is just in this objectification, in this rationalisation and reification of all social forms that
      we see clearly for the first time how society is constructed from the relations of men with
      each other'. Lukàcs 1988, p. 176.

This seems to be a deliberate misreading of *Capital*. In fact, one of Marx's charges against classical political economy is that its analyses stop short when it succeeds in uncovering the content concealed in the form of the commodity but refuses to examine the form itself.[141] For Marx, the commodity can tell us little about what labour is historically except to say that labour was not a commodity. Indeed, this seems to be the point of the Robinson Crusoe story found in Chapter One, Section Four of *Capital*.

When Marx talks of Crusoe, it is in the context of describing several modes of production. The point of the description is to demonstrate what is unique about each mode of production, including capitalism. For Marx each mode of production except for Crusoe's is taken as social; yet it is Crusoe's mode of production and its concomitant mode of consciousness that Lukàcs takes to be the closest to capitalism, despite his own claim that capitalist relations are the only really social mode of production. In fact, it is hard to know how Lukàcs reads the Robinson Crusoe story when he claims that bourgeois consciousness emerges in the form of a Robinson Crusoe, except to say that, like the classical political economist, Lukàcs takes this to be the case. But if Lukàcs is indeed asserting this, he must be missing the irony in Marx's little narrative about modes of production.[142] Perhaps, then, we can say that Lukàcs' history of the appearance of labour as historical object shares more in common with classic political economy in so much as it takes one side of the commodity and attempts to write history from there. This begins to suggest why Lukàcs reads Chapter One, Section Four of *Capital* as containing the whole of historical materialism and the whole self-knowledge of the proletariat. For Lukàcs, that chapter reveals the essence of history, not just the one-sided content of capitalist social forms.

I am not claiming here that Lukàcs posited history as a necessity independent of human action. Rather, the historical process for Lukàcs can be described as 'the logic of contents'.[143] If bourgeois thought fetishises the object as a unique thing-in-itself, it is Lukàcs' aim to reveal formal definitions of bourgeois objects and to fill them with the story of their human creation. History has a crucial role to play because it is the very force that wrenches an object

---

141   Marx writes: 'Political-economy has indeed analysed value and its magnitude, however incompletely, and has uncovered the content concealed within these forms. But it never asked the question why this content has assumed this particular form, that is to say why labour is expressed in value and why the measurement of labour by its duration is expressed in the magnitude of the value of the product'. Marx 1976, p. 174.

142   See Marx 1976, p. 170.

143   Lukàcs 1988, p. 144.

THE PROBLEM OF THE SOCIAL SCIENCES IN AFRICA

out of its unique particularity, revealing an object's content to be its structural principles, rather than what is immediately visible. For Lukàcs, each object is embedded in historical tendencies. This is not due to the object itself, but to its overall situation, which in turn is the result of the mediation of history.

The consequence of all of this is that, for Lukàcs, 'intellectual genesis must be identical with historical genesis'.[144] What is particular about bourgeois society is that the reality and the origin of society are linked through a totalised consciousness. At the bottom of the totalised consciousness is the secret that the proletariat is its producer, which means that in bourgeois societies history and genesis are linked though the totalising tendency of trans-historical labour, now expressed as the proletariat. It is this claim made by Lukàcs that Chakrabarty takes as Marx's own.

At the same time, what characterises even the best of bourgeois thought for Lukàcs is formalism devoid of content. This is expressed in the rigid dichotomy between subject and object, thought and praxis, nature and reason. Consequently, when in the last section of his essay Lukàcs remarks that 'classical philosophy cannot discover the concrete subject of genesis' nor 'the methodologically indispensable subject-object', it is clear that his recounting of the history of the proletariat neatly solves the problem of bourgeois formality. On the one hand, the consciousness of the proletariat solves the problem of 'how to deduce the unity of creation'.[145] On the other hand, it demonstrates that truth can only lie in the future: when the world is made whole by revolution and there is subject-object identity.

Lukàcs' 'logic of contents' suggests to us, then, that the proletariat solves the problem of bourgeois action by filling bourgeois forms with self-consciousness, and thus with praxis. Indeed, what the proletariat achieves is the actual establishment of bourgeois praxis. One will do well to listen closely to Lukàcs on this score:

> The great advance over Hegel made by the scientific standpoint of the proletariat as embodied in Marxism lay in its refusal to see in the categories of reflection a 'permanent' stage of human knowledge and in its insistence that they were the necessary mould both of thought and of life in bourgeois society, in the reification of thought and life. With this came the discovery of dialectics in history itself. Hence dialectics is not impor-

---

144   Lukàcs 1988, p. 155.
145   Lukàcs 1988, p. 140.

ted into history from outside, nor is it interpreted in the light of history (as often occurs in Hegel), but is *derived* from history made conscious as its logical manifestation at this particular point in its development ...

[I]t is the proletariat that embodies this process of consciousness. Since its consciousness appears as the immanent product of the historical dialectic, it likewise appears to be dialectical. That is to say, this conscious-ness is nothing but the expression of historical necessity. The proletariat 'has no ideals to realize'. When its consciousness is put into practice it can only breathe life into the things which the dialectics of history have forced to a crisis.[146]

What the 'logic of contents' tells Lukàcs is that it is a matter of life and death that the proletariat come to see that the world they live in is not *their* world. This puts into action a 'motor of class interests' that moves the object of society (the proletariat) to reflect on its immediacy.[147] This motor is for Lukàcs emin-ently practical, because as we have noted the proletariat are the secret subject behind all bourgeois forms. Reflection by the proletariat on the conditions of its existence is therefore always already action on itself. Embodied in the pro-letariat is the ability to bring about 'objective structural change in the objects of knowledge'.[148] Here we see that Hegel's goal of absolute knowledge is still valid for Marxists. This is because the particular as seen from the standpoint of the proletariat is no longer a segment of history; rather it begets the unravelling and bringing together of totality. The crux of Lukàcs' argument therefore rests on a philosophy of history.

When Lukàcs writes about the ontological status of the proletariat he does not see its realisation as inevitable, but neither does he see objective action as having to be formulated. Instead, objective action lies dormant in the prolet-ariat, and all that is needed is an aspiration towards reflection on the world: moving away from a reified structure of consciousness, the proletariat auto-matically becomes subject and so breaks the subject-object dichotomy that defines its historical moment.[149] Now, this would be true if trans-historical labour defined the proletariat's historical moment. But as we have argued, this in fact is not the case.

At first, then, the 'logic of content' delineated by Lukàcs may appear to fol-low Marx's methodology in so much as both are concerned with turning objects

---

146   Lukàcs 1988, p. 177.
147   Lukàcs 1988, p. 171.
148   Lukàcs 1988, p. 169.
149   Lukàcs 1988, p. 198.

back into processes. Yet, it seems that for Lukàcs the stages leading towards totality, rather than critical-practical thought, become the principle explanation of phenomena. Categories that exist in one historical stage or another become the points of transition towards a stadial notion of truth. Earlier, we started to ask how it is that Lukàcs could conflate the history of bourgeois philosophy with the genealogy of the universal subject. Now it becomes clear that for Lukàcs this is possible because their origin stems from the same historical and structural moment: the transformation of trans-historical labour into the proletariat.

5   Critical-Practical Thought

In his 'Theses on Feuerbach', Marx advises that the departure point for critical-practical thought should be the standpoint of 'social humanity', and perhaps this is where Lukàcs begins.[150] But for Lukàcs the standpoint of the proletariat is merely a necessity for a future where bourgeois forms are realised but not abolished; rather:

> [T]he proletariat is the identical subject-object of the historical process, i.e. the first subject in history that is (objectively) capable of an adequate social consciousness.[151]

This is why it is possible for Lukàcs to claim that the liberation of the proletariat lies in its mere coming to self-consciousness. Reading Lukàcs with Moishe Postone, we can therefore say that Lukàcs:

> [G]rasps capitalism essentially in terms of the problem of formalism, as a form of social life that does not grasp its own content. This suggests that when he claims the commodity form structures modern, capitalist society, he understands that form solely in terms of its abstract, quantitative and formal dimension – its value dimension. He thereby posits the use-value dimension, the 'real material substratum', as a quasi-ontological content, separable from the form, which is constituted by labour trans-historically understood.[152]

---

150   See thesis ten in Marx 1973, p. 423.
151   Lukàcs 1988, p. 199.
152   Postone 2003.

Previously, we had noted that Lukàcs wrote that for classical German philosophy history was overly formal, while for him it is full of human activity. Yet as we have just seen, the content of history for Lukàcs is separable from the form that is part of its ever-changing possibility. But if there is any point to Marx's 'Theses on Feuerbach', it is that praxis is the irretrievable coming together of form and content. This, we are told, is not a philosophical problem but is evident in all objective human activity. Indeed, for Marx all 'human sensual activity' is constituted by form and content together, and as such, 'all social life is practical' (here he is also talking about pre-capitalist societies).[153] To separate historical content from its form is therefore to be as one-sided as classical German philosophy. This is because it prevents critical thought from growing out of human sensuous experience; instead, we get a philosophy of history that is good for all time: a philosophy of history without much everyday history.

If this is the case, then the notion of praxis that Lukàcs offers us is hardly the 'sensuous human activity' that Marx describes as constituting all of human life. Rather, we get a one-sided praxis divided from itself. Following Lukàcs, the proletariat is both the motor and the mechanic of history; and yet the motor that they fix never belongs to them as human sensuous activity. This is because the motor is history; and history, for Lukàcs, always belongs to the past, never to the proletariat. Indeed, for Lukàcs the past becomes necessity, whereas the present is simply a transition to the future, in which the bourgeois problem of practical thought is resolved. This, of course, is the problem of historical transition that Chakrabarty has identified with Marxist thought. And this is why I have suggested that what Chakrabarty has identified with Marxist thought is rather only a manifestation of a form of Marxist historiography that is best exemplified by Lukàcs' essay. On the other hand, when Chakrabarty claims that we can separate History 2 (use value) from History 1 (the history of the law of exchange), he is committing the same mistake as Lukàcs but from the opposite direction: he takes use-value to be a quasi-ontological object that is separable from the transformations wrought by its relation to History 1.

In the 'Theses On Feuerbach', practical-critical thought is said to be revolutionary when it seeks the coincidence of self-consciousness and transformative activity by changing in 'theory and in practice' the conditions that gave rise to the contradictions that separate consciousness and changing circumstances in the first place.[154] To do otherwise would separate form and content: practical-critical thought could not combat the heteronomy that divides

---

153   See thesis eight in Marx 1973, p. 423.
154   See thesis two, three, and four in Marx 1973, p. 422.

'sensuous human activity' from itself. Given that bourgeois forms are the conditions for the contradictions of bourgeois life, revolutionary thought cannot seek to fill bourgeois forms with secret content; it must destroy them in theory and in practice. When Lukàcs locates human liberation in the totalising social forms of the bourgeois era he cancels this possibility. The proletariat, then, cannot be the location of human freedom; however, this does not mean that they are not the mystified content of capitalist social forms. It might be true that the totalising tendency of the law of equivalency subsumes consciousness; but to desire, as Lukàcs does, that the subject become self-conscious of this totalisation, and to call this freedom, can only mean that the subject continues to suffer under a form whose necessity was not of their choosing. Like Benjamin, it is better to remind ourselves that 'in every era the attempt must be made anew to wrest tradition away from a conformism that is about to overpower it'.[155]

In this sense, then, Chakrabarty is right in identifying a strain of Marxist thought where the realisation of bourgeois social forms is the end goal. He is also right in identifying this form of thought with a regressive social and political practice. Indeed, if Lukàcs was correct in his reading of Marx, we could see how the crux of Marx's argument would in fact lie in a historicist method and a Eurocentric telling of the history of capital; after all, the end point of Lukàcs' philosophy of history has the implication that all those who lie outside of bourgeois social relations (as those relations exist in Europe) actually lie outside of the unity of history. Thus, the notion of trans-historical labour embedded in Lukàcs' ontological assumptions about the proletariat assumes that the form bourgeois relations take in Europe will determine the future of humanity's freedom. Lukàcs' story of redemption thus leaves out most of humanity from the story of labour coming to be for itself. Perhaps this is also why Banaji needs to include the peasantry into the motor of world history. Here I think that Chakrabarty is right to point out that capitalism has not always produced what looks like bourgeois social relations in India or Africa.

In any case, as we have been arguing, there is no notion of trans-historical labour at the heart of Marx's theory of capitalism. In fact, it is my claim that such a concept grossly misreads the Marxian notion of social progress and social development. It is also my argument that, unlike Chakrabarty, we do not have to abandon a notion of social progress in order to have a non-Eurocentric history of capitalist development.

---

155   Benjamin 1968.

6   The Human as Subject and Object

According to Marx, the human is a living sensual creature, and thus both needy, conditioned, and limited by objects outside of his body.[156] If the human is to survive they must be able to subsume the objects of nature into their own nature.[157] But an important corollary to this basic observation, for Marx, is that if it is possible for living creatures to subsume objects then it must mean that these same objects also realise their nature through the process of being sub-sumed by objects outside of themselves.[158] Tracing out where subject begins and object ends can as a result become much more difficult. This is not because nature really is subjectivity alienated from itself, as Lukàcs posits, but because the human as a living object is a subject who must obtain his objects through becoming objectified for another in nature. Intelligibility as such does not determine the object for the subject; rather the subject has an object because the subject can be objectified.

Speaking of Hegel's subject, Marx asks us to 'imagine a being which is neither an object itself nor has an object'. He then goes on to tell us that such a being would be an impossibility:

> For as soon as there are objects outside of me as soon as I am not alone, I am another, a reality other than the object outside me. For this third object I am therefore a reality other than it, i.e., its object ... As soon as I have an object, this object has me for its object ... To be sensuous, i.e., to be real, is to be an object of sense, a sensuous object, and thus to have sensuous objects outside of oneself, objects of one's self-perception. To be sensuous is to suffer (to be subjected to the actions of another).[159]

Nature, then, provides a means to life in the sense that the subject receives physical sustenance from nature. Because nature also subjects human beings to actions outside of the subject, nature becomes that through which the human gets to know what they might be. Thus, Marx says that nature is 'man's inorganic body'.[160] This implies that the human's need 'to confirm his [sic] dispositions and capacities' in the world makes the human being into an always already suf-fering creature; but it is precisely through human suffering and neediness that

---

156   Marx 1973, p. 327.
157   Marx 1973, p. 328.
158   Marx 1973, p. 390.
159   Ibid.
160   Marx 1973, p. 328.

the human becomes objective.[161] If the human being did not suffer they would be entirely outside of the system of nature. As such, we can also say that it is through suffering that the possibility to realise one's nature remains open. From this it follows that the human being not only has their origins in human suffering, but that the human being continues to develop and transform themselves because they suffer. Marx therefore writes that the human is a passionate being, where passion is defined as 'man's [sic] essential power vigorously striving to attain its objects'.[162]

We have seen thus far that, for Marx, in order for there to be human subjectivity the human's essential nature must be objective, and this objectivity implies that the human's own nature is outside of itself. Objectivity is characterised as a relationship whereby the subject always exceeds what the subject is in its neediness. The third object created through the human's relation to nature is neither the purely subjective product of human powers nor is it an empirical object; it is rather mediated relationships. As a mediated relationship, that which is produced through the subject interacting with the object can never be fixed.

For Marx, human beings are constituted through relationships, and human need is always transformed by these relationships. Even though human neediness is what commands the human to seek objects, human sensibility is always already transformed through the very processes of objectification into a social activity. Since the human as a part of nature can only have a relationship to itself and to other humans precisely because the human can objectify nature, it must be that even in the most basic state of nature the individual is formed through relation, and is as such constituted by the social collective. Human need is therefore always something other than what it appears to be for itself.[163] When we speak of nature and human need we must speak of both as having a history, one whereby objects transform the subject; but since object and subject vary according to the perspective from which we view their relationship and yet are ultimately part of the process of transforming nature, we must take nature's history to be continuously transformative.

One might assume that this would make knowledge of the thing-in-itself impossible; after all, by definition what is knowable is that which can be fixed. But for Marx, even if objectification is relative, fluid and continuous, knowledge can grasp the fleeting and partial identification of subject and object that occurs through the process of objectification. Even if human beings' objective

---

161   Marx 1973, p. 389.
162   Marx 1973, p. 390.
163   Marx 1973, p. 391.

selves cannot be made obvious, their 'process of origin in *history*' is given to consciousness and can therefore be transcended.[164] For Marx the very possibility of knowledge is rooted in history; but this history is what constitutes social history – it is the history of human beings reconstituting themselves as objective being.

Another way of saying this is that the human being only has a relation to itself and to nature as objectified nature. For Marx the objects of the world, whether they are religion or property, are the history of the human objectification of nature. As society transforms itself, what it is transforming is the relation between subject and object. Such a transformation necessarily involves the development of different ways of appropriating nature. But this nature, which comes to us through human development, is the true nature of human history.

Nature thus exists as humans' existence for other humans.[165] Indeed, as Marx tells us, nature can only exist for humans precisely because humans are constituted as social creatures through nature. Marx therefore writes that nature exists for man as a bond with other men. In addition, Marx also declares that as social man, natural existence becomes human existence and nature becomes man for man: 'man's feelings and passions are historical and anthropological', but as such they are the 'truly ontological affirmations of his essence (nature)'.[166]

This is why Marx insists that the human is always the immediate object of both philosophy and natural science. Indeed, for Marx both the natural sciences and philosophy as they are constituted at the present moment are abstract and idealistic endeavours. This is because both of these fields of knowledge take nature to be something that can be cognised through trans-historical concepts. Yet if the human itself is constituted through the shifting relation between subject and object, then human perception must have a history that is imbricated in the history of nature as social being. To posit forms of cognition as trans-historical is to abstract human knowledge as outside of nature, but it is also to posit nature as outside of its very possibility.

At the same time, because reason's knowledge of the objects of the world is partial and historical, subject and object cannot be the same thing. After all, if they were to be the same thing there would be no relation between the two, and as such not only would the human's objectivity come to an end, but – since history is really human's relation to nature – history would also end. If the subject is to survive, the point is precisely to avoid taking human knowledge as a fixed

---

entity, for this would cancel out the very process that makes human objectivity possible. When Marx says that history is the only nature human beings can know, this should not be taken to mean that human knowledge is what allows human beings to maintain a dialogue with nature; rather, it is the human need to be objective that prepares nature to have a history for humans. Again, we can conclude that it is not human knowledge but human suffering that gives man access to nature, for 'suffering, humanely conceived, is an enjoyment of the self for man'.[167]

7   A Theory of Human Development

The process of alienating and conceptualising nature makes human thought a process of identity formation. But, in truth, what mediates this movement is the abrogation of necessity through human suffering (the desire for objectivity). What then allows for human activity is the paradoxical situation in which human beings can only produce knowledge when they take that which human thought objectifies as nature to be fixed; and yet history is the progressive movement of social being as non-identity.

Of course, this is not just the paradox of a few individual minds stuck with a stubborn form of thought. It is itself the problem of social life. If humans are social beings who know each other through the representation of nature that we create for ourselves, then it must be the case that the form of thought through which social life exists cannot be separated from its content. More specifically, we must say that the historical forms through which we represent ourselves – the objective tendencies of society – are correlated with social being. At the same time, if the progressive movement of history is the movement of subject and object as non-identity, then social being must necessarily contain a gap between the unity it has achieved and the plurality it must deny to that which is fixed and dominated. This gap must also be reflected in the real distance between subject and object that exists in the real world of praxis. Moreover, given that this gap between subject and object exists, we can say that history always contains its own negation. Social freedom must therefore involve tracing the historical shape of reason when it is absolutised.

We can conclude here that Marx takes as given that the human is the existence of nature for the human and that nature is the existence of the human for

---

167   Marx 1973, p. 351.

the human. Marx therefore refers to nature as an 'anthropological nature'.[168] This also means that rather than thinking about reason as the executor of history, we must follow Adorno and Horkheimer's suggestion in the *Dialectics of Enlightenment* and think of human reason as an epoch of natural history:

> [T]he brain or human intelligence is strong enough to form a regular epoch in the history of the world. The human race with its machines, chemicals and organization – which belong to it just as teeth belong to a bear ... – is the *dernier cri* of adaptation in this epoch.[169]

Following this, we can agree with Adorno and Horkheimer that abstraction is a part of human development, for if human beings are to produce knowledge they must take that which human thought objectifies as nature to be fixed. But, Adorno and Horkheimer warn, this means that the basis of the ego is the systematisation of the world according to its own self-image; that is, the 'I think' of human cognition (what Kant calls the transcendental self) takes itself to be eternal.[170] If we can say that human thought is inherently self-transformative, we must also conclude that the ego has a tendency to forget its own non-identity with the world; it forgets nature. The 'I think', which is developed and constituted through relations with the world is thus arrested in its very development. The implication of this for nature, which includes human life, is that it becomes a pure sign, whereby 'being is apprehended by administration'.[171] Alternatively, as Marx puts it, 'life itself appears only as a means to life'.[172]

Adorno and Horkheimer follow Marx in claiming that thought which fixes a connection between human thought and social freedom leads to historical and anthropological progress as well as to regression.[173] The problem with calling for subject-object identity is that it fixes the subject, which is then unable to

---

Marx 1973, p. 357.

169   Adorno and Horkheimer 1972.

170   Adorno and Horkheimer 1972, p. 35.

171   Ibid.

172   Marx 1973, p. 328.

173   That Marx sees social life up till now as both progress and regression is seen in his discussion of estranged labour in the first section of the *Economic and Philosophical Manuscripts*. Witness how he addresses this question: 'If the product of labour is alien to me and confronts me as an alien power to whom does it belong? The Gods? ... And what a paradox it would be if the more man subjugates nature through his labour and the more divine miracles are made superfluous by the miracles of industry, the more he is forced to forgo the joy of production and the enjoyment of the product out of deference to these powers'. Marx 1973, p. 330.

reflect on how it has come to have knowledge. Adorno and Horkheimer demonstrate that Marx's notion of 'dialectical anthropology'[174] differs from Lukàcs in so much as Lukàcs ultimately separates an historical form of subjectivity from its content and then posits it as trans-historical. Consequently, for Lukàcs the subject becomes the executor of history rather than something that is continuously constituted through historical relationships with nature and other human beings (as a part of nature). In Lukàcs both the form and the content of the self as a self-conscious subject are posited as having inherent qualities that can be set against the historical process. Concomitant with this is that for Lukàcs future actions can be predicted based on philosophical interpretations of the past. Indeed, Lukacs's interpretation of the past is based on projecting historically specific forms of human activity back into history as a whole.

Social revolution for Lukàcs becomes a process of discerning the movement of subject and object as framed by what he has constituted as real history. Lukàcs, therefore, demands more subject and object identity. But all that this can mean is that Lukàcs mistakes the finite for the infinite, and so demands the subsumption of all that is outside of domination into a historically specific form of human knowledge that has been erected as eternal. We learn with Adorno and Horkheimer that for a thinker like Lukàcs, thought becomes a mere means of enabling domination (subject-object identity) to become an end. Freedom, in this instance, does not transcend the given order, but rather ends up as 'a sanction of the world as its own yardstick'.[175]

We can argue, then, with Adorno and Horkheimer that the process of human development produces an over-valuation of the human mind. Consequently, domination of the object by the subject, which was once a means to achieve human ends, becomes an end itself: the human (who is nature) begins to posit their self-image of nature (domination) as eternal. Wrapped up in all this is the observation that human thought itself is both progress and regression at the same time:

> Mankind, whose versatility and knowledge become differentiated with the division of labour, is at the same time forced back to anthropologically more primitive stages.[176]

---

174 This phrase is taken from the Introduction to Adorno and Horkheimer 1972, p. xvii. However, it is my belief that the term is another way of talking about anthropological nature or a humanised nature, two terms Marx uses on numerous occasions in the 'Economic and Philosophical Manuscripts'.
175 Adorno and Horkheimer 1972, p. 26.
176 Adorno and Horkheimer 1972, p. 35.

Clearly, then, social life for Adorno and Horkheimer, as for Marx, contains a dual character, and that dual character is embodied in the dialectic of human activity as it develops through history. If we can say that in the early phase of human development adaptation demanded that human beings fix themselves in a manner similar to how they perceived the outer world, this also means that humans were able to represent life through their own self-images. When Lukàcs demands subject-object identity, what he is really demanding is that human life become its own frozen image: 'existence denied the light of reason, animal existence itself'.[177] I mean by this that life is unable to take as an object the process through which human activity comes to have a history. It is also for these reasons that Marx calls the attempt to reproduce social life under capitalism 'abstract labour' – it abstracts the human from their origin in nature. Marx therefore writes:

> The relation of private property contains latent within itself the relation of private property as *labour*, the relation of private property as *capital* and the connection of these two. On the one hand we have the production of human activity as *labour*, i.e., as an activity wholly alien to itself, to man and to nature, and hence to consciousness and vital expression, the *abstract* existence of man as a mere workman who therefore tumbles day after day from his fulfilled nothingness, into his social and hence real non-existence.[178]

And later:

> The cultivation of the five senses is the work of all previous history ... For a man who is starving the human form of food does not exist, only its abstract form exists; it could just as well be present in its crudest form, and it would be hard to say how this way of eating differs from that of animals.[179]

Together, these two quotes indicate to us that reason, for Marx, is the human species cognising its own self-creation as well as its alienation from its self-creation.

Earlier, we said that it is through suffering that human beings are able to cognise nature, and yet we see now that it is this very movement of human

---

suffering that undermines the human movement towards nature. However, we can now say that critical thought provides us a passage towards nature when the 'I think' of human perception measures the distance between its formality and its more substantive constitution as nature:

> The possibilities of reconciliation appear not in certainty unaffected by thought, in the pre-conceptual unity of perception and object, but in their considered opposition.[180]

Overall, then, I am claiming with Marx, as well as with Adorno and Horkheimer, that truth is revealed negatively, through exposing false absolutes. It follows from this that social being can only be explained through an examination of the image humans make of nature. This entails the examination of the historical relationship between subject and object. This is not a nostalgic move whereby the whole of nature would be made to appear to our present moment. Rather, progressive history begins with negating the eternal sameness that the human image of nature provides us with. This is not done in order to predict the future; instead it is an attempt, by means of a backward-looking gaze, to stop, in the future, the eternal repetition of today. Following from this, we can conclude that critical and revolutionary thought is not determined by an economic or a political crisis (as a Marxist Hegelian like Lukàcs might claim), nor by the unidirectional movement of history (as the so-called scientific socialists might claim); rather, it lies in opening up the contradictions of social being to self-critical thought.

Subjectivity is given to us when historically specific social forms organise experience. Human activity, then, is always both a social practice and a practice of the mind. When one experiences economic or political crisis, what one is experiencing is most certainly a crisis in thought, a crisis of language, and as such a crisis in the subject. An immanent critique of the way life is organised must therefore begin with an account of the production of human thought. Such an account would have to be a chronicle of both the manner through which human thought as subjectivity constitutes practice, and the practices through which thought is constituted.

Human life as historical life leads to a critique of knowledge. Human life as such contains within it an immanent obligation to become a critic of the social. The critical theorist must therefore ask: how can we transform the necessity of present conditions into a time where society can take its history as its own?

---

180   Adorno and Horkheimer 1972, p. 189.

The critical theorist begins their work by reconstructing the process through which humans experience the loss of an object. This is achieved by first historicising those objects that are taken as given. But as Horkheimer's essay on 'Materialism and Metaphysics' advises, where the relativist relates feelings of indignation, compassion, love and solidarity to a metaphysical worldview and thus to an absolute order, the materialist relates them to finite and historically produced phenomena.[181] Moreover, where the metaphysician reads the universal into the particular, the critical theorist reads the universal out of every particular. Obligation for the critical theorist must come from what is immanent to human knowledge – which is a social self that struggles to shape society and as such is aware of the relation between rational intention and its (failed) realisation.

At stake is the tricky terrain between theory and practice; and what we see is that the image of the present that we draw out does indeed matter. This is why in this research project I have been concerned with the social types, derived from the social sciences, that are deployed when trying to help all those poor Ethiopians. Yet, in another way, what matters is not people's self-understanding, but how this understanding is intimately part of the process of reproducing reality. As such, a description of one's social reality cannot help but also be a description of the social relations necessary to reproduce reality, and thus a particular way of being in the world. Within African studies, when we endlessly unravel local vs. colonial epistemologies we keep the conversation at the level of immediacy. But, in fact, what is more pressing are the ways in which these discussions remain untethered to a broader conception of reality and being: social forms and the content they produce remain divided in theory and in practice. But as such the individual's relation to his or herself, his or her activities, and his or her creativity also remains divided in theory and in practice. As we have been arguing, critical theory would need something more than this if it wants to truly engage the repressive practices embedded in social relations.

Walter Benjamin has written that human knowledge can only come from the 'air that we have breathed'.[182] This means that if something from the past comes to have historical necessity, it occurs posthumously through the struggles of

181 The overall description of the critical theorist that I have mobilised in this section of the current chapter is a paraphrase of the arguments contained in two essays by Max Horkheimer, 'Materialism and Metaphysics' and 'Traditional and Critical Theory', both in Horkheimer 1982. For a more specific discussion of a metaphysical description of life, see p. 23 of 'Materialism and Metaphysics'.
182 Benjamin 1968, p. 254.

generations that follow. The best human knowledge can achieve is the redemption of the past. For Benjamin, the historical-materialist must be concerned with the past, but only so that they can 'blast open the continuum of history'.[183] In so doing they ensure that what has been turned into a fact can be wrested from the victors and redeemed by those who appear outside of necessity. Indeed, for Benjamin, this is the obligation that the past renews with each coming generation: the obligation to be remembered, and as such to be redeemed for the future.

The point here is that when we delineate the transition of past, present and future as a linear process we imbue the present with a necessity that is not based in the air of human struggle. Instead, we get a one-sided history that reveals a content that might be good for the future, but which fails to address how the necessities of the past and present are established. Rather than an empty future ready to be fulfilled through human action, the cultural goods of the victors delimit the possibilities open to the losers of history. But this in turn cancels human freedom, for, following Benjamin, all that freedom should ever mean is the revelation of the contradictions of past human struggle and its redemption through self-conscious struggle in the present.

For Benjamin as for Marx, time as lived through anthropological nature is always out of joint with itself. The negation of anthropological nature is therefore immanent to the very notion of the anthropological flow of time. But while negation is immanent to anthropological nature it cannot just be assumed as an inevitable stage of history. Instead it must be conjured as a social practice through critical-practical thought. Benjamin's point in the 'Theses on the Philosophy of History' is that critical-practical thought must pry open the present flow of time through what is immanent to it: 'The past can be seized only as an image which flashes up at the instant when it can be recognised and is never seen again'.[184] This is to open homogenous empty time to potential futures sedimented within History 1. Our discussion of Benjamin here also returns us to Neocosmos and *Thinking Freedom in Africa*, since what we have been arguing in this chapter, alongside Neocosmos, is that to think freedom in Africa is to open up the future through halting what Neocosmos calls 'the reproduction of the regular and the habitual'.[185] Here we also see why a critique of African studies must rest on both a notion of social progress and a non-Eurocentric universalism.

---

183   Benjamin 1968, p. 252.
184   Benjamin 1968, p. 257.
185   Neocosmos 2016, p. 12.

Outdoing yesterday, shouldering on today,
Borrowing from tomorrow, renewing yesteryears,
Comes tizita (memory) hauling possessions.

8   Coda

As a concluding remark it might be useful to pause and consider how a recent
contribution to the Marxist historiography of revolution continues trends in
Eurocentric history-telling by presenting the case of the Ethiopian revolution
under the guise of historical necessity. I am thinking of Neil Davidson's book
How Revolutionary were the Bourgeois Revolutions?[186] In Davidson's rather large
book, which has something to say about nearly every major social movement
of the modern era, the Ethiopian revolution is posited as having merely acted
out a future that Ethiopian actors had little control in determining. Even if
Davidson is concerned with the contingent forces that shaped the origins of
capitalism, he argues that at a certain point in world history there comes to
be a moment of 'systemic irreversibility' in terms of how economies can be
organised.[187] Davidson locates that moment in the historical conjuncture created by the British victories in the Napoleonic wars, the collapse of European
empires in the Americas, and the emerging dominance of Britain and the royal
navy in international trade. He then goes on to argue that the rise of Britain
as a capitalist nation-state forced other European states to consider how to
support capitalist expansion and infrastructural coordination in their territories.[188] Davidson also shows that this stimulated a series of bourgeois revolutions from above, wherein the nation-state became the social and political form
through which to achieve a capitalist economy. For Davidson, this means that
most bourgeois revolutions after France in 1789 take on the character of reformist movements from above (perhaps with the exception of the American civil
war).[189]

   All well and good; however, towards the end of his book Davidson has a very
strange discussion of counter-factual history, where he goes to some length
to condemn historical studies that attempt to demonstrate that alternative
paths out of capitalist development have always existed within capitalism's

---

186   Davidson 2012.
187   Davidson 2012, p. 580.
188   Davidson 2012, p. 599.
189   Davidson 2012, p. 602.

history.[190] Under this rubric, Davidson discusses the work of historians such as Markus Rediker and Peter Linebaugh, whose well-known book *The Many Headed Hydra* documents multi-racial, anti-capitalist social movements during the revolutionary period in America. Davidson also discusses James Holstun's *Ehud's Dagger: Class Struggle in the English Revolution*, a work that among other things seeks to show that the Diggers were an important example of attempts to break with early forms of agrarian capitalism. Against these historians, Davidson argues that the real question raised by these case studies is whether these social movements could have been successful in 'their own right, rather than on behalf of the bourgeoisie'.[191] For Davidson, to posit marginal anti-capitalist social movements such as the Diggers as an alternative to the march of bourgeois history is to do counter-factual history, since the Diggers' confrontations with capitalism were never 'feasible'.[192] Davidson goes so far as to claim that our contemporary concern for these movements betrays a politics that is both voluntarist and distracting, since these movements at best reflect a backward-looking desire to escape capitalism rather than to confront capitalist social relations in the present. Thus, when Davidson says that the Ethiopian revolution was one of the last of the bourgeois revolutions, one assumes that what he means is that no confrontation with capitalism was 'feasible' in Ethiopia in 1974. Here, Davidson is implying that bourgeois revolution should be defined as that which removes the blocks to capitalist development; but he is also assuming not only that pre-revolutionary Ethiopia was pre-capitalist, but that a capitalist society must also be a bourgeois society. If our discussion of Jairus Banaji has taught us anything at all, however, it is that capitalist exploitation can happen under conditions where feudal lords remain as rulers.

For Davidson, to be a Marxist is to accept that only fully established bourgeois capitalism makes it possible to imagine a world where we can both overcome scarcity and organise the world as equals. The logic goes that, given that scarcity always trumps equality and is a beacon for hierarchy, until we have fully productive capitalism there will be inequality. Thus, while it might be important to have stories about anti-capitalist social movements, for Davidson, these stories are there only to remind us that once bourgeois relations are fully established our responsibility is to dredge up the past so as to 'wager' claims on behalf of the losers of history (and as such to wage social revolution).[193]

---

190   Davidson 2012, pp. 648–53.
191   Davidson 2012, p. 648.
192   Davidson 2012, p. 652.
193   See Davidson's discussion of Benjamin in Davidson 2012, p. 284.

Missing in Davidson's analysis is any sense that scarcity is subjected to changes in historical norms. After all, as we have seen, for Marx human needs are historical. For Davidson, it is only after bourgeois society is fully established that scarcity can be diminished. Of course, it is unclear when bourgeois society will be seen as fully established, and scarcity diminished, especially if our notions of scarcity are historical. When then is it 'feasible' to have a socially organised confrontation with capital? In 1848, 1917, 1989, or 2016?

Within Davidson's historiographical project there is very little need to deeply engage the reasons for the Ethiopian revolution or to ask how subsequent events played out, precisely because Ethiopia's relationship to world history is entirely derivative and rehearsed, and merely fits into a schema about the development of capitalist relationships. As a result, Davidson only needs a few lines to explain the vicissitudes of the Ethiopian revolution, thus emptying the Ethiopian struggle of any political content. Its future is simply someone else's past.

For us, while Davidson's historiographical project might be worthwhile in so much as it helps clarify how world-historical processes bear down on a poor country like Ethiopia, his work also forces us to ask if Ethiopia has lessons to offer the world when thinking about social change and the trajectory of world history. Is Ethiopia a part of the world or does the world just act on it, without it having its own lessons to give? Can the lessons be given both ways?

Bibliography

General Bibliography (Secondary Sources)

Abbink, J. 2006, 'Discomfiture of Democracy? The 2005 Election Crisis in Ethiopia and Its Aftermath', *African Affairs*, 105, 419: 173–99.

Adam, Achamyeleh Gashu 2014, 'The Challenges of Land Rights in the Transitional Peri-Urban Agricultural Areas of Ethiopia in the Era of Urbanization: A Property Rights Approach', presented at the 2014 conference on land policy in Africa, Addis Ababa, 11 November 2014.

Ademo, Mohammed and Hassen Hussein 2015, 'The Unrest in Ethiopia', available at http://africasacountry.com/2015/12/the-unrest-in-ethiopia/.

Adorno, Theodor and Max Horkheimer 1972 [1947], *Dialectic of Enlightenment*, translated by Edmund Jephcott, New York: Continuum.

Aglionby, John and Feng, Emily June 3 2018, "China Scales Back Investment in Ethiopia", *Financial Times*, available at: https://www.ft.com/content/06b69c2e-63e9-11e8-90c2-9563a0613e56

Akram-Lodhi, Haroon, Cristóbal Kay, and Saturino Borras 2007, *Land Poverty and Livelihoods in an Era of Globalization: Perspectives from Developing and Transition Countries*, London: Routledge.

Alemu, Ashebir n.d., 'Comments on John Markakis' "Amhara": What Is in a Name,' available at http://www.ethiomedia.com/courier/comments_on_markakis.html.

Amadiume, Ifi 1997, *Re-Inventing Africa: Matriarchy, Religion, and Culture*, London: Zed Books.

Amin, Samir 1972, 'Underdevelopment and Dependence in Black Africa: Origins and Contemporary Forms', *Journal of Modern African Studies*, 10, 4: 503–24.

Amin, Samir 1977, *Unequal Development: An Essay on the Social Formations of Peripheral Capitalism*, New York: Monthly Review Press.

Asad, Talal (ed.) 1973, *Anthropology and the Colonial Encounter*, Reading: Ithaca Press.

Bach, Jean-Nicolas 2015, 'New Trends, Old Views: The Ambivalent Centre-Periphery Paradigm of Ethiopian Studies', in *Ethiopian Studies – Proceedings ICES 18*, edited by Eloi Ficquet and Ahmed Hassan: 275–88.

Balsvik, Randi 1994, *Haile Selassie's Students: The Intellectual and Social Background to Revolution, 1952–1977*, Lansing: Michigan State University Press.

Banaji, Jairus 2010, 'Response to Arundhati Roy', available at http://kafila.org/2010/03/22/response-to-arundhati-roy-jairus-banaji.

Banaji, Jairus 2011a, *Theory as History: Essays on Modes of Production and Exploitation*, Chicago: Haymarket Books.

Banaji, Jairus 2011b, 'Fascism, Maoism and the Democratic Left', *Infochange News and*

Views, available at http://infochangeindia.org/governance/71-governance/analysis/ 8872-fascism-maoism-and-the-democratic-left.

Barchiesi, Franco 2012, 'Precarity as Capture: A Conceptual Reconstruction and Critique of the Worker-Slave Analogy', presented at the International Colloquium 'The Politics of Precarious Society', Johannesburg, 5 September 2012, available at http:// works.bepress.com/franco_barchiesi/36.

Bayat, Asef 2017, *Revolution without Revolutionaries: Making Sense of the Arab Spring*, Stanford: Stanford University Press.

Bayat, Asef 2017, *Revolution without Revolutionaries: Making Sense of the Arab Spring*, Stanford: Stanford University Press.

Bayart, Jean-Francois 1994, *The State in Africa: The Politics of the Belly*, London: Longman Publishers.

Benjamin, Walter 1968 [1940], 'Theses on the Philosophy of History', in *Illuminations*, edited by Hannah Arendt, translated by Harry Zohn, New York: Schocken Books.

Bennett, John 1983, 'Tigray: Famine and National Resistance', *Review of African Political Economy*, 10, 26: 94–102.

Bernstein, Henry 2004a, '"Changing Before Our Very Eyes": Agrarian Questions and the Politics of Land in Capitalism Today', *Journal of Agrarian Change*, 4, 1&2: 190–225.

Bernstein, Henry 2004b, 'Considering Africa's Agrarian Question', *Historical Materialism*, 12, 4: 115–44.

Bhattacharya, Tithi and Lise Vogel (eds.) 2017, *Social Reproduction Theory: Remapping Class, Recentering Oppression*, London: Pluto Press.

Brenner, Robert 1976, 'Agrarian Class Structure and Economic Development in Pre-Industrial Europe', *Past and Present*, 70: 30–74.

Brenner, Robert 1977, 'The Origins of Capitalist Development: A Critique of Neo-Smithian Marxism', *New Left Review*, 104: 25–92.

Brenner, Robert 1986, 'The Social Basis of Economic Development', in *Analytical Marxism*, edited by J. Roemer, Cambridge, UK: Cambridge University Press.

Brown, S.C. (ed.) 1979, *Philosophical Disputes in the Social Sciences*, Sussex: Harvester Press.

Caporaso, James A., and David P. Levine 1992, *Theories of Political Economy*, Cambridge: Cambridge University Press.

Carmody, Pádraig 2017, 'Variegated Capitalism in Africa: The Role of Industrial Policy', *Review of African Political Economy*, available at http://roape.net/2017/01/04/variegat ed-capitalism-africa-role-industrial-policy/.

Césaire, Aimé 2001 [1939], *Notebook of a Return to the Native Land*, translated by Clayton Eshelman and Annette Smith. Middletown: Wesleyan University Press.

Chabal, Patrick, and Jean-Pascal Daloz 1999, *Africa Works: Disorder as Political Instrument*, Bloomington: Indiana University Press.

Chakrabarty, Dipesh 2000, *Provincializing Europe: Postcolonial Thought and Historical Difference*, Princeton: Princeton University Press.

Chatterjee, Partha 1999, 'Nationalist Thought and the Colonial World', in *The Partha Chatterjee Omnibus*, Oxford: Oxford University Press.

Clapham, Christopher 1990, *Transformation and Continuity in Revolutionary Ethiopia*, African Studies Series 61, Cambridge: Cambridge University Press.

Clapham, Christopher 2005, 'Comments on the Ethiopian Crisis', available at http://www.ethiopians.com/Election2005/ChristopherClapham_CommentsonEthiopian Crisis.htm.

Cliffe, Lionel 2004, 'Obituary of Abdul-Mejid Hussein', *Review of African Political Economy*, 31, 101: 545–6.

Clifford, James and George Marcus (eds.) 1999, *Writing Culture: The Poetics and Politics of Ethnography*, Berkeley: University of California Press.

Cohen, John 1980, 'Analyzing the Ethiopian Revolution: A Cautionary Tale', *Journal Of Modern African Studies*, 18, 4: 685–91.

Connell, Dan 1982, '*Eritrea: Africa's Longest War* by David Pool', *Review of African Political Economy*, 9, 23: 111–12.

Connell, Dan 1993, *Against All Odds: A Chronicle of the Eritrean Movement*, Trenton: Red Sea Press.

Cowan, Nicola Anne 1983, 'Women in Eritrea: An Eye-Witness Account Briefing', *Review of African Political Economy*, 10, 27/28: 143–52.

Cooper, Frederick 1981, 'Africa and the World Economy', *African Studies Review*, 24, 2/3: 1–86.

Cowen, Michael 1998, 'Reviewed Work: *The History of Development: From Western Origins to Global Faith* by Gilbert Rist', *Canadian Journal of African Studies / Revue Canadienne Des Études Africaines*, 32, 1: 240–44.

Cumming, D.C. 1953, 'British Stewardship of the Italian Colonies: An Account Rendered', *Royal Institute of International Affairs*, 29, 1: 11–21.

Davidson, Neil 2012, *How Revolutionary Were the Bourgeois Revolutions?*, Chicago: Haymarket Books.

Davidson, Neil 2015, 'The Prophet, His Biographer and the Watchtower', *International Socialism Journal*, 104, available at http://pubs.socialistreviewindex.org.uk/isj104/davidson.htm.

Debray, Régis 1967, *Revolution in the Revolution?: Armed Struggle in Latin America*, translated by Bobbye Ortiz, New York: Grove Press.

Deininger, Klaus, Jin Songqing, Berhanu Adnew, Samuel G. Selassie, and Mulat Demeke 2003, 'Market and Non-Market Transfers of Land in Ethiopia: Implications for Efficiency, Equity and Non-Farm Development', World Bank Working Paper, Washington, DC: The World Bank.

Deininger, Klaus, Jin Songqing, Adnew Berhanu, Samuel G. Selassie, and Berhanu Nega 2004, 'Tenure Security and Land-Related Investment: Evidence from Ethiopia,' in *Proceedings of the First International Conference on the Ethiopian Economy*, edited by Alemayehu Seyoum, Addis Ababa: Ethiopian Economic Association.

Dobb, Maurice 1963, *Studies in the Development of Capitalism*, London: Routledge & Kegan Paul.

Donham, Donald 1999, *Marxist Modern: An Ethnographic History of The Ethiopian Revolution*, Berkley: University of California Press.

Donham, Donald and Wendy James (eds.) 1986, *The Southern Marches of Imperial Ethiopia*, Cambridge: Cambridge University Press.

Editorial Board 2016, 'Ethiopia Silences Its Critics with a Deadly Crackdown on Dissent,' *Washington Post*, available at http://wpo.st/Awh-2.

Edwards, Brent Hayes 2003, *The Practice of Diaspora: Literature, Translation, and the Rise of Black Internationalism*, Cambridge: Harvard University Press.

Escobar, Arturo 1995, *Encountering Development: The Making and Unmaking of the Third World*, Princeton: Princeton University Press.

Escobar, Arturo 1998, 'Imagining a Post-Development Future', In *The Power of Development*, edited by Jonathan Crush, New York: Routledge.

Eshete, Andreas 1981, 'On Fraternity', *The Review of Metaphysics*, 35, 1: 27–44.

Eshete, Andreas 1993, 'Implementing Human Rights and a Democratic Constitution in Ethiopia', *Issue: A Journal of Opinion*, 21, 1/2.

Evans, Richard J. 2014, '"What If" Is a Waste of Time', *The Guardian UK*, 13 March 2014.

Eze, Emmanuel Chukwudi (ed.) 1997, *Postcolonial African Philosophy: A Critical Reader*, Cambridge, Mass: Blackwell.

Fanon, Frantz 2004 [1961], *The Wretched of the Earth*, translated by Richard Philcox, New York: Grove Press.

Fanon, Frantz 2008 [1952], *Black Skin, White Masks*, translated by Charles Lam Markman, London: Pluto Press.

Freud, Sigmund 1955 [1919], 'The Uncanny', in *The Standard Edition of the Complete Psychological Works of Sigmund Freud*, translated by James Strachey, Volume 17, London: Hogarth Press.

G, Surafel, 2002, 'Ethiopia: Abdulmejid Hussein: Love for Public Service', *AllAfrica.com*, available at http://allafrica.com/stories/200106110310.html.

Gebre-Medhin, Jordan 1984, 'Nationalism, Peasant Politics and the Emergence of a Vanguard Front in Eritrea', *Review of African Political Economy*, 11, 30: 48–57.

Gebre-Medhin, Jordan 1989, *Peasants and Nationalism in Eritrea: A Critique of Ethiopian Studies*, Trenton: Red Sea Press.

Gilroy, Paul 1995, *The Black Atlantic: Modernity and Double Consciousness*, Cambridge: Harvard University Press.

Gordon, Avery 2008, *Ghostly Matters: Haunting and the Sociological Imagination*, Minneapolis: University of Minnesota Press.

Gyekye, Kwame 1987, *An Essay on African Philosophical Thought: The Akan Conceptual Scheme*, Cambridge: Cambridge University Press.

Gyekye, Kwame 1997, *Tradition and Modernity: Philosophical Reflections on the African Experience*, Oxford: Oxford University Press.

Habte-Selassie, Bereket, Lionel Cliffe, and Basil Davidson 1980, *Behind the War in Eritrea*, Nottingham: Spokesman.

Haddis, Ezana 2014, 'How Not to Make a Master Plan', *Addis Standard*, available at http://addisstandard.com/how-not-to-make-a-master-plan/.

Hagmann, Tobias 2006, 'Ethiopian Political Culture Strikes Back: A Rejoinder to J. Abbink', *African Affairs*, 105: 605–12.

Haile-Mariam, Yacob, 2009, 'We Were Not Capable of Fulfilling Our Duties and Responsibilities to the Ethiopian People', *Ethiopian Reporter*, 21 November 2009.

Halliday, Fred 1990, 'The Ends of the Cold War', *New Left Review*, 180: 5–24.

Halliday, Fred and Maxine Molyneux 1982, *The Ethiopian Revolution*, London: Verso.

Hammer, Joshua 2016, 'Berhanu Nega's War', *New York Times Sunday Magazine*, 4 September 2016.

Hammond, Jenny 1990, *Sweeter Than Honey: Ethiopian Women and Revolution: Testimonials of Tigrayan Women*, Trenton: Red Sea Press.

Hassen, Hussein and Adema, Mohammed November 11, 2017 "Ethiopia: Is OPDO the new opposition party? An Appraisal", *OPride*, available at: https://www.opride.com/2017/11/11/ethiopia-is-opdo-the-new-opposition-party-an-appraisal/.

Herbst, Jeffrey 2014, *States and Power in Africa: Comparative Lessons in Authority and Control*, Princeton: Princeton University Press.

Hiwet, Addis 1975, *Ethiopia: From Autocracy to Revolution*, London: Review of African Political Economy.

Horkheimer, Max 1972 [1968] *Critical Theory: Selected Essays*, translated by Matthew J. O'Connell and others, New York: Continuum.

Horton, Robin 1967, 'African Traditional Thought and Western Science', *Africa: Journal of the International African Institute*, 37, 2: 155–87.

Horton, Robin and Ruth H. Finnegan (eds.) 1973, *Modes of Thought: Essays on Thinking in Western and Non-Western Societies*, London: Faber.

Hountondji, Paulin J. 1983 [1976], *African Philosophy: Myth and Reality*, translated by H. Evans and J. Rée, Bloomington: Indiana University Press.

Hussein, Hassen and Mohammed Ademo 2016, 'Ethiopia's Original Sin,' *World Policy Journal*, 33, 3: 22–8.

Hydén, Göran 1980, *Beyond Ujamaa in Tanzania: Underdevelopment and the Uncaptured Peasantry*, London: Heinemann.

Hydén, Göran 1983, *No Shortcuts to Progress: African Development Management in Perspective*, London: Heinemann.

Idahosa, Pablo and Bob Shenton 2006, 'The Layers of Social Capital', *African Studies*, 65, 1: 63–78.

Inikori, J.E. 2002, *Africans and the Industrial Revolution in England: A Study in International Trade and Economic Development*, Cambridge: Cambridge University Press.

Isaacman, Allen 2003, 'Legacies of Engagement: Scholarship Informed by Political Commitment', *African Studies Review*, 46, 1: 1–41.

James, C.L.R. 1963, *Beyond a Boundary*, London: Stanley Paul.

Javed, Akram 2012, 'Bourgeois Democracy and Its Others: A Response to Jairus Banaji', *Sanhati: Fighting Neo-Liberalism in Bengal and Beyond*, available at http://sanhati .com/excerpted/5683/.

Jewsiewicki, Bogumil 1989, 'African Historical Studies Academic Knowledge as "Usable Past" and Radical Scholarship', *African Studies Review*, 32, 4: 1–76.

Kandil, Hazem 2014, *Soldiers, Spies and Soldiers: Egypt's Role to Revolt*, London: Verso.

Kebede, Messay 2008, *Radicalism and Cultural Dislocation in Ethiopia, 1960–1974*, Rochester: University of Rochester Press.

Khogali, Mustafa 1977, 'Editorial: The Horn of Africa,' *Review of African Political Economy*, 4, 10: 7.

Kifle, B. 1994, 'Class Struggle or Jockeying for Position: A Review of Ethiopian Student Movements from 1900–1975', in *The Role of African Student Movements in the Political and Social Evolution of Africa, From 1900–1975*, Paris: UNESCO Publishing.

Kitching, Gavin 2000, 'Why I Gave up African Studies', *Mots Pluriels*, 16, available at http://motspluriels.arts.uwa.edu.au/MP1600gk.html.

Lefort, René 1983 [1981], *Ethiopia: An Heretical Revolution*, translated by A.M. Berret, London: Zed Publishers.

Lefort, René 2007, 'Powers – Mengist – and Peasants in Rural Ethiopia: The May 2005 Elections', *Journal Of Modern African Studies*, 45, 2: 253–73.

Levine, Donald 1974, *Greater Ethiopia: The Evolution of a MultiEthnic Society*, Chicago: University of Chicago Press.

Leys, Colin 1996, *The Rise & Fall of Development Theory*, Bloomington: Indiana University Press.

Lukács, Georg 1988 [1923], 'Reification and the Consciousness of the Proletariat', in *History and Class Consciousness*, translated by Rodney Livingston, Cambridge, MA: MIT Press.

Lyons, Terence 2006, 'Ethiopia in 2005: The Beginning of a Transition?', Washington D.C.: Center for Strategic Studies.

Lyons, Terence 2007, 'Conflict-Generated Diasporas and Transnational Politics in Ethiopia', *Conflict, Security & Development*, 7, 4: 529–49.

MacLeod, Erin 2014, *Visions of Zion: Ethiopians and Rastafari in the Search for the Promised Land*, New York: NYU Press.

Mafeje, Archie 1997, 'Who Are the Makers and Objects of Anthropology?', *African Sociological Review*, 1, 1: 5–23.

Mafeje, Archie 2000, 'Africanity: A Combative Ontology', *CODESRIA Bulletin*, 1: 66–71.

Mamdani, Mahmood 1996, *Citizen and Subject: Contemporary Africa and the Legacy of Late Colonialism*, Princeton: Princeton University Press.

Marcus, George E. 1998, *Ethnography through Thick and Thin*, Princeton: Princeton University Press.

Marcus, George E. and Michael M.J. Fischer 1986, *Anthropology as Cultural Critique: An Experimental Moment in the Human Sciences*, Chicago: University of Chicago Press.

Markakis, John 1981, 'The Military State and Ethiopia's Path Towards Socialism', *Review of African Political Economy*, 21: 7–25.

Markakis, John 1996, 'The Horn of Africa', *Review of African Political Economy*, 30, 70: 469–74.

Markakis, John and Nega Ayele 1977, 'Class and Revolution in Ethiopia', *Review of African Political Economy*, 8: 99–108.

Markakis, John and Nega Ayele 1986, *Class and Revolution in Ethiopia*, Trenton: Red Sea Press.

Markakis, John and Lionel Cliffe 1984, 'Editorial: Conflict in the Horn of Africa', *Review of African Political Economy*, 11, 30: 1–7.

Marx, Karl 1973, *Karl Marx: Early Writings*, translated by Rodney Livingston and Gregory Benton, London: Penguin Books.

Marx, Karl 1976 [1867], *Capital, Vol. I*, translated by Ben Fowkes, London: Penguin Books.

Marx, Karl and Friedrich Engels 2006 [1848], *Manifesto of the Communist Party*, New York: Cosimo.

Masolo, D.A. 1994, *African Philosophy in Search of Identity*, Bloomington: Indiana University Press.

Mbembe, Achille 2001, *On the Postcolony*, Berkeley: University of California Press.

Mbembe, Achille 2002, 'African Modes of Self-Writing', *Public Culture*, 14, 1: 239–73.

Mbembe, Achille 2003, 'Necropolitics', *Public Culture*, 15, 1: 11–40.

McNally, David 2001, *Bodies of Meaning: Studies on Language, Labor, and Liberation*, Albany: State University of New York Press.

Mengestu, Dinaw 2011, *How to Read the Air*, New York: Riverhead Books.

Mengiste, Maaza 2010, *Beneath the Lion's Gaze: A Novel*, New York: W.W. Norton.

Merera, Gudina 2003, *Ethiopia: Competing Ethnic Nationalism, 1960–2000*, Addis Ababa: Chamber Printing House.

Mohan, Giles 1997, 'Radicalism, Relevance & the Future of ROAPE', *Review of African Political Economy*, 25, 76: 263–73.

Mudimbe, V.Y. 1983, 'African Philosophy as an Ideological Practice: The Case of French-Speaking Africa', *African Studies Review*, 26, 3/4: 133–54.

Mudimbe, V.Y. 1988, *The Invention of Africa: Gnosis, Philosophy, and the Order of Knowledge*, Bloomington: Indiana University Press.

Nega, Berhanu 2003, 'Ethiopia's Fate After One Generation', presented at the Vision 2020 Conference, Addis Ababa, available at http://www.ethiotube.net/video/11154/ESAT--Dr-Berhanu-Negas-famous-Vision-2020-Speech--Ethiopias-fate-after-one-generation. Accessed March 15, 2016.

Neocosmos, Michael 2016, *Thinking Freedom in Africa: Toward a Theory of Emancipatory Politics*, Johannesberg, South Africa: Wits University Press.

Oqubay, Arkebe 2015, *Made in Africa: Industrial Policy in Ethiopia*, Oxford: Oxford University Press.

Oruka, Henry Odera 1997, *Practical Philosophy: In Search of an Ethical Minimum*, Nairobi: East African Educational Publishers.

Osborne, Peter 1992, 'Modernity Is a Qualitative, Not a Chronological, Category', *New Left Review*, 192: 65–84.

Ottaway, David, and Marina Ottaway 1978, *Ethiopia: Empire in Revolution*, New York: Africana Publishing House.

Patnaik, U. 1990, 'Some Economic and Political Consequences of the Green Revolution in India', in *The Food Question*, edited by Henry Bernstein, London: Monthly Review Press.

Paulos Milkias, Haile-Selassie 2006, *Western Education and Political Revolution in Ethiopia*, New York: Cambria Press.

Poole, David 1980, 'Revolutionary Crisis and Revolutionary Vanguard: The EPLF (Eritrean People's Liberation Front)', *Review of African Political Economy*, 7, 19: 33–47.

Poole, David 1982, *Eritrea: Africa's Longest War*, London: Anti-Slavery Society.

Postel, Danny 2003, 'Out of Africa: A Pioneer of African Studies Explains Why He Left the Field, and Provokes a Firestorm of Debate within It', *Chronicle of Higher Education*, 28 March 2003, available at http://www.chronicle.com/article/Out-of-Africa/26109.

Postel, Danny 2015, 'Who Is Responsible: An Interview with Fred Halliday', *Open Democracy*, available at https://www.opendemocracy.net/danny-postel/who-is-responsible-interview-with-fred-halliday.

Postone, Moishe 2003, 'Lukács and the Dialectical Critique of Capitalism', in *New Dialectics and Political Economy*, edited by Robert Albritton and John Simoulidis, London: Palgrave.

Rahmato, Dessalegn 1984, *Agrarian Reform In Ethiopia*, Uppsala: Scandinavian Institute of African Studies.

Rahmato, Dessalegn 2008, 'The Voluntary Sector in Ethiopia', in *Civil Society at the Crossroads*, edited by Bahru Zewde and Taye Assefa, Addis Ababa: Forum for Social Studies.

Rahmeto (sic), Dessalegn, Belay Ejigu, Mesfin Wolde-Mariam, and Beyene Haile 1997, 'Roundtable Discussion on "Food Security and Rural Land Policy"', *Economic Focus*: 10.

Rigby, Peter 1992, 'Practical Ideology and Ideological Practice: On African Episteme and Marxian Problematic – Ilparakuyo Masai Transformations', in *The Surreptitious Speech: Presence Africaine and the Politics of Otherness 1947–1998*, edited by V.Y. Mudimbe, Chicago: University of Chicago Press.

ROAPE Editorial Board 1974, 'Editorial: Development In Africa', *Review of African Political Economy*, 1, 1: 1–8.

ROAPE Editorial Board 1985, 'Inside the Review of African Political Economy', *Review of African Political Economy* 12, 32: 95–101.

Russet, Peter, Joseph Collins, and Frances Moore Lappe 2000, 'Lessons from the Green Revolution', *Tikkun*.

Sall, Ebrima 2003, *The Social Sciences in Africa: Trends, Issues, Capacities and Constraints*, New York: Social Science Research Council.

Scott, David 2004, *Conscripts of Modernity: The Tragedy of Colonial Enlightenment*, Durham: Duke University Press.

Scott, David 2008, 'Introduction: On the Archaeologies of Black Memory', *Small Axe*, 12, 2: v–xvi.

Sekyi-Otu, Ato 1996, *Fanon's Dialectic of Experience*, Cambridge: Harvard University Press.

Serequeberhan, Tsenay (ed.) 1991, *African Philosophy: The Essential Readings*, St. Paul: Paragon Press.

Serequeberhan, Tsenay 1997, 'The Critique of Eurocentrism and the Practice of African Philosophy', in *Post-Colonial African Philosophy: A Critical Reader*, edited by Emmanuel Chukwudi Eze, Cambridge: Blackwell.

Sexton, Jared 2011, 'The Social Life of Social Death: On Afro-Pessimism and Black Optimism', *Intensions Journal*, 5.

Shivji, Issa G. 2006, *The Silences in the NGO Discourse: The Role and Future of NGOs in African*, Nairobi: Fahamu.

Sitas, Ari 2006, 'The African Renaissance Challenge and Sociological Reclamations in the South', *Current Sociology*, 54, 3: 357–80.

Sklar, Richard 1993, 'The African Frontier for Political Science', in *Africa and the Disciplines: The Contributions of Research in Africa to the Social Sciences and Humanities*, edited by Robert H. Bates, V.Y. Mudimbe, and Jean F. O'Barr, Chicago: University of Chicago Press.

Spivak, Gayatri Chakravorty 1998, 'Can the Subaltern Speak?', in *Marxism and the Interpretation of Culture*, edited by Cary Nelson and Lawrence Grossberg. Urbana: University of Illinois Press.

Sterling, Joseph Coleman Jr. 2010, 'No Independence without Sovereignty! The Resistance of Emperor Ḥaylä Śällase I to the British Occupation of Ethiopia (1941–1944)', *Aethiopica*, 13: 46–74.

Stevis-Gridneff, Matina 2018, "Ethiopia Opens Door To The World With Unprecedented Privatization Plan", *Wall Street Journal*, 6 June, available at: https://www.wsj.com/articles/ethiopia-opens-door-to-the-world-with-unprecedented-privatization-plan-1528275922

Sweezy, Paul 1976, *The Transition from Feudalism to Capitalism*, London: Verso.

Tareke, Gebru 2009, *The Ethiopian Revolution*, New Haven: Yale University Press.

Tareke, Gebru 2013, *Ethiopian Revolution: War in the Horn of Africa*, New Haven: Yale University Press.

Teferra, Hiwot 2012, *Tower in the Sky*, Addis Ababa: Addis Ababa University Press.

Tesfai, Alemseged 2003, 'Land & Liberation in Eritrea: Reflecting on the Work of Lionel Cliffe', *Review of African Political Economy*, 30, 96: 249–54.

Tiruneh, Andargachew 2009, *The Ethiopian Revolution, 1974–1987: A Transformation from an Aristocratic to a Totalitarian Autocracy*, Cambridge: Cambridge University Press.

Triulzi, Alessandro 2002, 'Battling with the Past. New Frameworks for Ethiopian Historiography', in *Remapping Ethiopia: Socialism and After*, edited by Wendy James, Alessandro Triulzi, and E. Kurimoto, Oxford: James Curry.

Tronvoll, Kjetil and Sarah Vaughan 2003, *The Culture of Power*, Stockholm: Swedish International Development Coordination Agency.

Tsegaye, Michael, 2011–12, *Future Memories*, available at http://www.michaeltsegaye .com/album/future-memories?p=1#14.

Vaughan, Sarah 2003, 'Ethnicity and Power in Ethiopia', PhD Dissertation, University of Edinburgh.

Wallerstein, Immanuel 1998, 'A Comment on Epistemology: What Is Africa?', *Canadian Journal of African Studies / Revue Canadienne Des Études Africaines*, 22, 2: 331–3.

Weibel, Jacob 2015, 'Let The Red Terror Intensify: Political Violence, Governance and Society in Urban Ethiopia, 1976–78', *International Journal of African Historical Studies*, 48, 1: 13–30.

Wibke, Crewitt and Korf Benedikt 2008, 'Ethiopia: Reforming Land Tenure', *Review of African Political Economy*, 35, 116, 203–220.

Williams, Raymond 1977, *Marxism and Literature*, Oxford: Oxford University Press.

Williams, Raymond 1979, *Modern Tragedy*, London: Verso.

Winch, Peter 1964, 'Understanding a Primitive Society', *American Philosophical Quarterly*, 1, 4: 307–24.

Winch, Peter 1970, 'The Idea of Social Science', in *Rationality: Key Concepts in the Social Sciences*, edited by Bryan Wilson, London: Basil Blackwell.

Wiredu, Kwasi 1996, *Cultural Universals and Particulars: An African Perspective*, Bloomington: Indiana University Press.

Wobshet, Dagmawit 2009, 'Tizita: A New World Interpretation', *Callaloo*, 32, 2: 629–34.

Wolde-Mariam, Mesfin 2002, 'The Spirit of America: A Moral Responsibility to Humanity', presented at Clark University, November 2002, available at http://www.mesfinw oldemariam.org/docs/MWM_Spirit_of_America.pdf. Accessed March 15, 2016.

Wolde-Mariam, Mesfin 2003a, 'Whither Ethiopia', presented at the Vision 2020, available at http://www.mesfinwoldemariam.org/docs/VISION2020.pdf.

Wolde-Mariam, Mesfin 2003b, 'One Cannot Make the Donkey Move by Beating the

Load. Breaking the Cycle of Recurrent Famine in Ethiopia', presented at the Christian Relief and Development Agency, Economic Commission for Africa, July 2003, available at http://www.mesfinwoldemariam.org/docs/MWM_CRDA_Famine_2003 .pdf. Accessed March 15, 2016.

Wood, Ellen 1990, 'The Uses and Abuses of "Civil Society"', *Socialist Register*, 26: 60–84.

Wood, Ellen Meiksins 2002a, 'Question of Market Dependence', *Journal of Agrarian Studies*, 2, 1: 50–87.

Wood, Ellen Meiksins 2002b, *The Origin of Capitalism: A Longer View*, New York: Verso.

Woubshet, Dagmawi 2010, 'An Interview with Andreas Eshete', *Callaloo*, 33, 1.

Young, John 1996, 'Ethnicity and Power in Ethiopia', *Review of African Political Economy*, 23, 70: 531–42.

Young, John 1997, *Peasant Revolution in Ethiopia*, London: Cambridge University Press.

Zeleke, Elleni Centime 2010, 'Addis Ababa as Modernist Ruin', *Callaloo* 33, 1: 117–35.

Zeleza, Paul Tiyambe 1997, *Manufacturing African Studies and Crises*, Dakar: CO-DESRIA.

Zeleza, Paul Tiyambe 2002, 'The Politics of Historical and Social Science Research in Africa', *Journal of Southern African Studies*, 28: 9–23.

Zewde, Bahru 2001, *A History of Modern Ethiopia, 1855–1991*, London: James Currey.

Zewde, Bahru 2002, *Pioneers of Change in Ethiopia: The Reformist Intellectuals of the Early Twentieth Century*, London: James Currey.

Zewde, Bahru 2004, 'What Did We Dream? What Did We Achieve? And Where Are We Heading?', *Addis Tribune*, 23 April 2004.

Zewde, Bahru (ed.) 2010, *Documenting the Ethiopian Student Movement: An Exercise in Oral History*, Addis Ababa: Forum for Social Studies.

Zewde, Bahru 2014, *The Quest for Socialist Utopia. the Ethiopian Student Movement, C. 1960–1974*, London: James Currey.

Zewde, Bahru, and Taye Assefa 2008, *Civil Society at the Crossroads: Challenges and Perspectives in Ethiopia*, Addis Ababa: Forum for Social Studies.

Reports

African-American Institute 1976, 'Final Report African Scholarship Program of American Universities', New York: African-American Institute.

Ambaye, Daniel Weldegebriel 2013, 'Land Rights and Expropriation in Ethiopia', Stockholm: School of Architecture and the Built Environment, Royal Institute of Technology.

Amnesty International 2005, 'Ethiopia: The 15 May 2005 Elections and Human Rights', available at http://www.refworld.org/pdfid/42ae98270.pdf.

Areda, Alemayehu 2007, *Maximizing Local CSOs Civic Engagement Potential in Ethiopia*, Addis Ababa: Organization for Social Justice in Ethiopia.

EU Election Observation Mission Ethiopia 2005, 'Final Report on the Legislative Elections', Brussels: EU.

Gorham, Roger 2014, 'Addis Ababa Urban and Metropolitan Transport and Land Use Linkages Strategy Review', Washington D.C.: World Bank Group.

Human Rights Watch 2008, 'Analysis: Ethiopia's Draft Civil Society Law', New York: Human Rights Watch, available at https://www.hrw.org/news/2008/10/13/analysis -ethiopias-draft-civil-society-law.

InterAfrica Group 1993, 'Genesis of the Ethiopian Constitution of 1994: Reflections and Recommendations from the Symposium on the Making of the 1994 Ethiopian Consitution – 17–21 May 1993, Addis Ababa, Ethiopia', Addis Ababa.

International Crisis Group 2009, 'Ethiopia: Ethnic Federalism and Its Discontent', Brussels: International Crisis Group, available at http://www.crisisgroup.org/africa/horn -africa/ethiopia/ethiopia-ethnic-federalism-and-its-discontents.

International Fund for Agricultural Development 2013, 'Smallholders, Food Security, and the Environment', Rome, Italy: International Fund for Agricultural Development.

International Monetary Fund 2018, 'Staff Report for the 2017 Article IV Consultation and Statement by the Executive Director for the Federal Democratic Republic of Ethiopia', Washington D.C.: International Monetary Fund.

Nega, Berhanu 2002, *A Research Report on Land Tenure and Agriculture: Development in Ethiopia*, Addis Ababa: Ethiopian Economics Association/Ethiopian Economic Policy Research Institute.

Newman, Carol and Page, John 2017, *Industrial clusters – The case for Special Economic Zones in Africa*, WIDER Working Paper 2017/15, Helsinki: United Nation University World Institute for Development Economics Research

Rahmato, Dessalegn, Akalewold Bantirgu, and Yoseph Endeshaw 2008, *CSOs / NGOs in Ethiopia, Partners in Development and Good Governance: A Report Prepared for the Ad Hoc CSO/NGO Task Force*, Addis Ababa: CDRA.

Vaughan, Sarah and Gebremichael, Mesfin 2011, *Rethinking business and politics in Ethiopia The role of EFFORT, the Endowment Fund for the Rehabilitation of Tigray*, London: Overseas Development Institute.

World Bank 2011, 'Ethiopia – Joint Staff Advisory Note on Growth and Transformation Plan (GTP), 2010/11–2014/15', Washington, DC: World Bank, available at http:// documents.worldbank.org/curated/en/2011/08/14822318/ethiopia-joint-staff-advis ory-note-growth-transformation-plan-gtp-201011-201415.

World Bank 2012, 'Ethiopia – Country Partnership Strategy (FY2013-FY2016)', Report No. 71884-ET, Washington D.C.: World Bank, available at http://documents.worldban k.org/curated/en/2012/08/16702735/ethiopia-country-partnership-strategy.

World Bank 2017, 'Ethiopia – Country Partnership Framework (FY2018-FY2022)', Report No. 119576-ET, Washington D.C.: World Bank, available at http://documents.worldba nk.org/curated/en/613041498788104835/Ethiopia-Country-partnership-framework -for-the-period-FY18-FY22

Ethiopian Student Movement Publications

Ayalew, Melesse 1965, 'Editorial: Revolutionary Renaissance', *Challenge: Journal of the Ethiopian Students Association in North America*, 5, 2: 1–6.

Ayalew, Melesse 1967, 'Review of Richard Greenfield, *Ethiopia: A New Political History*', *Challenge: Journal of the Ethiopian Students Association in North America*, 6, 1: 54–61.

Ayalew, Melesse 1971, 'Editorial: Imperialism and National Liberation', *Challenge: Journal of the World-Wide Union of Ethiopian Students*, 11, 1: 1–2.

Ayalew, Melesse 1971, 'Editorial Note', *Challenge: Journal of the World-Wide Union of Ethiopian Students*, 11, 2: 1–3.

Ayalew, Melesse and Dessalegn Rahmato 1965, 'Editorial: "All That Is Necessary for the Forces of Evil to Triumph in the World Is for Enough Good Men to Do Nothing"', *Challenge: Journal of the Ethiopian Students Association in North America*, 5, 1: 1–3.

Ayalew, Melesse and Dessalegn Rahmato 1966, 'Editorial: The Spirit of Solidarity', *Challenge: Journal of the Ethiopian Student Association in North America*, 6, 1: 1–3.

Ayalew, Melesse and Dessalegn Rahmato 1967, 'Editorial: Beyond an Ideology of Power-lessness', *Challenge: Journal of the Ethiopian Students Association in North America*, 7, 1: 1–8.

B., G. 1967, 'The Futility of Planning in a Feudal Society', *Challenge: Journal of the Ethiopian Students Association in North America*, 7, 1: 20–26.

Beshah, Girma 1966, 'The Making of a New Ethiopia', *Challenge: Journal of the Ethiopian Students Association in North America*, 6, 1: 41–53.

Eshete, Andreas 1970, 'The Problems of Regionalism and Religion: Some Theoretical Considerations', *Challenge: Journal of the World-Wide Union of Ethiopian Students*, 10, 1: 5–21.

Ethiopian Students Association in North America 1967, 'The Anti-Demonstration Pro-clamation: Introductory Remarks', *Challenge: Journal of the Ethiopian Students Asso-ciation in North America*, 7, 1: 9–11.

Ethiopian Students Association in North America 1970, 'Themes', *Challenge: Journal of the World-Wide Union of Ethiopian Students*, 10, 2: 1–3.

Ethiopian Students Association in North America 1973a, 'Analysis and Appraisal of the Ethiopian Student Movement', *Challenge: Journal of the World-Wide Union of Ethiopian Students*, 13, 1: 8–20.

Ethiopian Students Association in North America 1973b, 'Footnotes [includes Appendices A and B]', *Challenge: Journal of the World-Wide Union of Ethiopian Students*, 13, 1: 35–40.

Ethiopian Students Association in North America and Ethiopian Students Union in Europe 1970, 'Message From the Ethiopian Students Union in Europe to the 17th Conference of ESUNA', *Challenge: Journal of the World-Wide Union of Ethiopian Students*, 10, 1: 2–4b.

Ethiopian Students Association in North America, and Ethiopian Students Union in North America 1971a, 'ESUNA: The General Line', *Challenge: Journal of the World-Wide Union of Ethiopian Students*, 12, 1: 54–56.

Ethiopian Students Association in North America, and Ethiopian Students Union in North America 1971b, 'Resolutions of the 19th Congress of ESUNA', *Challenge: Journal of the World-Wide Union of Ethiopian Students*, 12, 1: 57–62.

Ethiopian Students Association in North America and Union of Ethiopian Students in Europe 1966, 'Resolutions: 13th Congress of ESANA; 5th Congress of ESUE', *Challenge: Journal of the Ethopian Student Association in North America*, 6, 1: 3–41.

Fulass, Haile 1965, 'Accusations and Prescriptions', *Challenge: Journal of the Ethiopian Students Association in North America*, 5, 2: 11–18.

Gouzo, Rejjim 1971, 'Mass Struggle Versus Focoism', *Challenge: Journal of the World-Wide Union of Ethiopian Students*, 11, 2: 67–76.

Habtu, Alem 1969, 'Themes', *Challenge: Journal of the World-Wide Union of Ethiopian Students* 9, no. 2: 1–2.

Habtu, Alem 1970a, 'Editorial', *Challenge: Journal of the World-Wide Union of Ethiopian Students*, 10, 1: 1.

Habtu, Alem 1970b, 'Regionalism and National Liberation: Some Observations', *Challenge: Journal of the World-Wide Union of Ethiopian Students*, 10, 1: 46–57.

Kassa, Belay 1965, 'Unveiling the Paradox', *Challenge: Journal of the Ethiopian Students Association in North America*, 5, 1: 14–18.

Lencho, Tumtu 1971, 'The Question of Nationalities and Class Struggle in Ethiopia', *Challenge: Journal of the World-Wide Union of Ethiopian Students*, 11, 2: 3–66.

Mabuza, Abo 1968, 'The Ethiopian Monarchical System', *Challenge: Journal of the Ethiopian Student Association in North America*, 8, 1: 7–16.

Mekonnen, Walleligne 1971, 'On the Question of Nationalities in Ethiopia', *Newsletter of the New York Chapter of Ethiopian Student Union North America*, March 1971.

Menkerios, Haile 1970, 'The Present System of Land Tenure in Ethiopia: An Introduction', *Challenge: Journal of the World-Wide Union of Ethiopian Students*, 10, 2: 4–24.

Rahmato, Dessalegn 1965, 'Art Betrayed', *Challenge: Journal of the Ethiopian Students Association in North America*, 5, 1: 18–22.

Rahmato, Dessalegn 1967, 'Review of Kwame Nkrumah, "Neo-Colonialism – the Last Stage of Imperialism"', *Challenge: Journal of the Ethiopian Students Association in North America*, 7, 1: 30–33.

Rahmato, Dessalegn 1968, 'Editorial', *Challenge: Journal of Ethiopian Students Association in North America*, 8, 1: 1–6.

Rahmato, Dessalegn 1970, 'Conditions of the Ethiopian Peasantry', *Challenge: Journal of the World-Wide Union of Ethiopian Students*, 10, 2: 25–49.

Takele, Tilahun 1971, 'The National Question ("Regionalism") in Ethiopia', *Newsletter of the New York Chapter of Ethiopian Student Union North America*, March 1971.

Tekle-Tsadik, Shimellis 1967, 'Letter to the Editor', *Challenge: Journal of the Ethiopian Student Association of North America*, 7, 1: 34–6.

Yesus, Hagos Gabre 1965, 'Land Reform: Plus Ça Change?', *Challenge: Journal of the Ethiopian Student Association of North America*, 5, 1: 3–14.

Yesus, Hagos Gabre 1966, 'Review of Donald N. Levine, "Wax and Gold"', *Challenge: Journal of Ethiopian Student Association of North America*, 6, no. 1: 62–73.

Yesus, Hagos Gabre 1970, 'Problem of Regionalism in Ethiopia', *Challenge: Journal of the World-Wide Union of Ethiopian Students*, 10, 1: 22–35.

Political Party Documents, Government Legislation and Proclamations

Ethiopian People's Revolutionary Democratic Front 1989, *A Democratic Alternative for Ethiopia*, London: EPRDF.

Ethiopian People's Revolutionary Democratic Front 2006, *Ethiopian People's Revolutionary Democratic Front Basic Program*, Addis Ababa: EPRDF.

Federal Democratic Republic of Ethiopia 1995, *A Proclamation to Announce the Coming into Effect of The Constitution of the Federal Democratic Republic of Ethiopia. Proclamation No.1/1995*, Addis Ababa: Federal Negarit Gazetta.

Federal Democratic Republic of Ethiopia 2002, *Re-Enactment of Urban Lands Lease Holding Proclamation, Proclamation No. 272/2002*. Addis Ababa: Negarit Gazeta, year 8, no. 19.

Federal Democratic Republic of Ethiopia 2005, *Rural Land Administration and Land Use Proclamation, Proclamation No. 426/2005*. Addis Ababa: Negarit Gazeta, year 11, no. 44.

Federal Democratic Republic of Ethiopia 2011, *Urban Lands Lease Holding Proclamation, Proclamation No. 172/2011*, Addis Ababa: Negarit Gazeta, year 18, no. 4.

Kinijit 2011, 'Coalition for Unity and Democracy (Kinijit), Party Manifesto (unofficial Party Translation)', available at http://zelalemkibret.files.wordpress.com/2011/11/kinijit-manifesto-english.pdf.

Ministry of Finance and Economic Development 2006, 'A Plan for Accelerated and Sustained Development to End Poverty (PASDEP)', Addis Ababa.

National Planning Commission, 2016 'Growth and Transformation Plan II (GTP II)', Addis Ababa.

Oromo Democratic Front 2015, 'Oromo Democratic Front Statement on the Killing
of Oromo Students & Civilians', available at http://oromodemocraticfront.org/odf
-statment-on-the-killing-of-oromo-students-civilians/.

Provisional Office for Mass Organization Affairs 1975, *Basic Documents of the Ethiopian
Revolution*, Addis Ababa: The Provisional Office for Mass Organizational Affairs;
Agitation, Propaganda and Education Committee.

Tigray People's Liberation Front 1983, 'The Constitution of the Tigray People's Liberation Front: Adopted at the Second Organizational Meeting of the TPLF', Addis
Ababa: Institute of Ethiopian Studies Archive.

Transitional Government of Ethiopia 1993, *A Proclamation To Provide For The Lease
Holding of Urban Lands No. 80/1993*, Addis Ababa: Negarit Gazeta.

Index

CPSIA information can be obtained
at www.ICGtesting.com
Printed in the USA
LVHW020747301020
669991LV00004B/4